HIMALAYAN HISTORIES

SUNY series in Hindu Studies

WENDY DONIGER, EDITOR

CHETAN SINGH

Himalayan Histories

ECONOMY, POLITY,
RELIGIOUS TRADITIONS

Himalayan Histories: Economy, Polity, Religious Traditions by Chetan Singh was first published by Permanent Black D-28 Oxford Apts, 11 IP Extension, Delhi 110092 INDIA, for the territory of SOUTH ASIA.

Not for sale in South Asia

Jacket photograph and design by Anuradha Roy

Published by State University of New York Press, Albany

© 2019 Chetan Singh

All rights reserved

No part of this book may be used or reproduced in any manner whatsoever without written permission. No part of this book may be stored in a retrieval system or transmitted in any form or by any means including electronic, electrostatic, magnetic tape, mechanical, photocopying, recording, or otherwise without the prior permission in writing of the publisher.

For information, contact State University of New York Press, Albany, NY
www.sunypress.edu

Library of Congress Cataloging-in-Publication Data

Names: Singh, Chetan, author.
Title: Himalayan histories : economy, polity, religious traditions / Chetan Singh.
Description: Albany, NY : State University of New York, [2019] | Series: SUNY series in Hindu studies | Includes bibliographical references and index.
Identifiers: LCCN 2018040339| ISBN 9781438475219 (hbk. : alk. paper) | ISBN 978-1-4384-7522-6 (pbk. : alk paper) | ISBN 9781438475233 (e-book)
Subjects: LCSH: Himalaya Mountains Region--History. | Ethnology--Himalaya Mountains Region. | Himalaya Mountains Region--Social life and customs.
Classification: LCC DS485.H6 S55 2019 | DDC 954.96--dc23 LC record available at https://lccn.loc.gov/2018040339

10 9 8 7 6 5 4 3 2 1

Contents

	Acknowledgments	ix
1	Introduction	1
2	Defining Spaces, Constructing Identities: Regional History and the Himalaya	13
3	Defining Community: Territory and Transformation in the Western Himalaya	34
4	Geography, Religion, and Hegemony: Constructing the State in the Western Himalaya	56
5	Nature, Religion, and Politics: Keonthal and Kumharsain	76
6	Myth, Legend, and Folklore in Himalayan Society	91
7	The *Dum*: Community Consciousness, Peasant Resistance, or Political Intrigue?	114
8	Between Two Worlds: The Trader Pastoralists of Kinnaur	124
9	Strategy of Interdependence: Gaddi, Peasant, and State	154
10	Migration and Trade in Mountain Societies	166
11	Pastoralism and the Making of Colonial Modernity in Kulu, 1850–1952	183
12	Diverse Forms of Polyandry, Customary Rights of Inheritance, and Landownership in the Western Himalaya	210

13 Thresholds in the Wilderness: Identities, Interests, and Modernity in Western Himalayan Borderlands 235

14 Riverbank to Hilltop: Pre-colonial Towns and the Impact of British Rule on Urban Growth 253

Bibliography 272

Index 295

Acknowledgments

SEVERAL QUESTIONS ABOUT Himalayan society have intrigued me over the past two decades and more. The fact that many scholars were exploring similar issues by looking at a variety of montane regions suggested that the questions had a wider import. It also became evident that research on previously marginalised mountain societies was gradually increasing and that over the years an impressive body of work around this subject had in fact emerged. In the course of finalising and polishing the essays that comprise this book it became clear to me that I had greatly benefited from my interaction with many outstanding scholars in a community that had focussed on our areas of common interest. And that there were others with varied academic interests who had brought diverse perspectives to the problems I sought to address.

Many thanks to Jon Mathieu for fifteen years of fruitful communications, conversations, and support. His infectious inquisitiveness initiated and sustained many shared research concerns on mountain societies. Laurence Fontaine, with her acute observations tinged with a delightful sense of humour, has been equally supportive and involved in many of these exchanges.

The articles that follow were discussed in detail when first presented in various conferences. I am grateful to the participants and friends whose perceptive observations and questions helped me revise: among them I wish to thank Shekhar Pathak, Richard Tucker, Sudha Vasan, Raquel Gil Montero, Bo Sax, Hermann Kreutzmann, Prashant Negi, Joelle Smadja, Luigi Lorenzetti, Pascale Dollfus, Daniela Berti, O.C. Handa, Jarjum Ete, P.D. Rai, Jaiwanti Dimri, Dinesh Saklani, Girija Pande, Hari Prasad Bhattarai, Ajay Dandekar, Bernard Derouet, Heraclio Bonilla, Siddiq Wahid, O.P. Tandon, and Claude Arpi.

Incisive comments by the late Jean-Francois Bergier always provided an alternative viewpoint to my own understanding, showing me other possible directions.

Colleagues and students at Himachal Pradesh University happily allowed me to draw upon their familiarity with local practices and beliefs. Among them I thank Laxman Thakur, R.S. Pirta, B.L. Mehta, Abha Malhotra, O.P. Sharma, Amrit Gandhi, Arun K. Singh, Dhirendra Dangwal, Jaideep Negi, Balkrishan Shivram, and Vidya Sagar Negi. Prem Raj, in the department office, always presented his earthy understanding of things in simple, straightforward language. I can recall some very meaningful exchanges on a wide range of subjects, including mountain development and Himachal society, with B.N. Goswamy, Karuna Goswamy, Mahesh Sharma, B.R. Sharma, Deepak Sanan, Ashok and Sarojini Thakur, Sanjeeva Pandey, Kanak Dixit, Vinay Tandon, Mamta Chander, Meenakshi Paul, C.K. Mathew, Arik Moran, Mark Baker, Peter Sutherland, Yogesh Snehi, and Aniket Alam.

Interactions with friends and colleagues at the Indian Institute of Advanced Study, Shimla, familiarised me with a wealth of enriching ideas and arguments. For those I must thank Peter deSouza, Tridip Suhrud, Ravi Palat, Gopal Guru, Bettina Baeumer, Madhavan Palat, D.L. Sheth, Sanjay Palshikar, Sundar Sarukkai, Sasheej Hegde, K. Satchidanandan, Meena Alexander, Radhavallabh Tripathi, Arindam Chakrabarti, Vrinda Dalmiya, Ghanshyam Shah, Rajesh Joshi, Jaya Tyagi, Anita Cherian, Kanchana Natrajan, Amba Kulkarni, Nirmal Sengupta, K.L. Tuteja, Anandita Mukhopadhyaya, Samir Banerjee, Varsha Ganguly, Priyambada Sarkar, S. Muralidharan, Satish Aikant, Gangeya Mukherji, B.V. Nemade, Om Prakash Valmiki, Udayon Misra, and many others whose presence at the institute made it the remarkable place that it was and continues to be. Prem Chand, the librarian at the institute, was very helpful and efficient as always. V.S. Rana provided useful secretarial assistance. It is possible that I have inadvertently overlooked some people and for that I request forgiveness.

Rukun Advani made this book possible, as he did the ones I have written earlier. His editing skills have helped rescue many authors from their own web of words. I have learnt much from him and would like to believe that some of this was reflected in the typescript I sent him.

Luxmi, Debu, Juhi, and Prithvi have in various ways – supportive and sarcastic, intentional and unintentional, fair and unfair – encouraged, goaded, and compelled me to complete this book. I fear they have conspired to continue this behaviour to keep me harmlessly preoccupied in future as well.

1

Introduction

FOR LONG STRETCHES in the past, historians and geographers collaborated when analysing or recounting the enduring facts about societies and civilisations. In these earlier times they brought diverse skills to the task, and the absence of rigid disciplinary divisions was a help. Humans and their natural surroundings were seen as interacting and influencing each other in bringing about long-term social and natural transformation.

But with the passage of time this collaboration became an unequal partnership. The increasing confidence of humans in their ability to alter and improve circumstances placed history in a dominant position. New theoretical perspectives accorded to history the increasingly exclusive privilege of narrating and elucidating the human saga. To geography, on the other hand, fell the muted task of providing physical props for this enactment.[1] The notion of spaces – particularly central to geography – came to be gradually and unfortunately disregarded by many of the social sciences as these were practised in the English-speaking world.

In critical social theory, too, the idea of space seemed to represent something dead and inert which contributed to society only as much as man purposefully chose to take from it. With the theoretical prioritisation of history over geography, scholars ignored the fact that their "lifeworld" was "creatively located not only in the making

[1] Soja 1990: 14. He points out how such thinking created a perspective wherein "An already-made geography sets the stage, while the willful making of history dictates the actions and defines the story line."

of history but also in the construction of human geographies, the social production of space . . ."[2] By the early years of the twentieth century, the idea of spatiality had been pushed to the fringes of the intellectual arena.[3] Territories and regions came to be regarded even more explicitly as the physical background or theatrical stages upon which historical actions were performed. Yet the enduring link between space and human relations could hardly be ignored. Thirty years ago, Lefebvre pointed out that "Social relations, which are concrete abstractions, have no real existence save in and through space. Their underpinning is spatial."[4]

One of the difficulties was, however, that history-writing had come to be a way of articulating national aspirations and asserting the primacy of the nation-state over its regions. In Europe, the roots of national and cultural unity were now traced to an ever more distant past. Regions and provinces became reduced concerns, seen as best left to lesser historians. Modernisation created national markets and the autarky of regions was gradually weakened. National political centralisation overshadowed local governance. Provincial loyalties yielded to the assertiveness of national cultures.[5] Regional scholarship, with its emphasis on local identity and political divergence, now seemed antiquated and reactionary.

Yet the relationship between the nation-state and regional history is not necessarily antagonistic. Regional political processes can be "constitutive – not always imitative – of the politics of the nation-state."[6] It is therefore important to see how regions differ from nation-states. In this context Foucault says: "It is surprising how long the problem of space took to emerge as a historic-political problem. Space used to be either dismissed as belonging to 'nature' – that is,

---

[2] Ibid.: 11, 25.

[3] Ibid.: Soja sees this arising partly from the rejection of the physical environment as a determinant of social processes. Society and history were seen as functioning autonomously, based on the theoretical assumption that human geography was only part of the "physical background of society".

[4] Lefebvre 1991: 404.

[5] Applegate 1999: 1163.

[6] Ibid.: 1172.

the given, the basic condition, 'physical geography', in other words a sort of 'prehistoric' substratum: or else it was conceived as the residential site or field of expansion of peoples, of culture, a language or a State."[7] Regions, because of their predominantly geographical nature, are perhaps closer to being an assertion of "physical geography". Explicitly demarcated borders of nation-states, on the other hand, are seen as an artefact of the political imagination. But the matter is immensely more complex, for regions too are the product of human engagement with the environment, not merely nature's platform. Equally, nation-states are not wholly the result of national aspirations but are powerfully forged by the forces of historical geography.

A series of conceptual shifts enabled regional scholars to proceed beyond geographical description and environmental determinism. The idea of a region moved closer to social anthropology and thus offered a valuable "frame of reference for the study of social phenomena and processes."[8] A region or area was no longer defined through "objective attributes"; it was, in fact, the "dynamic relationship existing between an area and the social processes and ideologies that give it meaning",[9] and was "thought of as such by its residents",[10] even in some manner created by people "in their experience and in their imagination."[11] This purposeful relationship of people with regions was essentially how Knight perceived the nature and transformation of territories: "In a sense, territory is not; it becomes, for territory itself is passive, and it is human beliefs and actions that give territory meaning."[12] To give such meaning to a territory was by no means easy. Lefebvre famously wrote: "It is not the work of a moment for a society to generate (produce) an appropriated social space in which it can achieve a form of means of self-preservation and self-representation, a social space to which that society is not identical, and which is its

[7] Foucault 1980: 149.
[8] Moore 1938: 474.
[9] Murphy 1990: 532.
[10] Feldhaus 2003: 4.
[11] Ibid.: 5, 211. She further argues that "People bring regions into being by moving across the landscape."
[12] Knight 1982: 515.

tomb as well as its cradle. This act of creation is, in fact, a process."[13] The changing and evolving character of processes makes the empirical study of such changes doubly complicated.

Differences obviously exist between the outsider's "etic" viewpoint and the insider's "emic" understanding. Nevertheless, points of convergence are possible to find.[14] More complex, however, are the divergent theoretical perspectives that emerge from the different academic disciplines. For regional geographers, "the roles of region and society are reversed: region as institutional shape, is the object; society is its property or attribute."[15] The challenge lies in adopting a multi-dimensional perspective of a region, one that combines spatiality with several other social variables. Even then, it would be almost impossible to describe a region in all its aspects.[16] For practical reasons, therefore, regions have been delineated on the basis of "convenience". The scale or size of the region chosen and the purpose of the study have, therefore, been the two main considerations.[17]

In her presidential address to the Panjab History Conference in the mid 1970s, Romila Thapar dwelt upon the "scope and significance of regional history". She suggested that this was particularly relevant in the study of interludes between the collapse and rise of empires.[18] Regional history in India could therefore be seen as "a corrective to the earlier tendency to generalize about the subcontinent . . ."[19]

---

[13] Lefebvre 1991: 34.

[14] Mandelbaum 1982: 1459. Mandelbaum attempts to resolve the problem by arguing that the "two types of regions" the different viewpoints generate are "not totally separate realities".

[15] Hoekveld and Hoekveld-Meijer 1995: 159.

[16] McDonald 1966: 518. He argues that "In many respects, the idea that a region is susceptible to total definition has been . . . an illusion which has led to a great deal of geographic nonsense."

[17] McDonald 1966: 524.

[18] Thapar 2004: 318. She argues that "The interest in regional history assumes greater historiographic potential, potential with which we are perhaps as yet not altogether fully familiar."

[19] Ibid.: 318.

These "inter-imperial" phases also saw the socio-political reordering of regions that once constituted the empire. The periodic fragmentation of imperial power encouraged the emergence of provincial elites and regional identities.

There was another dimension to the issue: the growth of nationalist writing in India had probably kindled interest in regional history, which had then encouraged a wide range of differing interpretations and explanations. New socio-political groups and identities emerged in response to subcontinental developments. Regional historians highlighted the significance of provincial events. But the larger context that stimulated their work was history written on a national scale.[20]

Such a development was not unique to India. The United States, too, witnessed the tendency, though "by the end of the 1960s, the study of national character and the respect for national myths was collapsing, not only in history but also in the other social sciences. The principal writers of consensus history were falling silent..."[21] Consequently, studies of the cultural diversities of the major regions of the United States declined.

The interlinkages between historiographies at different levels are fairly evident. The idea of the nation had certainly stimulated regional histories. Yet regions were not merely sites upon which national-level ideologies and processes were played out. Regional histories, while being influenced by a larger national history, were also equally a rejoinder to it. By implication, regional and national histories came to be mutually constructed.

In approaching their work as a political construct, regional historians often particularised national developments to accommodate provincial sensitivities. As a result, their histories resonated deeply within regional cultures. This engagement with mainstream developments could be either confrontational or participatory, depending upon the shifts in power equations in the region. Popular memory, has the ability to refashion historical characters or depict events in a different light. It therefore contributed substantially to the emergence of regional narratives and alternative histories. Precolonial events

[20] Ibid.: 317, 318.
[21] Higham 1994: 1298.

and political entities of subcontinental significance shaped regional traditions in the different parts of the subcontinent. Mewar's resistance to Mughal rule, for instance, and the long-drawn Sikh and Maratha struggle in the seventeenth century are an important part of popular historical memory in some parts of India. It is a memory enlivened by regional heroes who successfully defied imperial functionaries shown as being tyrannical and oppressive. Both in victory and defeat, Mughal power and its imperial image had a large presence in regional historical consciousness. Subsequently, under colonial rule and in recent times, too, national-level historiography has influenced regional historiography. The grand narrative and regional accounts have always been closely connected.

However, even counter-narratives and alternative histories were accounts of dominant politico-cultural elites, albeit at the regional level. Though the lesser or subordinated sections of society were indispensable in the emergence of a broad regional identity, they remained peripheral to the creation of the assertive regional consciousness which overshadowed the undercurrents that are invariably a part of historical processes. As a result, Rajasthan's history has largely been about the military exploits of Rajput rulers rather than the story of communities such as the Bhils, Meenas, Jats, and Gujjars who (together with the Rajputs) collectively gave the region its fundamental social character. Folklore in Maharashtra recalls the inspiring struggle of Shivaji and his Maratha warriors against Aurangzeb, but relatively little is written about the unstinted support they received from other sections of society that contributed critically to the growth of Maratha power. Here a word of caution is necessary. Historians and chroniclers have always been fascinated by dramatic events, military contests, the glory of victory, and the grandeur of power. This was the predisposition that the Subaltern Studies historians had originally set out to redress by unearthing many of the numerous smaller stories that collectively constituted the history of the nation.

Do we then need to replicate the Subaltern Studies endeavour for the regions? Subaltern scholarship had questioned and enriched the dominant national narrative by highlighting regional and local accounts. Does it follow that influential regional narratives too should incorporate the hitherto muted stories of communities lower in the social hierarchy? If writing a better history of the nation requires the inclusion of perspectives and contributions of the subordinated, should the history of regions not also require the same? It is hardly in doubt that provincial elites stifled weaker voices by dominating a region's history and defining its culture. As a result much has remained untold. More recently, thus, social scientists have examined minor cultural traditions more closely to provide a more inclusive picture.

Regional historians impeded by the lack of historical sources may possibly be prompted to adopt some of the research methods of the other social sciences. There is a need to go beyond political history and examine region-specific economic rationalities, repressed subcultures, and marginalised social practices and beliefs. Some pointed questions too need to be asked. Who speaks for the region and by what authority? Does the region have only one voice? Are there murmurs that one must try harder to hear and understand? What meanings can be attributed to the silences? In asking such questions, a more nuanced history becomes possible, one in which the social, the cultural, and the political are closely entwined. Such a history looks at the pervasive nature of power and its ability to permeate every relationship. It may moreover connect diverse polities to each other through a layered and complex arrangement, even if not all of them necessarily form a cohesive system.

Ecological historians have shown that ecology has always been a powerful influence on human history. In fact, most ecological histories have highlighted ecologically defined regions rather than political entities. Worster sees the history of a region as the history of "evolving human ecology". "A region", he says, "emerges as people try to make a living from a particular part of the earth." A region's history was about how a people "acquired" it, "perceived" it and "tried to make use of it".[22] Long term socio-economic processes that gave societies their divergent characteristics were the result of this interaction between man and nature. The question of how historical developments are perceived has, in fact, become a matter of growing

[22] Worster 1994: 27.

interest. More recently, scholarship in cultural studies has fostered a history-writing wherein "culture" has replaced "social" as a more inclusive term. The idea of culture seems to encompass questions embedded in the concepts of gender, race, ethnicity, language, and a host of other things that are sometimes quite intangible.

Along with the writing of large-scale histories of civilisations that was at times seen as a measure of serious scholarship, case studies and research on micro-regions, too, have remained a lively aspect of historical research. Local histories and the studies of specific and specialised nature are frequently very rich in description and detail. Collectively, they can more meaningfully explain some of the larger historical developments. Their grounded empirical nature can help support a vigorous theoretical framework to understand relatively abstract socio-economic processes.

The essays in this book explore aspects of history, religion, and culture in a part of the western Himalaya that today constitutes the Indian province of Himachal Pradesh. Before 1947, this area included British-governed Kangra and Shimla districts, and over two dozen principalities. The territories under the British were extensive and administered along norms established in the rest of Punjab province. Most principalities, on the other hand, were rather small and autonomously ruled by hereditary rajas and petty chieftains. Some chiefships were so tiny that they comprised only a few scattered villages. Notwithstanding their colonial government, the customary cultural practices and agro-pastoral system in the British districts were the same as in those of the neighbouring "native" states. Despite their indirect exposure to Mughal and Sikh rule, and subsequent subjection to intrusive colonial government, mountain societies clung doggedly to many age-old socio-political institutions. The latter were very important and integral to what these societies regarded as a sense of being.

The fact that the mountains were usually seen as peripheral frontier territories gave mountain people far greater freedom than those living in closely regulated "core" areas. The state's ability to intrude upon mountain societies was constrained by various factors. Geography was the most obvious and important of these. It accounted for the difficulty of access as well as the meagre resources that the state could possibly obtain from such areas. As a result, the administrative apparatus and institutions of political control in these frontiers were different from those in the plains. So was the manner in which life was organised. Even in states where formal institutions of governance existed – as in Chamba – there was much that escaped their purview. The ruler's pretensions to authority, approved by Brahmanical pronouncements, rested ultimately upon power that was disaggregated across communities. Loyalties stretched to the limit by a difficult terrain required periodic renewal. The political balance was always precarious and the state treaded softly in the countryside.

Some rulers of Chamba – situated in the far western mountains of the region – made land grants to temples and Brahmins. Grantees were explicitly given the income and resources of land in some villages where royal control was firmly established. But these grants reveal little about distant territories where the royal writ compromised with powerful local elites and where socio-religious institutions asserted the latters' autonomy. Inscriptions on large and elaborately carved memorial stones placed at natural springs by local *ranas* and feudatories are an important measure of their influence in distant places.

Historians of the region have few historical records to go by. This gives rise to several questions that a scholar justifiably asks. Did the state not have adequate means to maintain detailed records? Was the nature of mountain economy and society inherently incompatible with methodical record-keeping? The mountain villages of Himachal were primarily sustained by agro-pastoralism. Systematic transhumance was used to exploit the natural resources of a vast and difficult area. The constant movement of animals and people across political borders was a necessary part of such an economy. Resources were shared by people of different states that were in any case too small to provide adequately for their own population. Furthermore, transhumant agro-pastoralists were difficult to tie down. They could easily evade government monitoring of their products and income. They were not however entirely nomadic and possessed permanent houses and cultivated land to which they returned at certain times of the year. The state, therefore, enumerated the households and demanded a fixed amount of labour and payment in kind from each household. It was a rudimentary system and inexpensively harnessed the meagre surplus yielded by a difficult terrain to a hard-pressed peasantry. The task was, nevertheless, difficult and the Himalayan peasant was assertive enough to compel the ruler not to push too hard. Some of the essays in this volume are about how the rulers and the ruled made the system work and yet episodically tested where the limits lay.

The virtual absence of written sources makes it difficult to write a formal documented history of the region. The few political accounts available are in the form of poorly dated royal genealogies or panegyric compositions of heroic achievements in warfare and conquest. Petty rulers saw little sense in employing a professional bureaucracy to maintain official records in any meaningful detail. It was immeasurably easier to use the force of tradition to secure the consent of the peasantry than to try and coerce it into obedience. The latter was a risky gamble. Tiny mountain communities scattered across the landscape were guided by a collective memory of tradition and history, some of it specific to their village. These communities followed their respective customs and beliefs. But they did not exist in isolation. Numerous small traditions were linked to each other and were components of a network of widely understood myths and legends. From time to time, more expansive narratives were also created to serve a larger socio-political purpose and re-created differently as and when another occasion so required.

What does history mean to a society that sees as much – or more – value in the spoken word as in the written? How is one to understand people who regard collective memory as historical record and for whom past and the present virtually coexist in daily life? If oral traditions are the means by which a society understands the world and also explains itself to others, do they serve the purpose of history? Must historical research mean the relentless search for an elusive "objective" truth? Several similar questions have engaged scholars over the years. Some works (specially to do with the use of oral sources) have been very influential in defining the field.[23] Historians, however, have been rather wary of working with disciplines and methods that do not lend themselves to a sufficient level of chronological rigour. Yet the need to write the histories of societies that seemingly lack historical sources has never been more pressing. In an increasingly connected world, closer interaction has revealed the different ways in which humans have understood and experienced their surroundings. History as a means of remembering and recounting such experiences over time, too, has been diversely perceived.

It is not, however, my purpose here to engage in a theoretical or methodological discussion on this subject. While that is immensely important, my focus in this book is on using the available sources to create a historical understanding on a range of subjects pertaining to material and cultural life in the western Himalaya. The essays dealing with political economy and the "rational" organisation of material life seem strikingly at variance with the apparently "superstitious" beliefs that so strongly influence cultural practice. But people in the region never saw this as contradictory in the past: nor do they see them as such today. Ignorance and backwardness are not the reasons for this. After its creation as a distinct political unit of the Indian Union, Himachal Pradesh made impressive progress in almost every social indicator of development. Incomes are higher than the national average. The number of hospitals and educational institutions, in particular, has increased impressively. Literacy levels are amongst the highest in the country. However, none of this has diminished the faith of village communities in their local gods or weakened their own ability to implement collective decisions. Religion and rationality have hardly ever worked together. Therefore, the continued authority of village deities to decide important matters of secular (sometimes even political) concern in large parts of Himachal seems a bit of a puzzle. Perhaps, village folk do not see the religious and the secular as discrete domains, but as fluid components of a single sphere.

---

[23] It is not possible to mention the enormous amount of work that exists on the subject. However, the work of Vansina 1965 seems to have been particularly influential amongst historians.

Did centuries of dealing with the political power of the raja and the religious authority of the state deity nurture in the Himalayan peasant the skill to negotiate the precarious space between these two aspects of daily life? Though an attempt has been made here to provide some answers, the last word on the matter is still a long way off.

2

Defining Spaces, Constructing Identities
Regional History and the Himalaya

Few scholars can claim expertise over the history of the entire Himalaya; even the most reputed would find it difficult to discern new historiographical trends for a region so vast and varied. It is therefore usually necessary to restrict oneself to certain broad issues and concepts that seem critical to an understanding of society, culture, and history within a specific part of any large region. Some of these issues might appear to be especially true for the Himalaya, where the influence of the environment on man is perceived to have always been overwhelming and explicit.

Empirical information constitutes the core of historical research, but it is made meaningful by theoretical constructs; so, a new historiography can only emerge if we develop alternative theoretical frameworks that raise new questions compelling us towards different answers. We need, in short, to look closely not only at how historians have dealt with the ideas of territory and region – and the corresponding notions of identity that these create – but also at how other social sciences have evolved methods of dealing with such questions. Historians have much to gain from concepts and methods in other disciplines, especially geography, sociology, and anthropology.

In relation to the Himalaya, this is of crucial importance on account of an extreme paucity of historical sources. If much that is available appears to lie beyond the bounds of history, we need to free ourselves from the orthodox methodologies that straitjacket our discipline. Only a combination of academic methods can provide solutions to many of the problems that confront historians working on peripheral regions.

Defining Spaces and the Creation of Landscape

> "Landscapes and panoramas are not simply realities of the present but also, in large measure survivals of the past. Long-lost horizons are redrawn and recreated for us through what we see; the earth is like our skin, fated to carry the scars of ancient wounds."[1]

Unlike states and political entities, geographic regions are not usually accorded legal recognition. Geographers have for long defined regions as "natural" areas where human–nature interaction has over considerable periods produced social and physical landscapes that distinguish one region from another. Yet the problem is immensely complicated. Not all characteristics in a landscape produced by the man–nature engagement are specific or particular to it. Those that are shared with others frequently form the basis of a region's reorganisation, or the emergence of a new or redefined space.[2] Specific distinguishing criteria are often highlighted selectively to define a region for varying purposes. Depending upon the objective in mind, it is possible for completely divergent descriptions of a given area to emerge. Considerable energy is often invested, for instance, in delineating the borders of a "historical" region for political ends. Whatever the ultimate purpose, such motivated manoeuvrings of boundaries highlight the inadequacy of approaches that see physical surroundings as "objective realities" waiting to be revealed by purposive reasoning. Human interaction with the physical world requires, however, that the latter be seen not as "objective reality" – there being, in fact, no such thing – but as one half of an ongoing and changing relationship.[3]

[1] Braudel 1989: 31.
[2] Holland 1976: 4.
[3] Kobayashi 1989: 171.

For a historian, this means "a continuous interweaving of geography and history, achieved through cognition of the changing ecological components of the physical environment, of the role of environmental perception and natural resources (including time and space) as cultural appraisals, and the constant interplay of human and non-human forces . . ."[4]

The most compelling connection with physical surroundings began very early from a community's need to create the essential material conditions for its survival. This it usually did by claiming a territory that, Godelier argued, was "a portion of nature and therefore space". It was also "the site where its members are to find in perpetuity the material conditions and means of their existence."[5] While this frequently required some kind of partition of territory between various communities, it did not lead inevitably to the exclusion of all other communities. In fact, some societies were (many still are) not explicitly "territorial" in this sense: at times they shared the resources of their territory with others. On the other hand, there also exist communities that have access to the resources of several separate areas.[6]

There has been an attempt to see societies as being of two kinds, depending on the surrounding physiography. Those with access to the sea or navigable rivers are perceived as engaged in "transport", while those in areas devoid of such "opportunities of navigation" are seen as engaged primarily in "travel". The ability to "transport" enabled "societies or settlements to grow beyond their natural environmental constraints – to grow, that is, beyond the size that could be supported by the resources available to populations that commanded only human and animal energy." Societies of "travel", on the other hand, exchanged "money, men and messages" rather than goods.[7]

In addition to this broad division, there was the phenomenon of urbanisation. Towns of different sizes and importance contributed significantly to the prosperity of the region in which they were situated, including towns in landlocked regions. Such urban centres

[4] Baker and Gregory 1984: 6.
[5] Godelier 1986: 82, 83.
[6] Ibid.: 86–8.
[7] Fox-Genovese and Genovese 1989: 28, 236.

nurtured and developed certain areas of economic specialisation, thereby creating advantages that contributed importantly to the economy.[8] In the Himalaya, for example, the cities of Srinagar (Kashmir) and Kathmandu (Nepal) can be considered of particular prominence, apart from numerous other towns that were of political, economic, and religious importance. Towns, therefore, can be important signifiers of regional identity.

The impact of physical surroundings on people can hardly be overemphasised. Not only were these surroundings diversely interpreted by different people, they were also gradually transformed by them. Such transformation was obviously time- and place-specific. In the long-term construction of the landscape, therefore, a crucial role was played by "social conflict and social cooperation among individuals and groups" as they lived their lives in a given area.[9] Moreover, as individual and group relations grew and spread, they simultaneously altered the "sense of place" of those establishing these extended social connections.[10]

Constructing Identities

While recognising the historical importance of long-range migrations that continuously challenged political boundaries, one might suggest that this reaching out by societies was combined simultaneously with a strong notion of distinct geographical spaces. Most societies identified themselves with a particular area. Their long engagement and sustained struggle with the environment found expression in popular myths and symbols. Popular beliefs consolidated a sense of community rooted in an area that a society came to regard as its homeland.[11] This identification with an area was, however, not always explicit.[12] Nor were such territories distinctly marked and separated from each other. They overlapped and interacted at the fringes. It has

[8] Ringrose 1989a: 65.
[9] Baker 1984: 27.
[10] Ibid.: 26.
[11] Smith 1987: 183.
[12] Muir 1997: 33.

been argued that South Asian civilisation during the first millennium AD was a continuum of communities that helped define each other through a process of interaction.[13] How a large extent of territory is viewed can also, however, depend on what are regarded as its most essential constituents. The historian David Ludden, for instance, sees the Indian subcontinent "not as an aggregate of administrative or large-scale cultural territories, but instead as a large set of small-scale agrarian milieus."[14] In large parts of South Asia, the identity formation of communities occurred within the overarching context of politically dominant agrarian societies. At the fringes of the geographical imagination of the ordinary village peasant, the largest economically significant area was probably a region that included "interconnected villages, towns and cities", a place quite apparently "constructed" by peasant societies over a very long period. Ludden illustrates this by indicating that "new regions came to life in the Tamil speaking south as people used technology to make drainage water productive in communities along drainage basins."[15] He therefore emphasises the need to keep in mind both village- and region-level maps while studying peasant history. A disadvantage of focussing on the region, he suggests, is that "Our minds turn steadily towards major urban centres that hold the region together."[16]

Environmental diversities in South Asia also, however, sometimes encouraged social identities to be created via contrasts. The most significant of these was the symbolic contrast between the agrarian countryside of the ostensibly "civilised" society on the one hand and the unexplored wilderness of "savages" on the other.[17] The subcontinent was a vast space where agriculturists, pastoralists, and agro-pastoralists used, shared, and contested resources. It was a space both divided and united in many ways, depending on how it was used by those who lived off its resources.

It might, perhaps, be relevant to briefly mention the concept of

[13] Guha 1999: 26.
[14] Ludden 1989: 218.
[15] Ibid.: 204.
[16] Ibid.: 10–11.
[17] Guha 1999: 26.

"ethnie". The affinity of ethnie for a particular area did not necessarily arise from its actual possession of it. It may, as Anthony Smith argues, "be just a potent memory". Of importance was the idea that it was a symbolic geographical centre, a sacred habitat, a "homeland", to which it may "symbolically return, even when its members are scattered across the globe and have lost their homeland, centuries ago".[18] When Godelier argued that a society claimed both the "visible realities" and the "invisible powers" of a territory, he largely confined it to the "reproductive conditions of human life".[19] However, the influence of "invisible powers" was often believed to extend beyond the sphere of material production. Medieval Indian historians were convinced that land and environment chiselled the character of men. Abul Fazl was convinced that the climate of the Agra region made the people of that place "notorious throughout India for their turbulence, courage and recklessness".[20] Bengal, too, was seen as "a land where, owing to the climates' favouring the base, the dust of dissension is always rising".[21]

While geographical compulsions certainly influence the nature of social organisation, a society is much more than the territory it occupies. Spatial arguments provide only a partial explanation for the phenomenon of social consciousness. On the other hand, a host of non-spatial factors can combine to create a consciousness that comes to define a territory. Language, for example, is one such factor. As a means of interaction in daily life, language has been closely associated with geographical space. While delineating the borders of Kashmir, the Mughal emperor Jahangir remarked confidently that "the boundary of the country is the place up to which people speak the language of that country".[22] Yet in pre-modern times a social identity derived solely from a common spoken language – orally evolved – could not have existed over a region of very considerable geographical extent. Hobsbawm suggested that even the identification

[18] Smith 1987: 28.
[19] Godelier 1986: 83.
[20] Abul Fazl 1979: III, 327.
[21] Ibid: III, 427.
[22] Jahangir 1978: II, 141.

of nationality with "one platonic" language above all territorial dialects is "more characteristic of the ideological construction of nationalist intellectuals ... than of the actual grassroots users of the idiom. It is a literary and not an existential concept."[23]

The notion of a region therefore necessarily includes numerous non-material factors. Amongst these are ideas that constitute culture, community, and ethnicity, with all their fluidity and complexity. Seen from the perspective of historical geography, a region seems to evolve in accordance with "the social organisation of time and space".[24] This process is made possible and perpetuated by the continuity of certain cultural factors in a society: factors such as "memory, value, myth and symbolism" that have been particularly resilient and have permeated almost all cultural phenomena.[25] They both sustain and alter the structure of a society, and in course of time periodically provide to it new or altered meanings of identity, of the past, and of social values. These changes are more often transmutations rather than disjunctures, through which traditions of "memory, value, myth and symbolism" are transmitted in newly relevant forms to each new generation.

Territoriality and identity are autonomous socio-political concepts that draw upon each other to strengthen themselves. A "region" does not merely represent territoriality, just as an "identity" cannot emerge in isolation from its physical surroundings. Early English usage of the term "region" had a close affiliation with the idea of "rule". Even while it signifies a "large tract of land" or a "country", the concept of region has long-established links with the idea of "a realm or kingdom". Few would find the organic view of the state or nation still tenable. Anderson, interestingly, points out that the German geographer Fredrik Ratzel had argued that "states could be considered as living organisms and frontiers as equivalent to a skin".[26] While this may not really be considered acceptable any more, the intimate relationship between territoriality and identity is still central to our understanding of how regional histories have been written.

[23] Hobsbawm 1991: 57.
[24] Baker 1984: 18.
[25] Smith 1987: 3.
[26] Anderson 1996: 28.

Regional Continuities in India

Regions in medieval India that had over the long term emerged as geographic or cultural units were also constituted by the Mughals into administrative provinces. They appear to have acquired territorial identities, even though official documents refer to them simply by the name of the provincial capital. This, however, does not rule out the fact that *suba* Lahore was also known as Panjab, *suba* Kabul as Zabulistan, and that the term Gujarat was also used for *suba* Ahmedabad.[27] There was thus a considerable overlapping of geography, culture, and administration in the Mughal *suba*. Information from the provinces was obtained and systematically recorded by scribes under the head of each *suba*. Jahangir ordered that "the events of the *subahs* should be reported according to the boundaries of each". He mentions that he was following a rule established by his father Akbar and that "much gain and great advantage are to be brought about by it and information is acquired about the world and its inhabitants."[28] Prior to the establishment of Mughal rule, many regions that became *subas* had been independent kingdoms as well as distinct socio-cultural areas. For example, it was noted by the medieval Indian historian Nizam-uddin Ahmad that "the country of Malwa is an extensive country. Great rulers have always been [reigning] in that country."[29]

Moreover, most of the Mughal *subas*, even as they represented broad culture zones, were territorially very extensive units and enclosed smaller sub-regional (even regional) entities. Within the Mughal *suba* of Malwa, for instance, there was the territory of Garha, which Abul Fazl says "is a separate State, abounding in forests". Garha had substantial economic resources and the revenue was paid in "*mohurs* and elephants", its produce being "sufficient to supply both Gujarat and the Deccan".[30] In a letter to the Shah of Iran, Akbar said the Mughal empire covered an enormous geographical diversity, and that prior to his extensive conquests was "shared among so many

---

[27] Abul Fazl 1978: 129.
[28] Jahangir 1978: I, 247.
[29] Ahmad 1991: I, 466.
[30] Abul Fazl 1978: II, 201.

independent chiefs and martial rulers". Apart from the natural and political diversity of regions in his empire, Akbar recognised its cultural variety when he mentioned his conquest of "Afghan mountaineers, swift-careering, desert-dwelling Balucis and other forest dwellers", apart from many rajas and landowners.[31] Thevenot, a French traveller who came to India in 1666, learnt from his Indian informer that the Mughal empire consisted of twenty provinces. But the fact that the provinces overlay smaller and distinct entities seems to be suggested by Thevenot's comment that "I had rather call them Governments, and say that every Government contains several Provinces."[32] Another dimension was the social and geographical space between dominant political formations. In such spaces were probably to be found polities and communities which retained their separate identity even while being linked to or dominated by more powerful polities. The geographical location of the Bhils and the structure of their society has been seen in this manner, and the importance of the location of "peripheral ethnic communities with their homeland and its particular resources" has been emphasised.[33]

The various regions of the Indian subcontinent have therefore long represented different political economies that have time and again been politically and militarily united to form empires. Many of these regions, as indicated earlier, themselves incorporated diverse smaller socio-economic systems. Geographical diversity required specialisation, which in turn entailed a basic "difference" between communities. Most tribal areas differed economically from agrarian society on account of their greater reliance on pastoralism and forest produce rather than intensive agriculture. At the cultural level, the most important differentiating feature of tribal societies was the absence or weakness of a Brahmanised social structure. In the more extensive tribal areas these differences could possibly form the basis of a new regional identity, notwithstanding inter-tribal differences which were probably of reduced priority by being seen as matters of

---

[31] Abul Fazl 1979: III, 109.

[32] Thevenot 1686: Part III, Book I, Chapter III, 5.

[33] For the Bhils, Roy Burman 1993: 200–1; for peripheral communities, Smith 1987: 94.

"internal" negotiation.³⁴ The trope "awakening from sleep", used by new nationalisms in Europe to explain their social upheavals, might also partially describe the attitude of some of the leaders of regional movements in India. This awakening was closely linked to language consciousness, though logically it could also incorporate other cultural indicators of identity.³⁵ Even where striking geographical diversities did not lead to marked occupational differences, there emerged agricultural zones which "over time became ethnic zones and zones for dominant caste alliances". Ludden has further argued that the "symbolic identification of a caste with a particular territory would, of course, deepen with time as marriage networks become interwoven on the basis of status, power and interest inland . . . The identity of social groups and land would interpenetrate."³⁶ This could often involve the subordination of smaller and different areas and people by a regional elite. It has been suggested that Bengal, Tamilnadu, and Maharashtra are regions where, respectively, the *bhadralok*, Tamil Brahmins, and Chitpawan Brahmans formed regional elites.³⁷ Specific definitions of identity asserted by dominant social groups would nevertheless be challenged by new social forces that arose in the region from time to time.

It is quite possible that the regional elite could also propel a region (or in some instances ethnie) towards some sort of nationhood – following what Anthony Smith calls "a triple movement: from isolation to activism, from quietism to mobilization and from culture to politics."³⁸ This entry into politics by a region and its elite rules out the possibility of a return to the original state of isolation. It also encourages similar reassertions from other ethnic identities seeking to influence national policy and obtain greater benefit for themselves.³⁹ Mobilisation for such causes can often follow ethnic or lingual lines, especially in societies that become increasingly subject

---

³⁴ Basu 1992: 60.
³⁵ Anderson 1991: 195.
³⁶ Ludden 1989: 63.
³⁷ Basu 1992: 76.
³⁸ Smith 1987: 154.
³⁹ Ibid.: 156–7; Chadda 1997: 51.

to the intervention of external political and economic forces.⁴⁰ Support to the regional elite would probably come from a society that found itself alienated from its surroundings and forced at the same time to engage in politics to ensure its survival. Under such circumstances, "the stakes to politics . . . are no less than a recovery of self, of meaning and identity in a society where lay, tacit and local knowledge are systematically denied."⁴¹ The rapid globalisation of society and economy has now made the problem immensely more complex. But it has also compelled scholars to revisit the relationship between territory, environment, and identity.

Theoretical Trends in Mountain Studies

Unlike France and England, where human beings were supposed to have the upper hand over their natural environment, in Switzerland, at a time of considerable social uncertainty, people sought guidance from a rugged example of nature, which they found in their Alpine landscape. Intellectuals and portions of the intelligentsia portrayed this landscape as a relentless force capable of determining the character of their nation and of its inhabitants – an ideological pattern that I have termed the naturalisation of the nation.⁴²

It is within the broad universally relevant concepts of physical environment, identity, and region elaborated above that the study of mountain societies in general, and the Himalaya in particular, needs to be situated. For purposes of convenience I wish to reiterate here, in some detail, arguments that I have made elsewhere.⁴³ Scholars working on mountain societies have often assumed that mountainous physiography is, by itself, reason enough to delineate highlands as entirely distinct geographical regions. Another associated assumption is that mountainous terrains exert an extraordinary influence on humans and therefore nurture societies that see themselves as quite distinct from those in the lowlands. Even unconnected and distant

---

⁴⁰ Basu 1992: 12, 116.
⁴¹ Dickens 1996: 170.
⁴² Zimmer 1998: 659.
⁴³ Singh 2011.

highland cultures have sometimes, therefore, been viewed as sharing more with each other than with their neighbours in the plains. Briefly, mountains and mountain people all over the world are regarded as clearly different from people in the lowlands. Peculiarly, and not always for logical reasons, this difference has now come to form the basis of perceived similarities.

The apparently close relationship between man and environment in the mountains prompted anthropologists to attempt a comparison between different mountain societies. It was expected that comparable ecological conditions would evoke similar social responses. A broad comparative overview of the Alps, the Himalaya, and the Andes was attempted by Rhoades and Thompson. Their sweeping comparison was in contrast to the "tunnel vision" of earlier Alpine researchers who, focussing on specific cases and small communities, had refrained from making comparisons, prompting Rhoades and Thompson to call such an approach "ecological particularism".[44] Their study, by contrast, found a striking similarity in agro-pastoral transhumance, in the existence of fragmented landholdings at different altitude levels, and in the institutional allocation of both private and communal control over land and natural resources. Another remarkable resemblance was the manner in which even small communities constituted local authority and ensured responsive governance. There also existed obvious differences.

While the number of cultural studies increased impressively, it was the ecological significance of mountains that came to the fore. Mountain ecologies came to indicate a multifaceted interaction between people and their physical environment.[45] When Guillet first compared the Himalaya and the Andes, several attempts had already been made to grapple with the problem of the man–montane environment interface. Guillet concluded that because of the close link between social relations and material life on the one hand and the "production process" on the other, appropriate generalisations about environment and culture could be derived.[46] The approaches

[44] Rhoades and Thompson 1975: 536.
[45] Guillet 1983a: 561–7.
[46] Ibid.: 562–3.

that he examined include "geoecology", "vertical control", "cultural adaptation", and "*alpwirtschaft*" (agro-pastoral economy of the mountains based on local transhumance). He failed, however, to include history, political economy, kinship, value systems, religion, and several other aspects in his overview. It is now recognised that the "static and equilibrium view" needs to be discarded, and that the interaction between ecological and social sciences should become more dynamic and flexible. Scoones has pointed towards certain potential areas of "new ecological thinking" and indicated how this is beginning to influence the spheres of ecological anthropology, political ecology, and the old nature–culture debate – amongst other areas of research.[47] Guillet's self-stated purpose was "to show parallels in ecological adaptation in the Andes and the Himalayas".[48] Other important factors that could have contributed towards a more complete understanding were not brought into perspective. Guillet partly redressed this imbalance subsequently, admitting the "importance of incorporating history and political economy into human ecology", even though he focussed primarily on "montane productions strategy".[49]

The importance of "ecological adaptation" for explaining the actions of mountain people appears overstated and therefore needs modification. This has, to an extent, been done in the context of Alpine history. Mathieu has argued that "Even livestock economy and *Alpwirtschaft*, despite being cited as prime examples of adaptation, are subject to historical relativity."[50] He also suggested that "Of the two contexts – ecological, the one, and hierarchical-social, the other – which, according to Eric R. Wolf, held the key to understanding differences in family structures, the latter is far more important."[51]

It would be simplistic to argue that because mountain societies are somehow "different" from those of the lowlands, it is possible to

[47] Scoones 1999: 479, 484–6.
[48] Guillet 1983b: 571.
[49] Orlove and Guillet 1985: 10, 15–16.
[50] Mathieu 1999: 308.
[51] Mathieu 2000: 73.

provide a common theoretical model explaining this "difference". On the other hand, the search for comparability on several other important aspects of mountain life has been more realistic. Therefore, ecological, environmental, and livelihood issues now occupy considerable academic space.[52] The study of nomadism, urbanisation, and religion in the mountains, too, has attracted the attention of scholars.[53] This search for comparability has simultaneously nurtured the exploration for commonalities. International research trends have tended to highlight the larger number of similarities that connect mountain people in different parts of the world.

The Himalaya: Similarities and Diversities

> Beyond Kashmir there are countless peoples and hordes, *parganas* and cultivated lands, in the mountains. As far as Bengal, as far indeed as the shore of the great ocean, the peoples are without break. About this procession of men no-one has been able to give authentic information in reply to our queries and investigations. So far people have been saying that they call these hill-men *Kas*.[54]

The general tendency to juxtapose highlands in opposition to their "other" (i.e. the lowlands), apparent in the writings of Babur, is equally applicable to scholarship on the Himalaya. Five decades ago Berreman argued that the lower Himalaya – from Kashmir to eastern Nepal, where people had common cultural and historical traditions – could be considered a "culture area". He also argued that the people of this area "are considered by themselves and by others to be ethnically distinct", and spelt out several distinguishing characteristics that separated the Paharis (hill people) from the inhabitants of the plains.[55] Among these were the nature of inter-caste relations, marriage customs, the status accorded to women, religious practices, and dietary habits. Berreman noticed that the layering of multiple castes was not to be found in

---

[52] *An Appeal for the Mountains* 1992; *The State of the World's Mountains* 1992; Messerli and Ives 1997.

[53] Rao and Casimir 2003; *Histoire des Alpes* 2008; Bernbaum 1990 and 1997; *Mountain Research and Development* 2006.

[54] Babur 1979: 484.

[55] Berreman 1960: 774, 775.

the hills, where a simpler twofold division existed between the untouchables on the one hand and the Brahmins and Rajputs on the other. All castes here were unaverse to the consumption of meat and liquor. Unlike the lowlands, practices in mountain societies – such as bride-price, polyandry, divorce by mutual consent, widow remarriage, etc. – were widely acceptable. Hill women were active in various aspects of village life.[56] Berreman emphasised that within this milieu even the occasional contact between hill people was "more effective in accomplishing communication than more frequent contacts between Pahari and non-Pahari. The reason is that Paharis meet one another to a large extent on common cultural ground and on terms of equality. They understand one another not only in language but in total behavior patterns."[57]

Despite the fact that they appear to be metaphorically large in the popular imagination of most South Asian societies, the Himalaya have remained marginal in almost every other respect. For long, little was known about the region. This was partly because it was never drawn into the vortex of mainstream political processes in South Asia and was often the refuge of exiles and rebels. Economically, of course, the mountains were quite inconsequential to empire building when compared to the fertile North Indian plains. Fisher has pointed out that the centre versus periphery question runs through all other issues, and has been used by "Himalayanists" to challenge the "assumed centrality of lowland India or China to the north".[58] In fact, one might even suggest that the perception of the Himalaya being secluded and forbidding is an essential ingredient of the image in which these mountains have been cast. It was only traders, ascetics, or incorrigible adventurers who probably found it meaningful to enter such inhospitable terrain.

While a mystique has evolved around the Himalaya, linking them to mainstream beliefs of formal Hinduism in South Asia, this extensive mountain range is simultaneously considered (perhaps rightly) home to heterodox cults and nonconformist social practices.

[56] Ibid.: 777.
[57] Ibid.: 783.
[58] Fisher 1985: 108.

Over the last four or five decades, numerous anthropological studies have reinforced this perception. Fisher pointed out that scholars have tended to emphasise the particular and distinguishing characteristics of Himalayan societies. These characteristics, interestingly, are the ones to which Berreman had called attention in 1960. A considerable part of such research has, therefore, propped up typecast images of shamanism, polyandry, ecological determinism, and other peculiarities considered representative of mountain societies. There has also been an academic preoccupation with the study of isolated village communities, ethnic groups, and the caste–tribe engagement.[59] The singular effort of trying to differentiate mountains from plains has encouraged the emergence of a somewhat oversimplified picture, even though a broad differentiation of cultural zones within the Himalaya has been recognised. Berreman demarcated four distinct traditions in the Himalaya: (1) South Asian and (2) South West Asian, both termed Indo-Iranian; (3) Tibetan and (4) South East Asian, both termed Tibeto-Burman. The above description of Paharis would apply primarily to the South Asian tradition.[60] It goes without saying, however, that the Himalaya are manifestly more complex. Equally multifaceted are the social and religious institutions that have been stereotyped by scholars and made emblematic of Himalayan societies.

Even if we admit that mountain societies share "common cultural ground", does it necessarily follow that they have identical aspirations and ways of thinking? Studies of "non-Western societies" often generalise and impose a kind of uniformity on them. Peasant societies, too, are frequently subjected to a stereotyping that emphasises "typical characteristics" that serve to differentiate them.[61] While stereotyping gives the false impression of being useful in categorising different kinds of societies, generalisation conceals the multiplicity of social groups, practices, and worldviews that form part of these societies.

Though he emphasised a broad Pahari distinctiveness and recognised large cultural zones in the Himalaya, Berreman pointed to variations even in fairly small territories within the mountains. He

[59] Ibid.: 105–6.
[60] Berreman 1965; Karan and Mather 1976.
[61] Pelto and Pelto: 1975.

argued that these distinct cultural areas had evolved because varying degrees of isolation resulted in "greater opportunity for development of locally variant cultural forms". He saw that the vast expanse of the lower Himalaya was made up of smaller areas of "localised cultural variability". On the other hand, within these smaller areas was to be found "comparative cultural homogeneity across caste lines".[62] There was, in his view, a causal connection between culture areas (and the changes they underwent) on the one hand, and their varying degrees of isolation on the other.[63] He went on to suggest that "except for a very small educated elite, they think of themselves as citizens of nation states only in a very vague sort of way. Their identification tends to be with the people of their own immediate area, who speak their own dialect and with whom they interact frequently."[64] Internally, therefore, the Himalaya has always remained politically and culturally fragmented.

Even where recognisable political unity has been achieved, internal diversities have persisted. About Nepal (covering about 900 km of mountain territory), for example, Fisher argued that though the country had existed as an integrated political entity for more than two centuries, it encompassed "ethnic groups speaking literally dozens of mutually unintelligible languages, following a wide variety of religious beliefs and rituals, with different kinship and marriage systems, and dramatically contrasting ecological adaptations."[65] This is definitely true for the rest of the Himalaya. Layered diversities of an impressively complex nature can sometimes cause tension between different levels of representation: ranging from the broadly regional to the specifically local.

Is "Zomia" a Renewed Search for a Larger Commonality?

Diversities within the Himalaya have not, however, discouraged scholars in their search for commonalities that might possibly define

[62] Berreman 1960: 774, 778, 782.
[63] Ibid.: 788, 791.
[64] Berreman 1963: 290, 292.
[65] Fisher 1985: 101.

mountainous regions. In fact, the search has gone beyond nationally defined studies and moved towards a macro perspective on mountain regions that transgresses the territorial boundaries of countries. A recent development is van Schendel's argument that the enormous expanse of Asian highlands (including the Himalaya, the Tibetan Plateau, and the uplands of the South East Asian peninsula) becomes a noticeable region if certain characteristics and comparable historical experiences common to marginalised mountain areas are underscored.[66] The most significant aspect of these highlands, he contended, was their location at the periphery of large states that constantly sought to dominate them. While they reflected immensely greater cultural diversity than the more homogenised lowlands, all highlands were in contrast far less populated than the latter. He gave the name "Zomia" to this extensive and impressive macro-region that he had delineated, thereby generating considerable excitement and controversy.

This bold initiative received further support when James Scott made Zomia – both as a physical space and as an idea – the conceptual centre of his book, *The Art of Not Being Governed: An Anarchist History of Upland Southeast Asia* (2009). Scott's study is confined to the South East Asian Massif and does not extend to the whole of Zomia as defined by van Schendel. It is, nevertheless, extensive and includes the upland territories of several countries. Scott elaborates an interesting and provocative thesis out of van Schendel's original arguments, raising issues that are theoretically germane across academic disciplines and empirically relevant beyond the region of his focus. His pivotal contention is that the more significant organised human activities in the highlands were part of an endeavour to escape state domination, usually centred in the lowlands. Family organisation, community institutions, and economic strategies in the upland regions were, therefore, not determined simply by environmental conditions or cultural considerations. They were largely the result of certain options available after one initial conscious political choice had been made by people in the highlands.[67] This singular choice was to escape the stranglehold

---

[66] van Schendel 2002.
[67] Scott 2009: x, xi.

of powerful agrarian states by seeking shelter in the mountains. These marginalised areas of refuge, he argues, served as "shatter zones" adjoining states, havens where people were insulated from buffetings by the oppressive and violent processes of "state-making and state-unmaking".[68] A history of long-term resistance to state domination gave to highland societies the ability to change and adjust within a short span of time – "turn on a dime", as Scott puts it.[69] To sustain their resistance, they needed a social structure that could be easily "disaggregated and reassembled", and to achieve this purpose a "mixed portfolio of subsistence techniques yields a mixed portfolio of social structures that can easily be invoked for political as well as economic advantage."[70] Three key ideas were critical constituents of how hill people perceived themselves and their society: "equality, autonomy, and mobility".[71] The adoption of an oral tradition was yet another method of escaping state control. The virtual absence of writing and texts gave them "freedom of maneuver in history, genealogy, and legibility that frustrates state routines."[72]

For historians, however, this abandonment or refusal of writing has meant an inadequacy of source material. To overcome the problem, scholars have attempted to use oral tradition and folklore. Scott, however, argues that the ambiguity created by oral methods of remembering has given to mountain societies "multiple histories they can deploy singly or in combination depending on the circumstances." It was "in their interest to keep as many of their options open as possible, and what kind of history to have is one of those options. They have as much history as they require."[73]

Not surprisingly, a full special issue of the *Journal of Global History* is devoted to discussing the question of Zomia.[74] In his perceptive editorial introduction there, Jean Michaud stresses the need for historians and anthropologists to overcome disciplinary prejudices

[68] Ibid.: 7.
[69] Ibid.: 24.
[70] Ibid.: 211.
[71] Ibid.: 217.
[72] Ibid.: 226.
[73] Ibid.: 329, 330.
[74] *Journal of Global History* 2010, no. 5.

and collaborate in understanding marginalised societies and areas.[75] These regions have been neglected by historians, he says, because of their suspicion of oral sources, though anthropologists have listened to the remembered histories of such societies quite enthusiastically. The idea of Zomia is significant not only because it occupies a large geographical space that is both transnational and trans-regional in character, but also because it connects the political systems of different adjoining areas.[76] The great human diversity – cultural, social, economic, and political – within this expansive zone is obvious, and therefore questions arise about the necessity of conjuring up a region that has no common binding factors. Certainly, none of the numerous and marginalised mountain societies living here would possibly visualise any place on such a grand scale. It is argued, therefore, that the concept might serve better as an academic device: one that not only fulfils the "need for a macroscopic vision of large portions of humanity spreading over vast territories, but also of a desire to transcend political borders and disciplinary boundaries, in order to assess the current and future state of local societies differently."[77] Only time will tell whether Zomia (theoretical or empirical) and the notions of freedom and diversity that it is built upon will survive, or whether it will become more intimately bound to the polities of nation-states and a rapidly globalising world.

Irrespective of the outcome, the present discussion stimulated by Zomia offers an opportunity to researchers of different disciplines in the Himalayan region to review the perspectives that they have adopted. While sociologists and anthropologists have often ignored the political processes of state-making, historians have failed to recognise the significance of those elements of cultural, religious, and economic activity that remain outside the state domain. An appropriate balance of these two viewpoints might possibly enable us to develop a theoretical model acceptable across disciplines. Through her empirical study of the little-known Thangmis of the Central

---

[75] Michaud 2010: 187–93.
[76] Ibid.: 194.
[77] Ibid.: 213.

Himalaya, Shneiderman has explored the theoretical construct of the "non-state space" that is fundamental to the idea of Zomia.[78] Though she concludes on a somewhat cautious note, the structure of her study and its arguments implicitly accept the analytical framework of Zomia as a useful academic construct. Giersch, on the other hand, is somewhat more sceptical about the absence-of-state argument in Scott. His concept of Zomia is a space across which an intricate network of trade prospered, and which simultaneously facilitated the authority of states to "act at a distance". Not only were large parts of Zomia therefore penetrated in some manner by powerful states from outside, a multilayered power structure of local elites too came into existence at the local level.[79] Quite apparently, then, scholars have begun to explore and examine the concept of Zomia, not because it offers clear answers but because it raises significant questions of general relevance.

There is certainly much that historians can disagree about, not only in relation to the idea of Zomia, but also on the anthropologist's approach to oral traditions, the geographer's deference to the pre-eminence of environmental conditions, or the sociologist's disregard for the historical origins of social institutions. Yet I think it is time for us to admit that the cross-fertilisation of theories and methods amongst disciplines has become increasingly critical – especially for historians who see their discipline as an engagement with long-term changes in the human condition rather than as a testimony of elites (so unfairly over-represented in traditional historical sources). For the historians of the Himalayan region, more specifically, this seems to me a matter of great urgency.

---

[78] Shneiderman 2010: 289–312.
[79] Giersch 2010: 218, 229–30, 231, 236.

3

Defining Community

Territory and Transformation in the Western Himalaya

"In the majority of communities, the bulk of their populations remained in the area of their original or adopted territory... Their modes of production; patterns of settlement and folk cultures spring from their diurnal round of work and leisure, itself formed out of their ceaseless encounter with a particular environment."[1]

"Places in the past were peopled. Their changing landscapes contained within them social conflict and social cooperation among individuals and groups; and these relations should be seen as a vital part of the making of these landscapes."[2]

A set of physical and geographical conditions does not by itself constitute a territory – much as a mere grouping of people at a particular place does not create a community. A geographical area becomes a "territory" as a result of social thought and activity. Conversely, the material realities of geography influence in great measure the nature of activities and social organisation a society adopts. It has been observed that "a historical understanding of landscape formation is necessary to link the qualities of a particular landscape to both their social meanings and the technological means

Originally published as "Defining Community: A Historical Study of Territory and Transformation in the Western Himalaya", in Smadja 2014.

[1] Smith 1987: 183.
[2] Baker 1984: 27.

by which they are controlled."[3] With such understanding, a more explicitly recognised community comes into view, and it seems therefore that the emergence of community and the configuration of territory often occur simultaneously. By discussing one without the other we risk ignoring their essentially interdependent and complementary nature. The processes through which ideas of territory and community come into existence, and the manner in which they are perpetuated or altered, are thus inextricably connected.

How a community constructs its territory depends on how it structures itself. Individuals and families, Godelier suggests, have necessarily to be part of a community in order to "reproduce the conditions of existence of this community while producing their own". For this purpose, he argues, "space is distributed among these communities, each of them exploiting a territory whose bounds are known to the neighbours."[4] He nevertheless recognises that some societies do not claim any territory as their own, while some share their territorial resources with others.[5] It seems therefore that the nature of a geographical area and the necessity of evolving methods for procuring a livelihood from it caused societies to organise themselves variously. Yet from another viewpoint it can be argued that it was the diverse forms of social organisation that compelled societies to search for and claim the resources within different kinds of territories.

Mountain topography, by its very nature, provides to observers an apparent – clearly visual – depiction of interaction between human activity and physiographical space. One is tempted to believe the eye as it traces the likely contours within which community and territory might have interacted over the course of their historical development. But obvious appearances are often deceptive. Ideas and beliefs are no less significant influences upon the community than the compulsions of geography. In organising its physical surroundings, a community's response is often implicitly ideological – encompassing polity and social structure. What a particular landscape or territory means to it

[3] Kobayashi 1989: 164, 177.
[4] Godelier 1986: 54, 55.
[5] Ibid.: 86.

is as much a matter of physical realities as a question of mentalities and interpretations.

Small communities, especially in isolated areas, probably needed to develop a high degree of economic self-sufficiency. In pre-modern times this self-sufficiency was perhaps combined with considerable political autonomy. Such freedom is unlikely to have been enjoyed by individuals. In medieval ways of thinking, personal autonomy was perhaps not even a properly articulated concept. Allegiance to the "family, the village or the gild" preceded the notion of individualism.[6] Medieval law and polity recognised and interacted with not the individual but the group (family, community, etc.) as the primary and most significant entity. A village, therefore, was represented by a community whose members acted collectively, and only through the community or the social group was survival in the village possible. In turn, the ability of the community to retain its sphere of influence was likely to have been inversely related to a central authority's ability to assert power and restrict that of the community. As Nisbet puts it, "the solidarity of each functional group was possible only in an environment of authority where central power was weak and fluctuating."[7] And Anthony Smith sees the pre-modern *ethnie* as "usually made up of numerous clans or villages who practice nomadic pastoralism or a local, self-subsistent agriculture."[8]

Nevertheless, the authority of a community could hardly have been constructed entirely as an ideology of opposition to a hypothetical or real central authority. There were other means of creating authority. In settled agricultural or agro-pastoral villages, landholding families usually formed the core around which the community was consolidated.[9] Local histories were constructed to legitimise the dominance of landholding groups. Many pre-modern societies adopted this method of rationalising social control, among whom those in the Himalaya were no exception. Rooted as they were in a mixture of fact, myth, and legend, historicised "memories" of the community formed the basis of its worldview. Customs, norms, social

---

[6] Nisbet 1962: 81.
[7] Ibid.: 83, 84–5.
[8] Smith 1987: 31.
[9] Habib 1999; Kasturi 2002: 45.

hierarchies, and a host of other notions central to the integrity and survival of the community were derived from this worldview. These created "memories", or histories, also became the channel through which the local community linked and described itself to a world that lay beyond the limited confines of the village.[10] They enabled the community to locate itself in a larger – invariably unequal – grid of social and political relationships.

For present purposes, it may not be relevant to dwell upon the internal functioning of the village community. Of greater interest is the relationship that existed between the community and its constituting lineages and clans on the one hand, and the larger polity within which these operated on the other. It may be useful to understand how the lineages or clans effectively functioned as political organisations and thus successfully asserted explicit territorial claims, however small.

Majumdar's detailed study of polyandrous Jaunsari society (in present-day Uttarakhand) has attempted to reveal how the "lineage, locally known as *aal* or *thok*" served as the criterion for dividing society into groups. It was, he says, "on the basis of these groups that the villages have been established and maintained."[11] He makes a distinction between clan (for which he uses the term *gotra*) and lineage (what he calls *aal*), and argues that in Jaunsar the clan was completely absent. However, Majumdar comes to this conclusion because he mistranslates "*gotra*" as "clan", for it appears that the organisation of society along clans was important in the Himalayan region, especially considering the fact that large parts of it were politically dominated by a clan-based Khas population. Within the village, families belonging to a common sub-lineage resided in a common locality called *bhera*. Several villages were grouped together in a politico-administrative unit called *khat*.

Even as the affairs of the *khat* were managed primarily by the *khat sayana* (wise elder) they were usually done in consultation with the council (*khumri*) of village elders. Further, and most importantly, the temple of the village god was the central institution through which the collective identity of the community was constructed and

[10] Levine 1988: 21.
[11] Majumdar 1962: 70.

reinforced.[12] A more appropriate spelling of the word *bhera*, as used by Majumdar, would perhaps be *berha*. In the Himachal region, the village council is called *khumbli*.

In the adjoining mountains of Himachal, peasant society was strikingly similar. Far-flung hamlets with adjoining patches of cultivated land were too small to form viable administrative or political units of their own. They were therefore grouped to form a larger unit called the *ghori*. This did not, however, rule out the existence of some form of individual leadership in the village. Fraser, who travelled into the Shimla hill region in the early nineteenth century, refers to the fact that "In every village there is a man to whom they pay great deference, and to whom they refer all disputes; who, in short, is their chief, and who goes by the name of the *Seana* . . ."[13] Kashyap suggested that the smaller unit, in terms of social organisation, below the *khund* was the *barind*. This *barind*, he argued, was headed by a *sayana*.[14] In the Bashahr area, several hamlets grouped together were called a *ghori*, but in smaller states such a unit was called a *pargana*.[15] Sharma was of the view that a *ghori* consisted of ten or twelve villages.[16] Apart from the fact that in British times each *ghori* had a *lambardar* to look after its affairs (especially the task of revenue collection), a common grazing ground, shared by several hamlets of the *ghori*, was often an important integrating factor.[17] For an agro-pastoral society, the control and efficient management of pastures was a matter of survival. Not surprisingly, therefore, the *ghori* appears to have been a territorial unit dominated by a community of peasant-pastoralists. It was a community that could, and did, mobilise from within itself a group of warriors, or *khund*, to protect its interests.[18] In Kulu the comparable unit (though more explicitly for revenue purposes) was the *phati*.

[12] Ibid.: 25, 35.
[13] Fraser 1982: 217.
[14] Kashyap 2000: 120–1.
[15] *Shimla SG* 1911: Bashahr, 42–3.
[16] Sharma 1990: 136.
[17] *SHSG* 1911: Bashahr, 65.
[18] Sax 2006: 120–34; Sutherland 2006: 82–119.

II

The aggressive assertion of territorial claims by competing clans or communities through the use of force was only part of the story. Permanent control over an area – even at the local level – required legitimisation through a long-drawn but more widely acceptable social process. Gradually, the cosmic view of the community began to reflect the physiographical features and natural peculiarities of the area in which it resided. Occupation of territory was ideologically reinforced and legitimised through the mediating role of deities. Stories about the landscape and the supernatural actions of local gods were woven together into mythical sagas that passed for history. Through the power of myth and legend, communities legitimised their claim to territories. This simultaneously gave to deities "an identity and a place of their own". Western Himalayan myths about how deities acquired a domain for themselves often begin with their accidental discovery in a forest or a field. This is followed by a period of search, migration, and successful struggle for a territory and a people to rule over. Then comes the delineation of territories and subject village communities, and the creation of hierarchies. The new (i.e. now prevailing) socio-political order is thus seen as the outcome of a contest between gods: something that ordinary mortals could question only at great peril.[19] Moreover, the naming of many community gods after local physiological features converted the surrounding space into a meaningful place: one that *belonged* to a particular community, and the resources of which could justifiably be used by it.[20] Man, god, and nature were thus inextricably linked in a relationship that was, and remains, inherently political.

The institution of village gods thrived across the entire Indian subcontinent. Each local deity resided amidst its followers, often in a tiny village domain. Thus were created thousands of territorial spheres that consisted of either a single hamlet or a few closely associated villages.[21] Singh notes in his report that, "every village has a temple

---

[19] Rose 1970: I; Singh 2006: 328–35; Sutherland 2006: 91.
[20] Lovell 1998b: 55.
[21] Singh 1901: 49 Sec. 29.

of the *deota*. One *deota* cannot go into the area of another *deota*." This is perhaps an exaggeration, though it would certainly be true for *deotas* belonging to feuding village communities. The ubiquitous village god (*gram-devta*) was concerned primarily with the everyday "facts of village life", such as local rivalries, personal misfortune, and disease. It exercised no control over the more distant "great world forces" that impersonally shaped the destiny of multitudes.[22] The small gods exhibited entirely human characteristics – they were quick to take offence and become angry, but they were also easy to please through the sacrifice of animals.[23] Most importantly, the priests of the village gods were only occasionally drawn from Brahmin castes.[24] Yet, if exigencies required, Sanskritic symbols and rituals were used to portray these clearly local deities as manifestations of powerful Brahmanical gods.[25] There existed, as it were, two easily discernible socio-religious territories. One was the locality of the village god, non-Brahmin priests, and a constituency of small peasant communities. The other was the larger world of the Sanskritic gods, of Brahmin priests and ideologues, and of prosperous and powerful dominant classes.[26] Because of the unequal scale and significance of the concerns they addressed (and the kind of people they involved), the two "territories" seemed to emphasise difference.

We know, of course, that these were not exclusive zones. They interacted, merged, or separated from time to time and in different situations. So difficult indeed were they to demarcate, and so remarkable was the flexibility and dynamism they possessed that it seems only appropriate to regard them as part of a hierarchical continuum.[27] These socio-religious spheres were redefined as they followed the changing concerns of the "community". Conversely, the notion and description of community could be altered to correspond to a delineated territory. In effect, community and territory were both redefined as one moved up or down the social and spatial continuum.

[22] Whitehead 1921: 16–17.
[23] Ibid.: 17, 30.
[24] Ibid.: 30, 43–4; Srinivas 1965: 181; Klass 1995: 83.
[25] Srinivas 1965: 184.
[26] Ibid.: 60, 181, 185.
[27] Singh 2006.

A common linking factor, however, appears to have been the use of a religious idiom to articulate socio-political objectives.

There were, at the village level, countervailing forces contesting for domination. Srinivas has argued that while "caste has a tendency to stress horizontal ties", the economic compulsions of agrarian life pushed small communities in the direction of "vertical", village-based solidarity. While caste loyalties encouraged links between similar caste groups in different villages, the need to organise agricultural labour required that the collective interests of the village community be accorded priority. Long-lasting feuds between communities may possibly have been rooted in the primacy accorded to village loyalty. Srinivas suggests that only with the political integration brought about under the rajas did caste become an important political factor.[28] Community and territory, therefore, responded to historical and political developments occurring at a higher level, and were both gradually transformed in the process.

This shifting relationship between community, territory, and state can be illustrated by examples from the oral history of the Shimla hill region. Local accounts are embedded with collective memories of how village communities established new village gods, replaced old ones, or carried them along as they settled in distant places. The most common method of creating or legitimising a socio-religious territory was for a community to establish in its area the image of the principal state deity. But the new image would often be known by a name other than that of the principal deity – preferably after the person responsible for its establishment. In Keonthal state, Deo Chand, one of the ancestors of the Khanoga clan of Kanet peasants, installed a newly made image of the state god, Junga, in his village. This new local *deota* came to be named "Deo Chand" after the Khanoga ancestor and was ranked as one of the many gods subordinate to Junga. It is, interestingly, recorded that the new *deota* was established after the loan of the original Junga image to conduct a religious ceremony was refused to this ancestor of the Khanoga clan.[29] Similarly, the Chhibar clan of Kanets in Jatil *pargana* installed a Junga image in a separate temple,

---

[28] Srinivas 1965: 43, 69.
[29] Rose 1970: I, 447.

as did the Brahmins of Bhakar at a place called Koti, and the Rawal clan at Gaum.[30] We also have the instance of a smaller village god (Shaneti) being similarly established by the Shainti clan of Kanets as their own separate god. There are without doubt likely to have been many more such cases in the region as a whole.

Equally fascinating was the "displacement" of one god by another. Rose recorded the legend of how *deota* Junga became the state deity of the small principality of Keonthal after successfully displacing the now forgotten older god (Jipur) and taking over his temples and territory.[31] Even at the village level, folk legends record instances of such replacement. By implication, this was also a usurpation of the displaced god's domain. The cult of Kalaur in *pargana* Ratesh (Keonthal) that was associated with Brahmins was displaced by a *devi* (goddess) brought by two Kanets from the state of Sirmur. A god from Suket replaced *deota* Dharta in Jamrot *pargana* (the hill area of Patiala state) and this marked the beginning of the popular cult of Manuni. The appearance of new gods and their growing popularity perhaps indicate important underlying social change.[32] The growing popularity of a new cult at the expense of an older deity was not simply a cosmic reordering. It involved the shifting of social and political allegiances, and the redistribution of territories and real communities. For instance, tradition records that an image of Kaneti *deota* was stolen from Kawar by a section of the peasantry and first brought to Dodra. It was thereafter carried to the village of Dagon in Keonthal state. Here the new god, Kaneti, took over the temple of Jipur – the older *deota* – and also won over the *wazir* of Keonthal and the Bhaler clan that had previously been followers of Jipur.[33]

---

[30] Ibid.: I, 447, 448.

[31] Ibid.: I, 443. It is likely that the displaced god was Sipur and not Jipur. The temple of Sipur is located in the neighbouring principality of Koti with which the State of Keonthal has a close relationship. Legend has it that *deota* Junga was once a prince of Koti who disappeared in the forest, and was discovered later as a *deota*. There would, therefore, be reason enough for Junga to make a complete break with Sipur (who was closely associated with Koti) in order to establish his independence in the separate principality of Keonthal.

[32] Ibid.: I, 445.

[33] Ibid.: I, 446.

Stories of people and deities migrating from one place to another are also commonly told all over the hills. For most village communities, their initial arrival at the place where the village stands seems to mark a new beginning. When Kaneti *deota* travelled from distant Dodra to the territory of Keonthal, an entire community of followers – Kanets, Kolis, and Turis – accompanied him. These castes represented the main social sections that were to be found in a west Himalayan village. The state of Koti, adjoining Shimla, was quite characteristically home to gods brought in by their followers from different places. Klainu Deo of Kiar belonged originally to Kulu, while Sip Deo (Sipur) came with the ruling family of Koti from the Kangra region. Sharali Deo (of Sharal village) and Dhanu Deo (of Chhabrog) travelled along with their followers from the adjacent Keonthal state where they had formerly resided. Korgan Deo (of Chhabalri village) was brought from Sirmur by one of the princes of Koti and Nual Deo accompanied the people of Kogi village when they migrated to Kogi *pargana* from Suket state.[34] This is not merely a recounting of gods who migrated. More importantly, it signifies the movement of groups of people from one place to another. Such movements often required the reiteration of old, or the reconstruction of new, social identities. Local and community gods were used not only for this purpose, but also to legitimise the occupation of new territory. In the process, new communities emerged and new territories were delineated.

In large parts of the western Himalaya, it was through the local *deota* that village communities asserted a great degree of political autonomy. The local *deota* was often seen as a "ruler" in his own right, reigning over his followers, as would a king over his subjects. Collective – albeit unequal – participation in the periodic ceremonies of the village temple forged the community into a political unit.[35] For the Kulu villages we have the detailed description that Lyall made in 1872. Many of the important temples owned extensive and fertile agricultural land. They also possessed a *bhandar* (granary) where the *deota's* share of the grain from his land and other contributions of his

[34] *SHSG* 1911: Koti, 8.
[35] Sutherland 2006: 84; Sax 2006: 7–13.

followers were deposited. Several temples had large establishments. Lyall notes:

> Some of the large shrines have large fixed establishments, a *kardar* or manager, an accountant, one or more *pujaris* or priests, several musicians, several *gur* or *chelas*, i.e. interpreters of the oracle, standard-bearers, torch-bearers, blacksmith, carpenter, florist, watchman, messenger, carriers of loads & c., to all of whom *barto* or land rent-free in lieu of pay, are assigned out of the temple endowment. Most have a *kardar*, a *gur*, and musicians.[36]

He also observed that the village temple in Kulu was "owned, served and managed" by the peasantry of the area over which its *deota* wielded influence. This could range from a small hamlet to an entire *kothi* (a revenue division consisting of several villages). Notably, however, the influence of Brahmins – so common in the lower hills and the plains – was almost entirely absent. Most of the temples had for centuries been the recipients of revenue-free land (*muafi*) from the raja or state. What this meant in actual terms Lyall clearly understood when he prepared his revenue settlement report for the Kulu territory of Kangra district. He commented perceptively that "the *zamindars* of a hamlet or hamlets, who are themselves the only worshippers of the shrine and who distribute the office of *kardar*, *pujari*, *chela* & c, among themselves, eat up the proceeds in periodic feasts. The *zamindars* themselves are in fact, in some degree, the real *muafidars*."[37] Through their close association with the *deota* and the temple, the dominant sections of the peasantry not only controlled the *muafi* land, they effectively held sway over the entire territory of the *deota*. In small states where the position of the ruler was somewhat weaker, the proportion of *muafi* land controlled by the temples may have been considerable. For example, the land revenue settlement report of 1901 of Keonthal records that, of the total of seventy-five revenue-free (*muafi*) holdings in the state, forty-two were held by temples. In terms of revenue, these temple lands accounted for 71 per cent of the total revenue assigned towards *muafi*.[38]

[36] Lyall 1889: 83–4.
[37] Ibid.: 84.
[38] Keonthal SR 1914: Table, *Goshwara Muafiyat*.

Control over temples, associated offices and institutions, as well as over the large temple landholdings gave to the Kanet peasantry considerable political influence. The recognition thus accorded to leading Kanet clans bound them ever more closely to the monarchical state. In Keonthal the heads of six large Kanet clans acted as chief functionaries of the state by rotation.[39] Though the English version of the report uses the word *"wazir"* for the office they occupied by rotation, the published Urdu version of the settlement report uses the phrase *"virasat ka kam"* (hereditary work).[40] It also mentions, nevertheless, that the influence of these Kanet clans was considerable and that they were greatly respected in the state. The system in Bashahr state was quite similar, where the office of the *wazirs* was hereditary and held by Kanet families.[41] Their control over land and their ability to act collectively with the approval and support of their deity made the Kanet peasantry rather difficult opponents to deal with. The Keonthal Settlement Report notes that "They sometimes take oath in the temple of their god to accomplish a certain matter and having done so, they can with difficulty be induced to give up their oath till they have succeeded in the object. The other castes also have to join them, otherwise the Kanets would go against them and the other castes are always at their mercy."[42] Interestingly, this is perhaps what Sutherland may have implied while defining the *khund* as a "political community" that included Khas-Rajputs, Brahmins, and Kolis.[43] Peasant protest movements in the western Himalaya during pre-colonial times were therefore likely to have been well organised and highly effective. It was only subsequently, in colonial times, that the rajas could – with British support – successfully resist the pressure that their influential Kanet subjects had traditionally exerted on them.[44] Yet more often than not the hill rulers would have found it wiser to obtain the silent approval of their assertive yet obedient peasantry. It was the support of their subjects in normal times that

[39] Ibid.: Para 29.
[40] Singh 1901: 19, Para. 29.
[41] Chatur Bhuj 1928: 23.
[42] Keonthal SR 1914: Para 29.
[43] Sutherland 2006: 88.
[44] Singh 2002.

gave to many petty rajas a prestige and primacy that they could hardly have otherwise acquired. Their military power and wealth – or rather the lack of it – rested upon a polity that ultimately drew its strength from territorially defined communities.

III

While such communities enjoyed considerable political autonomy, it would be simplistic to see them merely as a collection of autochthonous village kingdoms ruled by their respective gods.[45] The "theistic sovereignty" of the local deity emphasised by recent work on the subject is somewhat exaggerated.[46] The image that this seems to create is one of segregated local communities engaged in ruthless and unending feuds. Robbery and bloodshed are projected as a way of life and the absence of a dominant political authority is by implication seen to be the cause of this.[47] Fascinating though it is, this picture is only partly correct. We need to recognise that there existed a larger system within which gods, *khunds*, and communities in general negotiated a complex network of relationships and hierarchies. Deities between whom there was believed to be a familial relationship (usually as brother or sister) often visited each other along with their followers. Those that were not "related" in this manner gathered at larger congregations of *deotas* that were periodically held. In order to obtain a broad semblance of order, it was not always a precarious *equality* that was "ritually made and unmade", as Sutherland has argued.[48] A similarly tenuous *inequality* – in the form of a hierarchy – also needed to be intermittently negotiated. Sutherland's suggestion of "equality among peers" may have arisen in the first instance less because *khunds* admitted an inherent equality *per se* amongst themselves, and more because they were commonly subjected to a larger system or a higher authority. Within this broad equality of a shared subjection were conducted the more nuanced ritual and political transactions of *inter se* status between *khunds*.

[45] Sutherland 2006: 88.
[46] Ibid.: 91.
[47] Sax 2006: 123.
[48] Sutherland 2006:110.

The relationship between monarchy on the one hand, and local communities and their deities on the other, was an extremely complex one. It was also one that influenced how territory and kingship came to be perceived by different groups. At the local level, the *deota* took on the veneer as well as the authority of a ruler (raja). Not only did the deity possess the material regalia of the raja – umbrella, mace, flags, drums, trumpets, palanquin, etc. – it actually functioned as one. The deity's will and command were expressed through its *gur* (oracle or medium). In important temples this royal status of the *deota* was further strengthened by a host of functionaries who acted as its ministers, courtiers, and officials to enforce the divine writ. Interestingly, while the *deota* asserted his rule by adopting the appearance of a raja, the raja legitimised his authority by claiming to be divinely ordained – or being some form of divinity himself. There was thus a close conceptual interdependence between *deota* and raja. Contrary to what is sometimes suggested, it appears unlikely that local communities – little kingdoms – ruled by *deotas* represented a form of political organisation that preceded the emergence of the larger kingdom. In fact, the forceful social enactment of the *deota* as a ruler assumes a familiarity with (and the prior existence of) the monarchy. It seems to be a local imitation of the power of the raja whose political influence prevailed over the domains of many village *deotas*.

Subtle divisions of territory and varying levels of allegiance could exist within a monarchical system without creating serious contradictions. Folklore in the region occasionally indicates how loyalties shifted in different circumstances. The legend of "Dhar Deshu" recalls the invasion of the state of Keonthal by raja "Mahi" Prakash of Sirmur. As Mahi Prakash prepared to attack the village of Balag, he was approached by a Brahmini of Balag who offered him a goat and a necklace to ward off the attack.

Mahi Prakash then inquired, "Who are your enemies [*boiree*] here?"

The Brahmini replied: "In Keonthal, enemies walk around everywhere. The people of Palwi – they graze their sheep and goats in [my] hayfields. When [these animals] go to [drink] water they tear up the pathway [with their hooves]."[49]

---

[49] Ramdayal 1973: 230–1.

She then lamented that one Homiyan Mian (a local village chief) had even built a platform (*thada*) in the village of Sainj. This act of constructing a *thada* was apparently symbolic of creating a separate centre of power – an assertion of authority and autonomy. For the Brahmini, therefore, quarrelsome and inconsiderate neighbours or an overbearing village chief occupied the place of *boiree* (enemies; *vairi* as derived from *vair* or feud).[50]

But this dispute with her neighbours and her unhappiness with the village head were matters to be resolved by her or by the ruler of Keonthal. When, however, Raja Mahi (of Sirmur) offered to teach these "enemies" of the Brahmini a lesson, her feudal loyalties came to the fore. She advised the raja to return to his home (Nahan), because the *rana* of Keonthal would not submit and was all too eager for battle. She described the kingdom of Keonthal (where she had moments earlier said "enemies walk around everywhere") as a place where complete peace prevailed:

> [Where] the lion herds the sheep and goats,
> [Where] the cat churns the butter-milk.
> The small kingdom of Junga [Keonthal],
> is like the Delhi of the Turks.[51]

It is evident, then, that for the Brahmini of Balag feuding neighbours were lesser enemies than an invading raja. Mahi Prakash and his army were clearly seen as outsiders – "*dakkhaniye*" (Southerners) – against whom the *rana* of Keonthal successfully mobilised not only the different clans within his state, but also warriors from neighbouring states of the north and towards the Satlej river.[52] The battles between

---

[50] Sax 2006: 124, 126; Ramdayal 1973: 250–1. William Sax makes two very relevant points. First is that the "*khund* is closely associated with pastoralism", with "much of the feuding between the various territories centred on pastoral disputes". The second is the importance of a structure called the *that* that was constructed in large villages and associated with a *that* goddess, and which was "the source of the warriors' martial power and energy". The protective power of s similar structure called the *thod* is also referred to in the legend of Dhar Deshu recounted by Ramdayal.

[51] Ramdayal 1973; Dhar Deshu: 232–3.

[52] Ramdayal 1973: 240–1, 244–5.

the two contending forces – with the active participation of numerous *devis* and *deotas* who fought (and fled!) alongside the opposing armies – are graphically recounted.

IV

Despite its apparent economic self-sufficiency and considerable political autonomy, the mountain peasantry was never insular. Its peculiar construction of village polity – as part reaction and part appendage to a larger Sanskritised worldview and overarching monarchical system – gave to it an ambivalent position. This ambivalence became explicit when the relationship between village polities (premised on a broad notion of equality) was altered into a politico-religious hierarchy whenever they interacted with the state. The emphasis on equality between communities prioritised local social and economic issues, but the recognition of a hierarchy underlined the political and cultural dominance of a more extensive, more complex world.

Hierarchical systems – where peasant communities are usually placed quite low in the scale – emphasise the fact that peasant culture is not complete in itself. It is, as Redfield argues, "an aspect or dimension of the civilisation of which it is a part. As the peasant society is a half-society, so the peasant-culture is a half-culture . . ." He elaborates: "the peasant village invites us to attend to the long course of interaction between that community and centres of civilisation. The peasant culture has an evident history; we are called upon to study that history; and the history is not local; it is a history of the civilisation of which the village culture is one local expression."[53] In India, particularly, apart from serving as a "safety valve mechanism for regulating relationships between villages", the regular convening of congregations, *jatras*, and other forums of collective activity symbolised "the weaving together of local, regional and pan-Indian traditions".[54] By their very nature, therefore, large gatherings of a socio-religious nature reiterated, as well as transcended, territorial boundaries. Small village communities

[53] Redfield 1989: 40, 41.
[54] Beals 1964: 105, 110.

asserted distinct local identities, yet perceived themselves as integral and active constituents of a vast social network.[55] This consciousness of a hierarchical (sometimes theoretical) system of social relations did not entail a negation of a "sense of community" that was rooted in its immediate surroundings. Unlike the experience of some other societies, a "breakdown" of traditional territories and identities was not here a prerequisite for the transformation of linkages "beyond the immediate locality and into the regional, the national and even international arena".[56] Linkages of a fairly extensive nature were in fact embedded into the structure of village communities. Smith argued that for "*ethnie* to move towards nationhood" required "a triple movement: from isolation to activism, from quietism to mobilisation and from culture to politics." And further that "Any *ethnie*, then, that aspires to nationhood, must become politicized . . ."[57] But what we need to consider is that societies might also disguise activism as isolation, present mobilisation as quietism, and practice politics as culture.

By collectively withdrawing from all dealings with the state and its functionaries, the hill peasantry's customary method of protest – despite its outward appearance of withdrawal – represented a high degree of organised activism. The *dhoom* or *dum*, as such protests were called, gave to the peasantry a decisive influence in the affairs of the pre-colonial state.[58] It also temporarily, and for purposes of mobilisation, transformed numerous territorially defined village communities into a larger integrated political entity. More importantly, such methods of mobilisation resurrected the underlying idea that, despite their scattered nature, local communities – especially Kanet clans – communicated with each other in a common socio-religious idiom. They conceptualised the larger epochal world in the language of the great Brahmanical tradition, but told the humbler intimate tales in the dialect of local beliefs and identities.

[55] Conzelmann 2006: 14–38; Berti 2006: 39–61; Luchesi 2006: 62–81; Sutherland 2006: 115–18; Goswamy 2006; Goswamy 2007.
[56] Alan Baker 1984: 25, 26.
[57] Smith 1987: 154, 156.
[58] Singh 2002.

There were other, more peaceful, occasions during which perceptions of territory underwent a transformation. Perhaps the most conspicuous were the customary celebrations of Dashehra and Sivaratri, at which the centrality of the monarchy and the state deity were asserted. These were also occasions when representatives (and *deotas*) of distant communities reaffirmed their political and ritual allegiance to the monarchy. Small territorial domains were for the moment subsumed by the Brahmanic state. The tiny divine kingdoms of the *deotas* became, as it were, a part of the empire of Visnu. Even as they acknowledged their subservience to the raja and the principal deity, however, the large number of assembled village communities tried to acquire a higher political standing through this annually enacted cultural drama. It was their proximity to, or distance from, the ritual centre that determined their status. Despite the disappearance of princely states in independent India, the social importance of this ritual enactment has persisted. An interesting example of such a contest for a higher ritual status is the ongoing dispute between two Kulu *deotas*, Balu Nag and Shringa Rishi, to occupy a position to the right of Lord Raghunath during the Kulu Dashehra procession. The assertion of local identities and the political significance of this long-lasting confrontation are still all too evident to local observers. It appears that the importance of Shringa Rishi of Chehni Kothi (Banjar) began growing after the former raja of Kulu was elected from Banjar constituency as a BJP member of the state legislative assembly in 1982. The neighbouring Ani constituency – the territory of *deota* Balu Nag – was apparently a Congress Party stronghold.[59] It seems that the devotees or "*haryans*" of Balu Nag were at a subsequent date prevented by the administration from participating in the Dashehra *rath yatra*. In 2006 even Shringa Rishi did not participate in the procession.[60] Subsequently in 2007 the Kulu Dashehra Committee chose not to invite either of the deities for the *rath yatra*, so as to avoid a confrontation.[61] Particularly interesting here is that, even in

[59] Chauhan 2004.
[60] *Tribune*, 3 October 2006; *Hindustan Times*, Chandigarh, 3 October 2006.
[61] *Hindustan Times*, Chandigarh, 22 October 2007.

contemporary political circumstances, the area that once constituted the former kingdom of Kulu remains the territorial context of this struggle.

V

Post-Independence India has witnessed the emergence of new political regions and provinces. The creation of Himachal Pradesh as a state of the Indian union has been one such development. It would appear logical therefore that the territorial dimensions of politics should have been radically transformed in this western Himalayan region. Socio-economic processes of subcontinental dimensions have prompted rapid and unprecedented change in this area, which was once regarded as peripheral in almost every respect. The possibilities arising from accompanying these processes are larger and more complex than those that western Himalayan society has ever confronted before. Have these developments prompted a reorganisation of local political and social territories? Has the language of politics changed or have the methods of political mobilisation been altered?

The prolonged Shringa Rishi–Balu Nag dispute in Kulu points towards the persistence of the traditional socio-political concept of territories defined through a hierarchy of *deotas*. Rivalry over contemporary political issues is the underlying reality of what has taken the appearance of a disagreement between *deotas* over status. Cultural celebrations have perhaps always carried political content. But this certainly does not mean that society and polity in the region has defied change. While outwardly the boundaries of territorial units and methods of local mobilisation display the continuity of tradition, often the nature and content of the debate engages with political polemics that are almost entirely contemporary.

A case in point is the proposal by an American company to establish a Himalayan ski village, i.e. a winter sports resort, in Kulu. Numerous village communities and their *deotas* opposed this proposal at a large congregation (*jagati pat*) convened by the former raja of Kulu. As in the case of the Shringa Rishi–Balu Nag disagreement, once again religion does not appear to be the most important issue at stake in the ski resort project. Neighbouring communities have instead raised questions about the likely economic and environmental impact of tourism of such huge proportions in a fragile mountainous area.[62] Certainly, some long-established interest groups in the region too feel threatened by a more powerful rival. The promoters of the project and their supporters have argued, on the other hand, that it will contribute substantially to the state exchequer and create rather than take away a large number of jobs for the local people.[63] For present purposes it is significant that local communities continue to be territorially defined by their traditional allegiance to a *deota*. They are, at the same time, engaged in a contemporary debate involving crucial issues of development and government policy. More importantly, the collective decision of community members is taken through the *deota* and his *gur*, and then communicated not to a government or elected representative but to the former raja of Kulu within whose kingdom the area of the concerned villages once fell. It appears therefore that while the territorial units and methods of political mobilisation retain pre-modern characteristics, the essential nature of political debate is modern. The contemporary language of developmental and environmental discourse is used with considerable sophistication by the *deota's* functionaries.

More recently, local opposition to a large hydroelectric project in Kinnaur has also been articulated through the *deota*. Local communities have resisted the construction of the 1000 megawatt

---

[62] *Hindustan Times*, Chandigarh, 10 January 2006; *Hindustan Times*, Chandigarh, 20 January 2006. NGOs opposing the project have raised questions pertaining to the destruction of forests, soil erosion, pollution, loss of traditional rights of local communities, the danger to folk culture, and a host of other related issues. "Annul MoU in Ski Village: NGO", *Hindustan Times*, Chandigarh, 10 January 2006; "Another NGO Raises Voice against Ski Village", *Hindustan Times*, Chandigarh, 20 January 2006.

[63] *Hindustan Times*, Chandigarh, 9 February 2006. Dile Ram Shabab, a former member of the State Legislative Assembly representing the Banjar constituency criticised Maheshwar Singh for convening a "*jagati* conclave" of *deotas* for this purpose and demanded that the issue be discussed by "political leaders" and "elected members" of village bodies. "'Ski village' project: Ex-MLA opposes jagati conclave", *Hindustan Times*, Chandigarh, 9 February 2006.

Karcham-Wangtoo Hydel Project on the Satlej river on the grounds that the tunnelling of the mountain would have an adverse environmental impact, including on their villages. At the forefront of this agitation has been Maheshwar Devta of Chagaon, an important deity of Kinnaur. In fact in October 2006 the *deota* "summoned" the chief minister of the state through the district magistrate of Kinnaur to "discuss" the matter. It was reported in the *Tribune* that the district magistrate "went to the deity temple at Chagaon . . . to hold talks with the deity on behalf of the State government seeking grant of permission to the company to start the construction work on this mega project."[64] Not much progress seems to have been made in these negotiations, and the agitation of the Karcham-Wangtoo Sangharsh Samiti led by the *deota* continued for several days. It finally turned violent and the police resorted to firing on the agitators to prevent matters getting worse. The district magistrate observed that the villagers who failed to participate in the agitation against the project were fined Rs 500 to Rs 1000 by their community leaders, who claimed to be acting on behalf of the *deota*.[65] Escalating tension drew political parties into the agitation. Subsequently, the Bharatiya Janata Party (BJP) attempted to make it a political issue in the state assembly elections of December 2007.[66] However, it is not the environmental implications of the mega power project that were sought to be raised by the BJP in this confrontation, for it seems unlikely if even the BJP government (formed in January 2008) will reverse the decision to build the project. An attempt was made to arouse local sentiment on the question of the "humiliation" and "insult inflicted a year ago on Maheshwar Devta of Chagaon".[67] This recognises the fact that traditional loyalties to *deota* and locality remain strong and relevant.

How has a remarkably diverse range of complex questions come to be effectively debated and decided upon by traditional village communities that remain territorially defined along distinctly pre-modern

[64] *The Tribune*, 14 October 2006.
[65] *Hindustan Times*, Chandigarh, 19 December 2006.
[66] *Hindustan Times*, 19 December 2006; *Hindustan Times*, 11 November 2006; Ashwini Sharma 2007.
[67] Ashwini Sharma 2007.

criteria? Logically, the socio-economic transformation experienced by modern India should have compelled radical social and territorial restructuring at every level. In Himachal Pradesh, however, other than the political merger of the princely states, such a transformation does not appear to have occurred on any great scale. One possible reason for this may be that shifting notions of community and territory have always been historically articulated for varying purposes. Culturally established norms of interaction between different levels of the political hierarchy may have something to do with the continued existence of traditional territorial divisions in Himachal.

It goes without saying that South Asian society has constantly changed through dynamic exchanges between what scholars have called the Great and Little Traditions. But there are few areas where the legitimising process of state formation itself has been as powerfully influenced by the Little Tradition as in Himachal. Long-term historical processes have combined with environmental circumstances to give small mountain communities the political autonomy to engage with the state from a position of considerable strength. Even after the emergence of the monarchical state, village communities remained important centres of power and exerted considerable collective influence over state functioning. The pre-colonial polities of the region carried this socio-political structure along with them when they merged to constitute Himachal Pradesh. As was the case earlier, the collective political influence of local communities has ensured that they continue to remain at the centre of government policies. This strength of village communities is indicated by the fact that, despite the remarkable socio-economic development that Himachal has witnessed over the last many decades, it remains even today the least urbanised state in India.

4

Geography, Religion, and Hegemony
Constructing the State in the Western Himalaya

Introduction

Through several historic periods in the North Indian plains, expansive military campaigns were crucial within empire-building activities. Watching these imperial endeavours from their fringes in the western Himalaya, the rulers of this region's various mountain principalities must have been alarmed. They may have seen, in addition, that military power alone does not ensure the longevity of empires and kingdoms: conquests have to be consolidated by legitimising the hegemony of a small ruling elite. This, they will have noticed, could apparently be achieved through the clever use of religion. The Himachal hill rulers realised quite early the power of non-military, hegemonic control. The complex relationship between diverse local cults and Brahmanic religion evident in their territories was in part a consequence of the process of political domination that was set in motion.

The "great tradition" of Brahmanic Hinduism used to be seen as a superimposition upon local non-Brahmanical belief systems, though its doctrinal supremacy was neither complete nor unquestioned. While many essential elements of Brahmanical beliefs certainly permeated

Originally published as "Constructing the State in the Western Himalaya", *Journal of Punjab Studies*, 2013, 20 (1&2): 3–21.

folk religious practices, the latter too transformed Brahmanic religion in various regions by compelling it to adapt and change.[1] In this context McKim Marriott makes this interesting argument:

> ... for understanding why Sanskritic rites are often added on to non-Sanskritic rites without replacing them, the concept of primary or indigenous process of civilisation again offers useful guidance. By definition, an indigenous civilisation is one whose great tradition originates by "universalisation" or a carrying forward of materials which are already present in the little tradition which it encompasses. Such an indigenous great tradition has authority in so far as it contributes a more articulate and refined statement or systematisation of what is already there.[2]

So influential, indeed, seem to have been the varied local traditions that one can hardly talk of a homogenised Hinduism. Despite the overarching influence of Brahmanism on them, there appears to have been no reduction in the astonishing number of folk cults that flourished across South Asia. But this does not indicate that there existed explicit distinctions between folk and Brahmanic traditions. The gods and rituals of the two "traditions" usually addressed different, yet overlapping and complementary, concerns. Mandelbaum has termed these "transcendental" and "pragmatic".[3] He explains: "In India, the gods charged with the cosmic verities are not expected to attend to a baby's colic or a lost cow. Yet both baby and cow must be cared for, since they are part of the grand design. In India, the answer is through specialisation of function and hierarchical arrangement among supernaturals, as among men."[4]

More specifically, such hierarchies amongst gods and their wide range of functional specialisations (within the instrumental and spiritual aspects of life associated with the "little" and "great" traditions,

---

[1] Srinivas 1965: 167; Berreman 1964: 55; Gonda 1976: 88.
[2] Marriott 1955: 197.
[3] Mandelbaum 1964: 11; Klass 1995: 57.
[4] Mandelbaum 1964: 11; see also Singh and Joshi 1999: 12; Herzfeld 1990: 320. In the context of the mountain villages of Crete, Herzfeld sees the "dialectic" between doctrinal and local concepts of Orthodoxy" as part of a "more general dialectic between structure and strategy".

respectively) formed the general structure of socio-political organisation in Himachal. The state, too, was part of this terrestrial reflection of the cosmic order. In the overlap between governmental authority, social organisation, and religious sanction the rulers of the Himachal principalities played a central role. Upon them rested the responsibility of creating and maintaining an ordered world. Naturally, the manner in which monarchical authority was locally constructed varied. There were several points of difference between the larger states and the tiny chiefdoms of the region.

Geography and Political Expansion

The large states of Himachal were Chamba, Kulu, Mandi, Kangra, Bashahr, Kahlur, and Sirmur. Perhaps the oldest and least mountainous of these was Kangra. It remained a dominant power in the area for most of the medieval period, till its annexation by Jahangir in the early seventeenth century. Throughout the seventeenth century Kangra was subject to direct Mughal rule. Because of its liminal position between the Panjab plains and the mountains, Kangra did not fully represent the typical Himalayan state. Chamba was another ancient state, but clearly more representative of a western Himalayan polity than Kangra. Originally, the rulers of Chamba seem to have controlled only Brahmaur in the upper Ravi valley. Under Meruvarman (AD 680), and later under Sahilvarman (AD 920), the kingdom of Chamba established control over numerous adjoining chiefdoms lower down in the valley.[5] It was here, on the right bank of the Ravi, that the capital town – Chamba – was finally established.

Most of the other large states, however, expanded during the medieval period through a long-drawn-out process of territorial conquest. The chronology of political expansion suggests that they originated as chiefdoms that first brought the main river valley under their control. Thereafter, the smaller tributary valleys were incorporated.

---

[5] Hutchison and Vogel 1982, I: 13, 279, 283. The Chamba rulers consolidated their position much before the others. It is argued here that in "Chamba state alone, with an area of 3216 square miles. There must have been more than 100 petty chiefs in ancient times." Sahilavarman "brought under his sway all the petty Ranas who still held the lower portion of the Ravi Valley."

As the expanding state reached out to these secluded valleys, the tiny political entities (*thakurais*) located within it were either extinguished or incorporated as feudatories of newly emerging monarchical states like Suket, Mandi, Kulu, and others.[6] There are references in the Chamba inscriptions of as early as AD 1160 and AD 1170 to some *ranas* having already acknowledged the suzerainty of Raja Lalita Varman. It is possible that these *ranas* also served as functionaries of the state. Under Balbhadra (AD 1589–1641) a large number of land grants and gifts were made to Brahmins. This certainly indicates that the formal "Brahmanisation" of the state political system had already taken place.

State formation in Kulu has a long history. But its expansion in medieval times took place under Raja Sidh Sen (AD 1500). His first victory was over a local *thakur* and this enabled him to capture territory that lay above the village of Jagatsukh, on both banks of the river Beas. Local tradition asserts that he was thereafter elected Raja of Waziri Parol. Subsequently, a rapid and significant expansion of the state occurred in the reign of Raja Bahadur Singh (AD 1532). During this period, the control of the Kulu ruler extended to Waziri Rupi, Shainshar Kothi, Makarsa in Hurla Khad (which actually functioned as Bahadur Singh's capital), and Chaini Kothi. During the reign of Raja Jagat Singh (AD 1637–72) the area lying on the right bank of the Beas – that was then the small kingdom of Lag – was annexed to Kulu. Kulu state therefore controlled extensive territory lying on both banks of the Beas. It was at this time that the sanskritisation of state polity apparently took place. Lord Raghunath became the state deity and was established as the ruler of the state while the raja was declared his first servant. The capital, too, was transferred to Sultanpur from Naggar in about 1660.

The state of Mandi expanded in a strikingly similar fashion. It grew out from the village of Manglaur (in Kulu) where the estranged brother of the raja of Suket had earlier established himself as the *thakur*. Local tradition asserts that it was Kalian Sen (AD 1300) who

---

[6] Ibid.: II. For the process of expansion in Mandi, see vol. II: 378–86. In Kulu, the struggle that its rulers Sidh Singh (AD 1500) and Bahadur Singh (AD 1532) had to engage in against the *ranas* and *thakurs* remains deeply embedded in folk memory, see ibid.: 442–56. For the subjugation of the *thakurs* in Suket state by Bir Sen, the founder, see vol. I: 343–5.

first acquired the land at Batahuli across the river from Mandi. It was here that "Old Mandi" was first established. Between 1332 and 1470, under Hira Sen and his successors, the endeavour of suppressing the numerous *ranas* and *thakurs* continued. The area that finally came to constitute the principality of Mandi was largely annexed by Ajbar Sen (AD 1500), and Mandi town was established in AD 1527. However, till as late as the reign of Narain Sen (AD 1575) several *ranas* remained in control of their separate territories, and it was only through the efforts of Raja Suraj Sen (AD 1637) that most of these *ranas* were finally defeated. During his reign – in a manner very similar to Kulu and at almost the same time – Lord Madho Rai was deemed as the formal ruler of the state of Mandi in 1648.

The expansion of each of these states brought within their political ambit geographically distinct areas and people with different and long-established socio-religious traditions. As mentioned earlier, people and territories could be militarily subjugated by the state. Establishing permanent dominance over vanquished people, however, presented an immensely more complex problem.

Religion: The Mainstream

The large states of Himachal invariably controlled an extensive part of an important river valley. The state capital was usually situated on the bank of the main river. Chamba town is situated on the Ravi River. Mandi and Sultanpur, the capital towns of the states of Mandi and Kulu respectively, were on the banks of the Beas. Bilaspur, the capital of Kahlur, and Rampur, the winter capital of Bashahr, were located on the Satlej. It was here that the raja resided and held court, and from where he exerted political control over the state. The centres of formal religious authority, too, were located in the main valley. Indeed, most of the important temples dedicated to Brahmanical deities were initially built in the main river valleys. The earliest examples of *nagara* temples, it has been argued, came up along trade routes passing through Himachal and linking Garhwal with Kashmir. These locations, interestingly, are also along the major rivers or important tributaries: Nirmand on the Satlej, Jagatsukh and Bajaura on the Beas, Hatkoti on the Pabbar – a tributary of the Yamuna. A temple dedicated to Lakshana Devi was built in the seventh century AD in the Ravi valley at Brahmaur, the ancient capital of Chamba.[7] By the tenth century AD the temples of Mani Mahesh and Narasimha too had come into existence. At Chhatrarhi, also in the Brahmaur area, a Shakti Devi temple was constructed in the seventh century. With the shifting of the capital to Chamba town, a large and impressive complex of temples dedicated to Visnu and Siva was raised at the new capital roughly between AD 920 and 1000.[8] Three of the temples in this complex were dedicated to Visnu, and three others to Siva. Even in Kulu state, several important Siva temples were constructed quite early at Jagatsukh, Bajaura, Naggar, and Dashal – all places located in the main Beas valley. In the Satlej valley were built the Sun temple at Nirath and the Dattatreya (Visnu) temple at Datnagar. Even the ancient village of Nirmand – with the temples of Parsuram, Ambika Devi, and Dakhani Mahadeva – is situated in the Satlej valley. Political authority and religious orthodoxy were almost always located in the central valley along which the larger monarchies expanded and exercised complete control. Virtually all the extant copper plates of the Chamba rulers recording the grant of land to various individuals and institutions pertain to villages located in the Ravi valley.[9] The largest number of beneficiaries must have been either from the politically central areas of the state or Brahmin immigrants in the service of the raja. This uneven distribution of copper plates certainly indicates the complete administrative control of the Chamba rulers over the Ravi valley, but it does not mean that their influence did not extend to the tributary valleys.[10]

---

[7] Lakshana Devi is a form of Mahishasurmardini, who is in turn a form of Shakti.

[8] Thakur 1996: 44.

[9] Vogel 1911: 40. Vogel writes that: "In Lahaul not a single specimen has come to light; in Pangi only one is known to exist . . . In the Churah division comparatively few copper plates are found belonging to the Muhammadan period. In the main Ravi, on the contrary, such documents are exceedingly numerous. The pre-Muhammadan plates all belong to this region."

[10] Thakur 1996: 130–1. Chamunda Devi temple was a large proprietor holding land in villages beyond the Ravi valley even though some of the original grants are not available. See also Peabody 1991a: 45, who refers to the use

We also need to factor in the possibility that religious processes that asserted the dominance of Brahmanic deities could follow on the heels of larger subcontinental political developments. Brahmanism was not merely consequential to the emergence of large local states. Some land grants and temples at Nirmand and Nirath can be attributed to regional feudatories (*samantas*) who owed allegiance not to any hill ruler but to an imperial power outside the region. In such cases, the areas falling under the sway of Brahmanism were situated at the fringes of an imperial authority located in the North Indian plains.

As a result of the Brahmanisation of the main river valleys, there was a difference between a section of the ruling elite that resided in the capital and the influential groups and clans that inhabited the more distant territories but owed allegiance to the raja and the state. This was not simply a difference in access to political power. A social distinction was probably sought to be made. The elite in power claimed a higher caste status and adopted sanskritised socio-religious practices, and its closer association with Vaisnavism seems to have distinguished it from the peasantry.[11] This was true of Chamba, but even more so of states such as Mandi, Kulu, and Bashahr. Visnu, in one or other incarnation, was the presiding deity of many of these states and enjoyed a position superior to that of any other deity.[12] So close

---

of the *mandala* schematic by Tambiah 1985: 252–86, which when applied to the polity creates a "conception of territory as variable space, control over which diminished as royal power radiated form the centre."

[11] Marriott 1955: 209. In his study of Kishangarhi (Haryana) Marriott observed that "Sanskritic deities of the great tradition play a larger part in the bloc of high castes in Kishangarhi than they do in the devotions of the lower castes." Even so, the importance of non-Sanskritic beliefs is evident from the facts that only "45 per cent of the deities worshipped even by Brahmans are Sanskritic." Atkinson 1976: 141, recorded that "Amongst the peasantry of the highlands the cult of Visnu is little known." *Chamba SG* 1910: 179, 191, mentions that the Rajputs in Chamba town worshipped Visnu, though it also notes that "Visnu, though commonly worshipped in Chamba city, has but few shrines in the State."

[12] *Mandi SG* 1920: 110 informs us that Madho Rao, an incarnation of Visnu, was the "national God of the State" in Mandi. In Kulu, Lord Raghunath

indeed was the association of the ruling elite with Vaisnavism, and so clear its demarcation from popular religion, that the worship of Visnu does not appear to have spread beyond a few politically important centres. Though this cult was probably introduced into Chamba as early as the tenth century, it remained virtually confined to the town of Chamba.[13] This seems to have been the case in Mandi as well.[14]

In addition to an incarnation of Visnu being declared as the supreme deity in most of the large states, each of the ruling families owed personal loyalty to a tutelary goddess (*kulaj*). The family goddess of the Chamba ruling house was Champavati,[15] that of the Mandi rajas was Sri Vidya.[16] Tripura Sundari of Naggar (and perhaps even to a greater extent Hidimba) occupied this position in the case of the Kulu rulers. The rulers of Bashahr state, which bordered Tibet and had a substantial Buddhist population, worshipped Bhima Kali as their family goddess.

From amongst the deities of the Hindu pantheon, Siva was by far the most extensively worshipped in the hills. Siva worship apparently prevailed in the region prior to the coming of Vaisnavism. Temples dedicated to Siva are found spread over a much wider area than those of any other deity.[17] It appears that local heterodox

---

occupied this position; see *Kangra DG (Kulu)* 1918: 63. The importance accorded to Visnu in Chamba is apparent from the large temple complex in the heart of Chamba town.

[13] *Chamba SG* 1910: 179.

[14] *Mandi SG* 1920: 110. Vaishnavism is mentioned as "being clearly an innovation to which only conventional adherence is given".

[15] *Chamba SG* 1910: 191. The prevailing tradition suggests that the goddess was of local origin. She is said to have been the daughter of the raja who established the town of Chamba and named the town after her.

[16] *Mandi SG* 1920: 110, notes that "Sri Vidya known also as Rajeshwari is depicted as having four arms and holding the top of a man's skull (*pakha* or *pasha*), an elephant goad (*ankush*), and bow (*dhanush*) and an arrow (*ban*); she wears red garments and has a half moon on her forehead. She is supposed to be the giver of wealth and happiness."

[17] *Chamba SG* 1910: 181, 191. Interestingly, the clan god of the Gaddis of Brahmaur (where the kingdom of Chamba originated) is Siva, not Raghunath, as in the case of the Rajputs. See also *Mandi SG* 1920: 110.

beliefs and practices, so typical of Himalayan Hinduism, were quite receptive to the growing popularity of Siva. Numerous village gods and local cults in Himachal became, by association, "instrumental" extensions of a higher and more distant "spiritual" Siva.[18] Through these linkages with smaller cults, Saivism established deep roots and became entwined with a network of diverse indigenous beliefs that collectively constitute what is sometimes called the "small tradition".[19] In their occasional interaction with the Brahmanical order, these cults claimed a position within the Saivite tradition. At the village level, however, non-Brahmanical religious practices were central to the belief system of the community. They enabled the common peasant to approach the local deity to expeditiously address his immediate, rather mundane, concerns.[20]

[18] *Sirmur SG* 1907: 42. Two of the most influential Siva cults in Sirmur and the Shimla Hill States area are those of Mahasu and Shrigul. The *Sirmur SG* observes that "the direct worship of Shiva is not very popular in the hills . . ."

[19] Gonda 1976: 95. About Hindu thinkers having little difficulty in "absorbing anything extraneous into their own system", Gonda argues that this was often done by "reinterpreting its mythology, symbolism and metaphysics and accepting its god as a servant or manifestation of their Highest Being." See also Marriott 1955: 215. Beals 1964: 105, in his study of *jatras* in Yadgiri *tahsil* of Karnataka, argues that "The myth and ritual of these *jatras* involve a weaving together of local, regional and pan-Indian traditions . . . The worshipped deity is regarded as local in origin even though identified with less parochial Hindu and Muslim deities." Srinivas 1965: 184.

[20] Klass 1995: 109; Mandelbaum 1964: 8; Berreman 1964: 67; Atkinson 1976: 40. Klass argues that village gods deal essentially with matters pertaining to what Mandelbaum has called the "pragmatic" dimension (immediate human problems) of religion rather than the "transcendent" (universe-maintaining) religious dimension that the greater deities were concerned with. But he also emphasises that the importance of these gods lies not so much in their position in a theological order as in "their role or roles in the particular community's religious universe". Many of the local practices were conducted not by priests but by shamans who, Mandelbaum observes, "deal with the exigencies of daily life, with the immediate and worldly welfare of their clients." Berreman makes the very interesting argument that "Shamans and other non-Brahmanical practitioners are not with the great tradition of Hinduism, but they are all-India in spread and hence are part of the pan-Indian

The Hidden Valleys

In the distant and almost hidden valleys of Himachal, then, a pragmatic religion had been cobbled together. It centred on the village *deota* (god) and was rooted in the daily life and social organisation of the peasantry. Yet it reflected a worldview that recognised the pre-eminence of the great gods of the Hindu tradition and the political system they legitimised.[21] A functional hierarchy of gods (*deotas*) is the most striking feature of Hinduism as it was, and still is, practised in Himachal. In this

> The key-stone is undoubtedly the *kul ka devta* or family god, and it is, therefore, unfortunate that the normal translation of *devta* as godling has obscured the prominent part he plays in the religious system of the hills. *Devta*, it is true, means literally a small god; but it is used not in the contemptuous sense conveyed by the expression godling, but to distinguish the minor deities from the *Devs* or mighty divinities who are too far removed from the daily worship of the people, whose religion centres round the ancestral god. The jurisdiction of the latter is both personal and territorial. He exercises sway over the hamlet, group of villages or valley recognised from time immemorial as his domain . . .[22]

Hindu vernacular, or little, tradition." About the Himalayan peasantry, as he saw it in the early years of the nineteenth century, Atkinson wrote: "Siva and Visnu and their female forms are the principal objects of worship, but with them either as their emanations or as separate divine entities, the representatives of the polydaemonistic cults of the older tribes are objects of worship both in temples and in domestic ceremonies."

[21] Sharma 1990: 136. In the Shimla area, a village god was usually worshipped by a cluster of ten or twelve villages called *ghori*.

[22] *Mandi SG* 1920: 119; Rosser 1969: 80, 81, 88. Rosser's study of the isolated village of Malana in Kulu, where *deota* Jamlu reigned, is quite representative of other village gods, though the hold of Jamlu over his domain is somewhat stronger than of most other *deotas*. The village council controls temple affairs in Malana. All land is owned by Jamlu and the Malana peasants consider themselves tenants of the god. Rosser argues: "Jamlu can be regarded as the deification of the village, and as the apotheosis of the village."

The mountain peasantry perceived and ordered the spiritual universe in the only way it knew – as an image that mirrored the temporal social order. Just as village headmen (*seanas*) were subservient to their *ranas* and *thakurs*, who in turn owed allegiance to the raja, so it was that village *deotas* were subordinate to a more powerful territorial god.[23] Territorial gods in turn offered obeisance to the supreme deity of the state. In some instances, an influential *deota* even had lesser *deotas* acting as his ministers, officials, and door-keepers (*wazir, kotwal, dwarpala,* etc.). The latter, too, had shrines of their own and their importance is not to be underestimated. In the early decades of the nineteenth century (and this is also true today) it was observed that

> The *wazir* is sometimes a being of great importance, his shrine containing more votive offering than that of his master; but this is as it should be, for, as they say, the *wazir's* business is to deal with the ordinary affairs of the ordinary people and so relieve the god of the petty importunities of his subjects. If the underlings are sometimes arbitrary and tyrannical, they only follow the examples of their human counterparts.[24]

Hegemony

Not surprisingly, an astonishing multiplicity of folk cults flourished and held sway in different parts of each state.[25] There also existed visible differences between the beliefs and practices of the ruling elite

---

[23] Redfield 1989a: 59. These territorial gods might in some respect be what Robert Redfield calls "deities that are intermediate between great and little traditions, being local forms of the one and universalized forms of the other."

[24] *Mandi SG* 1920: 120; *Kangra DG (Kulu)* 1918: 61. The *Kangra DG* observes that "if the people are questioned as to their private worship, they will say that they render dues to the Thakurs and other big foreign gods but for every day wants and troubles they go to their nature deities."

[25] *Sirmur SG* 1907: 38; *Mandi SG* 1920: 110. This variation could be marked both in terms of territory and caste. In parts of Himachal there is an interesting overlap even of territory and caste. For example, in Sirmur the Giri River was taken as the territorial demarcation between orthodox Brahmanical Hinduism and what was then regarded by observers as the "primitive" type. The *Mandi Gazetteer* notes a threefold division of (i) orthodox practices of superior Brahmans, Khatris, and some higher Rajput clans; (ii) the religion of

on the one hand, and the common people on the other. The political predicament before the state, therefore, was how to incorporate two apparently diverse worldviews into one recognisable and acceptable cosmic order. This would then be an order that the monarch would claim to obey, uphold, and implement in the material world. An effective solution to this problem emerged gradually in the form of a hegemonic but flexible socio-political system that drew heavily upon religion and religious symbolism.

This hegemonic system became possible because, for the hill peasant, the worlds occupied by *deotas* and mortals were not insular. The devotees of a *deota* were regarded as his subjects (*raiyat*), and temporal relations between the subjects of different *deotas* were closely interwoven with the relationship of their respective *deotas* with each other.[26] Village *deotas* were invariably subordinate to a more powerful territorial deity even if there were occasional disagreements between them. As a result their followers too were drawn into a corresponding position of subservience. This was not where the matter rested. At the top of the pyramid of political and religious authority were situated the raja and the reigning deity of the state.

The annual Dushehra festival at Sultanpur in Kulu is the clearest exposition of how this sovereignty of the raja and the state deity over their realm was symbolically established and renewed. Thakur Raghunathji, the supreme deity of the state, mounted his chariot and was escorted by the raja to an open ground where all the *deotas* of the realm were assembled in their traditionally allotted places in a manner quite similar to courtiers. Obeisance was paid and allegiances were

---

agricultural groups in areas adjoining the Kangra foothills; (iii) "the religion of the hills".

[26] *Kangra DG (Kulu and Saraj)* 1899: 41; *Kangra DG* 1918: 59. Folk tradition is replete with stories based on the familial relationship between village deities and their quarrels and friendships. The very human nature of their grudges is reflected in the hostility that has always existed in the Kulu valley between *deota* Kalinag and *deota* Narayan, because the former eloped with the latter's sister! The *Kangra DG* argues that "The social system is kept up by the rules of caste, by the numerous visits paid by *deotas* to each other accompanied by their people, and by gatherings on occasions of joy and grief."

extracted. The traditional relationship between Lord Raghunath, the raja of Kulu, the *deotas*, and the common subjects was reconfirmed at this annual enactment. It has been aptly described in the district gazetteer of 1917:

> Once a year there is a great parade of all the *deotas* of Kulu in honour of the god Raghunath at Sultanpur, the ancient capital. In olden days, they were brought in by the express command of the *Raja*, who seems to have been lord paramount of the gods as well as of the men of his kingdom, and this subservience of church to state still continues in the neighbouring independent state of Mandi. Doubtless it is based on the fact that the temples of the *deotas* possess endowments of land revenue which were held at the king's pleasure. The revenue of about one-seventh of the cultivated area of Kulu is alienated in this way, but now that it is held during the pleasure of the British Government the *deotas* are not so careful to pay their annual homage to Raghunath as formerly...[27]

An intricate network of hierarchically ordered deities stretched out to the remotest corners of the Himachal monarchies. Through it the rajas exercised influence of a kind, and in a manner that even the most efficient administrative methods could hardly have matched. Former subjects of the isolated *thakurais* – once politically independent – were now politically bound to their monarchs, and their village *deotas* (or their territorial god) subordinated to the presiding deity of the state. This linking of Brahmanical Hinduism to the extremely influential cults of the "little tradition" ideologically reinforced the dominance of the upper castes and the political authority of the monarchical state. This entwining of the raja's political pre-eminence with a "spiritual hierarchy" between superior and inferior gods was probably based upon an older tradition, one that preceded the formation of a clearly monarchical state. In fact, there were some parts of Himachal where this older tradition appears to have persisted.

Chiefdoms and Intermediate Societies: Legitimacy and Legend

It would be useful to look more closely at some of the smaller political entities. They apparently retained the characteristics of the old

---

[27] *Kangra DG (Kulu)* 1918: 65–6.

thakurais (chiefdoms) that had in many parts of Himachal been subsumed by the larger, expanding monarchies. To stretch the argument further, the political organisation of these small *thakurais* probably represented a polity that preceded the larger states.[28] The difference between the two was not simply the extent of territory they controlled. The smaller states – or *thakurais* as they were termed – continued to draw legitimacy from local politico-religious traditions. These were folk traditions – as folk traditions often are – particularly rich in myths and legends.

An essential constituent of a society's historical consciousness is the constant need to establish an unbroken link with antiquity. In most pre-modern societies myth, legend, and folklore contributed significantly to the construction of this continuity. A collective "memory" of the past, despite being rooted in myth and legend, commonly came to be accepted by society as its history.[29] Despite the differences that may exist between myths and legends an important factor common to both is that they are believed by the society in which they are prevalent to be an honest recounting of the past.[30]

The links between folklore, legend, and myth can conceivably result in the emergence of a "history" and a set of beliefs with which a community closely identifies and upon which it bases its

---

[28] Hutchison and Vogel 1982 describes in detail the position of the *ranas* and *thakurs* "who exercised authority, either as independent rulers or under the suzerainty of a paramount power" in the hills (vol. I: 12–40). The Chamba kingdom originated in the small territory of Brahmaur in the upper Ravi Valley (ibid.: 278). Similarly, Bahu Sen the founder of Mandi, quarrelled with his brother the raja of Suket, and became the *rana* of Manglaur. Thereafter, his successors expanded the territory into a large kingdom (ibid.: 375). In Kulu, Behangamani the founder is believed to have been "successful in gaining a footing in Upper Bias Valley by overcoming some of the local petty Chiefs. This as we know was the way most of the other Hill States were founded . . ." (ibid.: 431)

[29] Trompf 1989: 648 wonders "whether the early practice of history . . . was originally only possible because of myth".

[30] Bascom 1984: 9 says myths are sacred accounts and deal with a remote past in which the main characters are animals, deities, and culture heroes. Legends, on the other hand, are secular in nature and narrate stories of humans living in a world that is not very dissimilar from what it is today.

socio-political system.[31] Communities acquire ethnic identities to distinguish themselves from other groups, but they also simultaneously create distinct norms and practices to facilitate their own internal integration. Defined geographical territory and a common language and forms of expression do contribute importantly to the initial emergence of ethnicity, even though the historical circumstances in which ethnicities have been nurtured are curiously diverse. In all societies, however, "the imagining of the past was an ongoing creative process."[32] The episodic reconstruction and reassertion of a common past by a community enabled it to pronounce itself an entity rooted in antiquity. Like the sacred myths through which a society's links with antiquity were traced, its norms and values, too, were closely associated with folk tradition. The political order in the *thakurais*, especially the position of the chief, was strengthened by the legitimacy provided to it by popular cults.

The medieval *thakurais* of Himachal that had managed to survive as autonomous political entities till the early nineteenth century were administratively clubbed together by the British government as the Simla Hill States. While Bashahr (a large state included among the Simla Hill States) was the exception that controlled territory on both sides of the Satlej, the petty chiefdoms occupied only the watersheds of small tributaries of either the Satlej or the Giri rivers. Physiographically therefore these *thakurais* were either in the nature of a few mountain ridges and their flanks, or an almost bowl-like tract drained by small rivulets. They were difficult to access from the main river valleys and often occupied secluded niches that made them militarily and economically unattractive prizes for conquest by the larger states. This explains, albeit partly, their continued survival as *thakurais*. The example of one of the bigger chiefdoms – Keonthal – can be used to explain how the interweaving of religion, politics, and geography created intermediate socio-political entities such as chiefdoms.

[31] Kirk 1984: 58, provides an interesting argument about the forms and functions of myths.

[32] Talbot 1995: 713, 721, however, points out that in pre-modern Europe ethnicity also developed amongst a widely spread out aristocracy by cutting across territorial boundaries.

Keonthal *Thakurai*

With the arrival of the British in the region during the first decade of the nineteenth century, the boundaries of some of the hill states changed. Keonthal came to consist of eighteen *parganas* spread over six detached tracts.[33] This territorial fragmentation was the result of the *rana* surrendering some territory to the British as payment for military assistance provided him for expelling Nepalese invaders from Keonthal. In 1823, however, the detached *pargana* of Punar was given to Keonthal by the British government in lieu of additional land that the latter had taken over from the chiefdom. Sometime later the British obtained some more land from Keonthal for the expansion of the newly established hill station of Simla. As compensation, the *pargana* of Rawin was given to Keonthal in 1830.[34] The *pargana* of Rawin had originally been a separate *thakurai*.[35] It had a long historical tradition of its own, and its late incorporation into Keonthal prevented it becoming part of the hegemonic system that had historically evolved in the larger entity.

The original territory of Keonthal consisted of two geographical tracts. The southern tract (Halka Janubi) in which the state capital of Junga was situated, consisted of ten *parganas*. Further north was Halka Shumali or the northern tract. The villages in the core southern tract of Keonthal coalesced around the religious cult of Junga. It was through this cult that the Keonthal rulers exercised a hegemonic influence over their chiefdom. Folk tradition traces the mythical origins of *deota* Junga to a disgruntled prince of Kutlehr. The prince left his home and came to Koti (where a branch of the Kutlehr family had earlier established a separate state) which shares its southern boundary with Keonthal. Subsequently, he disappeared mysteriously while crossing a forested ridge that separated the territories of Koti and Keonthal, only to reappear as a spirit. This marked the manifestation of *deota* Junga, who then proceeded to displace Jipur, the family deity (which was more in the nature of a *jathera* or ancestor) of the Keonthal *ranas*.

[33] Rose 1970: I, 444; Keonthal SR 1914: 1.
[34] Keonthal SR 1914: 1.
[35] *SHSG* 1911: (Jubbal Tributaries).

By this usurpation Junga became the state deity: the suzerain of all other *deotas* in Keonthal.³⁶

Village Gods and Communities

There were twenty-two important village *deotas* – also called *tikas* (translated locally as "sons", but could also mean princes) – in Keonthal who stood immediately below *deota* Junga.³⁷ These *deotas*, or *tikas*, of Junga were situated in the various territories of Keonthal over which they wielded immense influence through clans of followers. However, even today no celebration or religious function can begin in the shrine of any subordinate *deota* without the permission of *deota* Junga. This consent is granted only after the customary dues from the *tikas* have been deposited in Junga's treasury.

There existed a close connection between a dominant peasant clan and its *deota*. This association acquired a territorial dimension from the fact that a single clan of Kanet peasants was often concentrated in contiguous villages or in a specific area.³⁸ Even the religious rituals and practices in many of the village temples were conducted not by Brahmans but by a Kanet peasant acting as a priest.³⁹ Territory, clan allegiance, and religious affiliation therefore often overlapped. Festivals at the *deota*'s shrine were occasions on which large yet well-knit congregations from adjoining villages assembled. The Kanet peasantry exerted considerable influence over the manner in which the *thakurai* was governed. In order to maintain a political balance between the different clans, Kanet clan leaders occupied, by turns, the

---

³⁶ Rose 1970: I, 443. Jipur is now no longer remembered. Quite possibly, Rose confused Jipur with Sipur. Sipur *deota*, however, was connected with the Koti *thakurai* rather than Keonthal. Interestingly, his temple is quite near the place where the Kutlehr prince is believed to have disappeared.

³⁷ The term *tika* came to be understood during Mughal times as a mark (*tika*) that signified the succession of a chieftain to the *gaddi*. Chieftains within the Mughal empire had to obtain the consent of the Mughal emperor before applying the *tika*. Subsequently, the heir-apparent of a hill state came to be addressed as *tika*.

³⁸ Singh 1998: 210–11.

³⁹ Cf. Klass 1995: 83.

important administrative positions of the chiefdom.[40] This periodic redistribution of public office probably prevented any single clan from becoming too powerful. But a subtler, more powerful, force bound the Kanet peasantry to the *rana*. This was the spiritual authority of the chief deity Junga over the gods of the different peasant clans.

Ethnographic information recorded in the late nineteenth century about most of the twenty-two *tikas* of Junga further illustrates the interconnections mentioned above.[41]

Tikas of *Deota* Junga

Junga Cults	Location of Temple	Followers
1. Kalaur	Village Charej, *pargana* Ratesh	
2. Manuni	Hill of Manun (Manun is Mahadev)	Brahmins of Parali and Koti *dhar*
3. Kaneti	Village Dagon, by replacing Jipur	Bhaler clan of Kanets
4. Kulthi	Village Kawalath	Chibhar clan of Kanets
5. Dhanun	Village Neog	Brahmans
6. Dum	Village Katian, Phagu *tehsil*	Subordinate to *deota* Junga but independent elsewhere
7. Raita	*Pargana* Parali	
8. Chanana		Doli Brahmans
9. Gaun	Village Rawal	Image of Junga established by the people
10. Biju		
11. Deo Chand		*Jathera* (ancestor) of the Khanoga clan of Kanets
12. Shaneti		Dispute between two groups of Kanets (Painoi & Shainti). The latter established Shaneti

(*Contd.*)

[40] Singh 1901: para 29. Singh's settlement report of Keonthal mentions six classes of Kanets and notes that "The head of these tribes used to be the *wazir* in the State by turn."

[41] Rose 1970: 445–50.

(*Contd.*)

	Junga Cults	Location of Temple	Followers
13.	Mahanpha	Jatil *pargana*	Chibhar Kanets
14.	Tiru		*Jathera* (ancestor) of the Jatik sect of Brahmans
15.	Khateshwar	Village Koti	Brahmans of Bhakar
16.	Chadei	Village Charol	Nawan clan of Kanets
17.	Shanei and Jau	Village Koti	
18.	Dhuru	Jai *pargana*	

Territorial Allegiance

All *deotas* with shrines within the territory of Keonthal were subordinate to Junga.[42] This is of particular significance because some of the larger and more popular folk cults had followers and temples spread across two or more *thakurais*. For example, shrines dedicated to Dum *deota* existed not only in Keonthal and the neighbouring *thakurai* of Kumharsain, but also in the chiefdom of Kotkhai and the state of Bashahr. This could logically have created complications in the hierarchical structure of *deotas* in a state. The problem was overcome by the stratagem of asserting the supremacy of the respective state deity over the different manifestations of Dum *deota* enshrined within their territories. Thus, Dum *deota* in Katian village (no. 6 in the table) of Phagu *tehsil* in Keonthal was subservient to *deota* Junga, while the Dum *deotas* with temples situated in Kumharsain were under the suzerainty of their own state deity – Kot Ishwar Mahadev. Similarly, Biju *deota* (no. 10 in the table) seems originally to have been an alien deity subordinate to *deota* Bijat of Jubbal state. After he was brought over by some of his followers who migrated to Keonthal, Biju began to owe allegiance to Junga.[43]

[42] If, hypothetically, Keonthal had been incorporated by conquest into a larger state (as happened to many *thakurais* in earlier times), then *deota* Junga would probably have been subservient to a deity of Brahmanical Hinduism.

[43] Rose 1970: I, 449; *Simla DG* 1908: 39; Lovell 1998: 54–5. In the area of Punar, that was added much later by the British to Keonthal state, the

Conclusion

The emergence of monarchical states along the riverine areas of Himachal was accompanied by the Brahmanisation of their ruling elite. Territorial expansion was gradually achieved through numerous small albeit hard-fought battles. But long-term political consolidation was immensely more complex. Large areas and populations in these mountain monarchies tenaciously retained socio-religious traditions and political identities that were diverse and clearly different from the Brahmanised areas. The limited economic resources of the hill states did not allow them to maintain large standing armies to enforce the allegiance of clans and communities located in distant territories. It was here that religion was particularly useful as an instrument of social control. Political incorporation of newly conquered territories was reinforced by ideological domination. Temporal hierarchies of authority in the state were replicated in the relationship between the deities of the kingdom. Territorial and village gods were hierarchically arranged down to the lowest levels. Their peasant followers, too, were politically and ideologically bound to the raja and the state deity. This convergence of politics and religion created a hegemonic system that ultimately outlasted even the monarchies that had initially created them.

---

deotas naturally had no history of being subordinate to Junga. Within Punar, nevertheless, the territories of different *deotas* had been historically delineated. Nihagu *deota* of Jaili village presided over Agla Punar while Pichhla Punar was under Baneshar *deota* of Chohag village. The establishing of a shrine to their deity in a new place may have been one of the means by which the followers also laid out a territorial claim. This clearly reiterates the connection between clan, deity, and territory.

5

Nature, Religion, and Politics
Keonthal and Kumharsain

MANY INDIGENOUS COMMUNITIES in rural South Asia contextualise their position in a larger world within oral traditions rooted in pre-modern times. These traditions are socially constructed memories of the past – an amalgam of myth, folklore, and legend – that usually serve also as history. Such societies, without a chronologically ordered view of the past, are sometimes considered devoid of a sense of history. Many pre-capitalist social systems have been similarly viewed, especially because of their alleged lack of internal dynamism for change. Instead of being seen as active, autonomous participants in global historical processes, they have been regarded as societies "upon whom history acts".[1] Of course, not many would seriously argue today that there are "people without history". Even the simplest societies nurtured history in the form of recollections of a collectively experienced or remembered past. Such recall was often entwined with a cosmic view that virtually functioned as religion. While the need for a secular history – devoid of religious rationalisation – was never seriously felt, religion itself became mundane, everyday practice. Political organisation and religious ideology were seen as crucial components of a single public sphere. This was a domain where both religion and politics were used

---

A substantial part of this article was published earlier as C. Singh 2006.
[1] Comaroff & Comaroff 1992: 24, 25, 97.

in constantly shifting combinations – a stratagem that practically erased the distinction, where there was any, between religion and politics.

For the study of mountain societies, a third factor – physiography – seems to be of vital importance. It adds a new dimension that has exerted considerable influence on the evolution of ideologies of governance, religious belief, and social organisation. The Indian montane state of Himachal Pradesh offers appropriate conditions for examining the historical interaction between nature and culture. In its rugged territory, large and fast-flowing rivers with numerous tributaries created small, semi-isolated valleys separated by high mountain ranges. These small-river valleys were accessible through the main river valley. Geographical divisions of this nature engendered the emergence not only of political territories, but also of the religious domains of different deities.[2] The region's history is marked by dynamic exchanges between nature, religion, and political organisation.

In the absence of literary texts or "histories" in the region, an attempt is made here to explore aspects of a "believed" folk history. For the inhabitants of the region the traditions explored here have long represented history in its fullest sense. They embody a social truth to which village communities tenaciously continue to anchor their lives. Folklore and legend are clever devices for creating community identities and legitimising political structures. While the long-term logic of this essay has to do with pre-colonial times, the instances specifically discussed pertain to the more recent period between the mid-nineteenth century and the early decades of the twentieth. Furthermore, the essential nature of the relationship between nature and culture ensures that many arguments made here remain relevant to contemporary Himachal society.

II

Pre-modern Himachal was divided into numerous monarchies and petty chiefdoms (*thakurais*) that had been fostered by its topography.

---

[2] Singh 1998.

They remained independent over the centuries and retained considerable administrative autonomy even under British rule. This long tradition of political freedom was complemented by the almost uninterrupted dominance of a few interrelated ruling lineages.[3] Geographical seclusion and relative poverty made many of these states unattractive to invaders. It also saved them from the socio-political upheavals usually wrought by external aggression. But these facts alone cannot explain the political longevity of the ruling clans or the stability of the traditional social order. Both material and ideological factors combined to establish the hegemonic authority of dynastic rulers as well as the continuity of local traditions.

An essential theoretical function of monarchical authority in India was the establishment of dharma (righteousness), and the preservation of a *dharmic* order. The acceptance of a monarch's political authority by his subjects also implied their submission to a *dharmic* or moral code of social organisation.[4] Despite the apparent harmony between kingship and dharma, and the Brahmanical approval that monarchy received, the king's rule ultimately rested upon the acquiescence of his subjects – who might on occasion disagree with their ruler. He was, as a result, compelled to "perform a precarious balancing act between forcefully proclaiming his own writ to be *dharma* and, on the other hand, following unassumingly what his subjects tell him to be *dharma*."[5]

---

[3] Hutchison and Vogel 1982.

[4] Drekmeier 1962: 251, 245, 269. Drekmeier also examines the relationship between kingship and divinity and mentions the shift in the basis of legitimisation of monarchy from "capricious and amoral Vedic gods" to "sacred tradition as revealed in the Vedic hymns". This shift increased the powers of the Brahmins as interpreters. The latter is what Heesterman calls the "king-Brahmin 'model' of Indian civilization". See Heesterman 1998: 18.

[5] Ibid.: 21, 22. Heesterman points out the contradictions confronting the monarch. The customary law of a conquered population was not to be altered or suppressed even if it was contrary to *dharma*; nor were the king's own subjects to be forced to abandon their customs even if they were contrary to the Vedic system. On the other hand, the king's authority is emphasised by instances where the *dharma* decreed by him was supreme and in some cases the "royal edict" was considered superior to *dharma*.

For this reason, the divinity of the Hindu monarch had to be continuously rejuvenated through rituals that functioned as weapons in an everlasting contest between good and evil.[6] However, as Inden observes:

> There was ... never a question of eliminating forces of darkness, evil or destruction, but rather of domesticating and placating them. Nor was this a job that could be done once and for all. It had to be done over and over again. Battles between gods and anti-gods, between contenders for the position of cosmic overlord and their terrestrial supporters had to be fought anew not in order to return India to some primordial *status quo ante*, but because circumstances themselves, including human knowledge of divinity continued to change.[7]

Through Brahmanical rituals the king sought to ensure his ascendancy. Yet contestations – both theoretical and actual – occurred at different levels of the political hierarchy. The local community, its economic resources, and social organisation were where such primary confrontations took place. Newly emergent social groups and beliefs had necessarily to negotiate with village institutions that may as a result have responded with considerable flexibility. Village communities usually enjoyed considerable autonomy, and their functioning also varied in the different regions.[8] Conflicts between villages could, however, be frequent, and violent enough to prompt state intervention. Because they formed the primary unit upon which the socio-political structure rested, the state endeavoured constantly to establish greater influence over village communities. Apart from exercising administrative control, a subtler way was to manipulate religious beliefs and traditions. To exert influence without actually appearing to do so was perhaps an essential characteristic of the hegemony that rulers sought to establish. Hegemony – so much like religious belief – "consists of things that go without saying: things that, being axiomatic, are not normally the subject of explication or argument. This is why its power seems to be independent of human

---

[6] Peabody 1991a: 33; Heesterman 1998: 24.
[7] Inden 2000: 238.
[8] Drekmeier 1962: 293.

agency, to lie in what it silences, what it puts beyond the limits of the thinkable."[9]

An essential facet of the moral order prevalent in western Himalayan kingdoms was the complex network of hierarchically placed deities that stretched out from the political capital to the remotest village. Despite its apparent rigidity, the hierarchy of deities was occasionally contested and even reordered. Because of the intimate bonds between the village folk and their god, this reordering of the position or privileges of particular deities was a likely indicator of social transformation occurring in the villages. The ruler (as the representative – even embodiment – of Lord Vishnu) was usually the arbitrator in disputes involving the lesser gods in his realm. Such situations certainly provided the raja the welcome opportunity of asserting his ideological supremacy.

As monarchical states expanded, the people and territory of the smaller chiefdoms (*thakurais*) were annexed; but more importantly even their village or territorial *deotas* were ideologically subordinated to the presiding deity of the monarchy. The ensuing pre-eminence of Brahmanism over subordinated indigenous cults legitimised the superiority of the upper castes and the political authority of the expanding monarchical state. By using religion as a political instrument, the rulers of the bigger states were in reality exploiting the strength of the socio-political framework of territorial and clan deities upon which the *thakurais* rested.

III

One apparent difference between *thakurais* and monarchies was that while the latter often controlled the territory on both banks of the major river of the region, the former occupied a niche in the smaller

[9] Comaroff & Comaroff 1992: 28–9. They have argued that "Hegemony . . . is that part of a dominant ideology that has been naturalised and having contrived a tangible world in its image, does not appear to be ideological at will." As a result, "The more successful any regime, the more of its ideology will disappear into the domain of hegemonic practice; the less successful, the more its unspoken conventions will be opened to contest." Ibid.: 30.

tributary valleys. Moreover, the monarchies attempted to follow scriptural prescriptions of governance while the *thakurais* subscribed to indigenous religious traditions particularly rich in myth and legend. These legends often grew out of the physical environment of the state and related to places and people within it. Like origin myths that linked society with an ancient past, norms and values too derived from folk tradition. Not unexpectedly, the socio-political order in the *thakurais* was closely entwined with the creation and rejuvenation of popular cults.

For purposes of convenience the British clubbed most of the cis-Satlej *thakurais* of Himachal into a loose administrative group called the Simla Hill States. These petty chiefdoms occupied the watersheds of tributaries of either the Satlej or the Giri rivers. Physiographically, therefore, the *thakurais* were either in the nature of a mountain ridge and its two flanks, or an almost bowl-like area drained by rivulets. They were difficult to access from the main river valleys and militarily and economically unattractive for conquest by the larger states. Of these autonomous states, the present study of the nature–culture interaction is restricted to Keonthal and Kumharsain.

Keonthal *Thakurai*

The capital town of the *thakurai* was Junga, so named after the state deity around which had grown a cult central to the political order of the chiefdom. The mythical origins of *deota* Junga are traced to a disgruntled prince of Kutlehr who left home and arrived at the *thakurai* of Koti, adjoining Keonthal. Subsequently, the prince disappeared inexplicably while passing through a forest between Koti and Keonthal. He then seems to have become a spirit and resided in a tree within the forest, till discovered by a resident of Keonthal. The fortuitous discovery of a hidden or buried god is common in the region, and perhaps common as well to other pastoral and semi-pastoral societies.

The new spirit discovered in the wilderness came to be recognised as *deota* Junga. Thereafter, Junga displaced Jipur – the state deity of Keonthal who was a *jathera* (ancestor) of the Keonthal *ranas* – and became suzerain of all other *deotas* in Keonthal.[10] The historical events underlying the emergence of *deota* Junga as the state deity are a matter of conjecture, but his elevation does seem to mark a new beginning of sorts. Significantly, *deota* Junga was not a Sanskritic deity, but one closely connected with the natural surroundings of the state. He seemed to represent a spirit that had been retrieved from the wilderness.

The mountainous terrain further divided Keonthal into small territories controlled by a sub-clan of the dominant Kanet peasantry or occasionally by a *jati* of Brahmans. Clan leaders also occupied important administrative positions in the state by rotation. The periodic redistribution of public office enabled the *rana* to retain a clan's loyalty and prevented any one of them from becoming too powerful.[11] But another powerful factor bound the peasantry to the *rana*. Every territory and clan in this patchwork of territories was the domain of a particular local deity. There were, in Keonthal, at least twenty-two regional *deotas* – also called *tikas* (translated locally as "sons") – subordinate to *deota* Junga.[12] In many cases they were a form of the god Junga himself. While considerable freedom was permitted in local issues, the celebration of important religious occasions at the shrine of lesser *deotas* required explicit permission from the state deity. This consent was granted only after followers of the lesser gods deposited the customary dues in Junga's treasury. The spiritual authority of Junga over territorial gods could readily be translated into control by the *rana* of peasant clans.

This is made clear by the fact that folk deities with shrines in two

[10] Rose 1970: I, 443. If, hypothetically, Keonthal has been incorporated by conquest into a larger state (as happened to many *thakurais* in earlier times), then *deota* Junga would probably have been subservient to a deity of Brahmanical Hinduism.

[11] *Keonthal SR* 1901: para 29. The report mentions six classes of Kanets and notes that "The head of these tribes used to be the *wazir* in the State by turn."

[12] The term *tika* came to be understood during Mughal times as a mark (*tika*) that signified the succession of a chieftain to the *gaddi*. Chieftains within the Mughal empire had to obtain the consent of the Mughal emperor before applying the *tika*. Subsequently, the heir-apparent of a hill state came to be addressed as *tika*.

or more *thakurais* were subordinate to the state god within whose territory the shrine was situated. For example, temples of Dum *deota* existed in all the adjoining states of Keonthal, Kumharsain, Kotkhai, and Bashahr. In each of these states the supremacy of the respective state deities was asserted. Dum *deota* in Katain (Gathan) village of Phagu *tehsil* in Keonthal was subservient to *deota* Junga, while the Dum *deotas* with temples in Kumharsain were under the suzerainty of their own state deity – Kot Ishwar Mahadev. Similarly, Biju *deota* was originally a deity subordinate to *deota* Bijat of Jubbal state. But after he was brought over by followers who migrated to Keonthal from Jubbal, Biju began to owe allegiance to Junga.[13] A difference in status existed even amongst the smaller *deotas*, and the case of *deotas* Shanei and Jau in Koti village of Keonthal is illustrative. Junga is believed to have himself ordered the construction of their temples in the village but to avoid disputes between their followers Shanei was given a higher status than Jau.[14]

Very unlike *deota* Junga, who dwelt like a monarch in the state capital, was the goddess Tara whose temple overlooked the *rana's* capital from the edge of a towering ridge. While Junga was surrounded by the tumult of socio-political life, Tara stood majestically aloof. She wielded influence over the entire state, not as a suzerain over smaller gods but as the essence of cosmic power. Tara was also the *kul* (family) deity of the Keonthal rulers.[15] While Junga was of indigenous origin, Tara, as a form of Shakti, signified the supremacy of Sanskritic religion in the state.[16] The official celebration of the annual Durga *ashtami* by the ruler at the temple was an occasion for reiterating the *rana's* legitimacy as a ruler.[17] Quite frequently, powerful devis occupied uninhabited mountain tops that were difficult to access and their

---

[13] Rose 1970: I, 449; *Simla DG* 1904: 39; Lovell 1998b: 54–5.

[14] Several considerations usually went into deciding the status of the *deotas*, not the least important of which was the influence wielded by the followers and their caste affiliation.

[15] *SHSG* 1910, Kumharsain: Appendix, viii.

[16] The State Gazetteer (Keonthal) says *jogi* Tara Nath, who was responsible for placing the idol of the *devi* in the temple, did so "according to rules set forth in the Hindu *shastras* for *asthapan*", i.e. establishment of an idol.

[17] *SHSG* 1910, Keonthal: Appendix, ix.

shrines were sometimes little more than a pile of stones.[18] While village gods lived with the people and addressed their common problems, the mountain *devis* were usually approached by worshippers with a sense of awe nurtured by their greater power and the aloofness of their shrines.

Kumharsain *Thakurai*

The picture in Kumharsain was more complex. Kot Ishwar Mahadev, whose temple was located at Kothi Mandholi, was the state deity.[19] Like *deota* Junga of Keonthal, Kot Ishwar too seems to have replaced an older god of the area, known now as Burha Dev, who is also installed in Kot Ishwar's temple in Kothi Mandholi.[20] The hierarchy of gods followed the usual pattern. While Kot Ishwar and Shakti (the family goddess of the ruling family) were the two deities that held sway over the whole of Kumharsain, there were some that controlled an entire *pargana* (revenue district).[21] The large majority were, of course, village

[18] Ibid., Bashahr: 27; *Simla DG* 1904: 35. The Bashahr Gazetteer observes that "the tops of hills are usually sacred to Kali", while the *Simla District Gazetteer* notes that "Divinities are believed to dwell on the mountain tops."

[19] *SHSG* 1910, Kumharsain: 9.

[20] Interview with Surinder Shaunik, priest of Kot Ishwar temple, 20 September 2004, during fieldwork at Koth Mandholi over the Chaar Sala Mela, Kumharsain (19–21 September 2004).

[21] *Simla DG* 1904: 36; Lovell 1998b: 55. The important territorial *deotas* of Kumharsain who controlled large areas, were:

Deota	Location	Territory
1. Mananeshar	Kot	The *deota* of Sihal territory
2. Dum	Sharmala	The *deota* of Upardes territory
3. Nag	Bagi	The *deota* of Chajoli territory
4. Marechh (Malendu)	Malendi	The *deota* of Chebishi *pargana*

Lovell makes an interesting observation that seems quite relevant in the present context: "Locality is constructed through the intermediary of deities which are themselves extensions of natural and environmental features. By providing these deities with names, a place is created for humans to dwell in, and the gods are simultaneously provided with an identity and place of

deotas. This hierarchy among deities is illustrated by a local tradition recounting the arrival of seven *deotas* – the Marechh brothers – in the region. According to popular belief, three settled in the principality of Kumharsain, two chose to stay in the state of Shangri, and one each in the territories of Kotgarh and Kulu.[22] The three Marechh *deotas* who chose to stay in Kumharsain were: (1) Dithu of Dholaseri, (2) Marechh (or Malendu) of Malendi, (3) Bareog of Kumharsain.

The story of Malendu's appearance in the Chebishi area of Kumharsain is especially interesting. We are told that

> the seven Marechh brothers came from the Mansarover lake [located in the Tibetan plateau] and fought with Bambu Rao ... After his overthrow, they came to Hatu, whence they scattered. Malendu went to Chhichhar forest and after a time flew to the top of the Dertu hill above Chebishi *pargana*. A Kali or Kalka called Bhagwati, who lived on this peak, received him kindly, but after a while she desired him to acquire a territory where he could be worshipped and recommended to him the Chebishi *pargana*, as it was subsequently named. So this *deota* Marechh left the Kalka and came to Lanki forest. Thence he descended to the Nala and reached Janjhat . . .[23]

Here Malendu revealed himself to a Brahman as a serpent that subsequently transformed itself into an idol. The Brahman took the idol

---

their own ... The action of naming a deity therefore imbues a space with a sense of place, no longer an anonymous feature in the environment. Yet, the identity of humans and that of their gods are intricately linked, as is their relationship with nature."

[22] Rose 1970: I, 454.

[23] Bambu Rao: A demon who is believed to have ruled the entire region before the *deotas* established themselves and rid the population of the terror and misrule to which they were subject. Hatu: the highest point in Kumharsain. The peak overlooks the Satlej valley and provides almost a bird's-eye view of the entire area (including Kulu, Kotgarh, and Shangri) over which the seven Marechh brothers are settled. Rose 1970: I, 455; cf. Srinivas 1965: 234–6. Rose has provided a fairly detailed account of this myth. Cf. Srinivas, who refers to the story of seven deities – six brothers and one sister. Three brothers settled in Malabar as deities while four others (including the sister) moved into Coorg and became deities in different villages.

to the *mawannas* (village chiefs) of Bashera and Pharal, apparently the most influential persons of that area. Thereafter, the state god Kot Ishwar was informed of the arrival of Malendu (Marechh) within Kumharsain territory. Kot Ishwar gave the new god the Chebishi *pargana* to rule, and four villages for his maintenance. Marechh was to follow all norms prescribed for a subordinate. Subsequently, the chiefs of Bashera and Pharal built a temple for Marechh at Malendi.[24]

How is one to interpret this story? It is not without significance that a Brahman first discovered the idol of Malendu. Nor is it surprising that the two most powerful persons of the area should approach *deota* Kot Ishwar (the state deity closely associated with the *rana*) about the matter and then proceed to establish the shrine of Malendu in this area. The origin myth of Malendu seems to have enabled the people of the Chebishi territory to find an appropriate place for themselves in the socio-political order of Kumharsain. As the chief worshippers of Malendu, the *mawannas* negotiated with the *rana* who represented *deota* Kot Ishwar.[25] But a hierarchy was accepted and reiterated when Kot Ishwar granted the newly arrived god Marechh (Malendu) a territory to rule and some villages for his maintenance.[26] By accepting these grants, Malendu also acknowledged his inferior yet powerful position.

As a territorial deity, Malendu in turn had several smaller gods within his area of influence. Among these were

> two *bhors* Jhatak and Lata.[27] Jhatak is a *deota* of an *uch* or superior caste while Lata is a *nich* or low caste. Jhatak lived at Urshu, a place also called Jhaila; so he is also called Jhaila at Urshu.

[24] Rose 1970: I, 455.

[25] Jaishree Joshi n.d. In a report on the affairs of Jubbal, a chiefdom of the Simla Hill States, William Hays, Deputy Commissioner of Simla, wrote, "Power in the Hills . . . May be said to be shared by the chiefs and the custodians of the *Deotas* of temples. Where there is no chief or the chief is a weak man, the *Deota* is all powerful."

[26] It is equally relevant to remember that Kali or Bhagwati (a goddess more easily identifiable with the important Hindu deities) also seems to have had a role in Malendu settling in Chebishi.

[27] An exact translation of this may not be available. A *bhor* was an assistant or sentinel who often accompanied the superior *deota* on journeys and even

Some say that Kot Ishwar gave Jhatak as *wazir* to Malendu. On one occasion Lata left Malendu and fled to Kot Ishwar, but on Malendu's complaint Kot Ishwar restored him to his master [Malendu] who took him back to Malendi.[28]

The status of *deotas* seems to reflect the inequalities of society. Lata a "low-caste *deota*" was ordered by Kot Ishwar to return to serve his master Malendu. Like a landless cultivator customarily obliged to serve his landlord, Lata was bound to Malendu.

Amongst the territorial *deotas* were two others that were particularly powerful in their respective areas. The first was Mananeshar Mahadev (or Manani), the *deota* of Sihal *pargana* (district). The second was Dum *deota*, with an important temple situated in Sharmala village – also located interestingly in *pargana* Sihal – even though he was actually the *deota* of the Upardes (Oobades) *pargana*.[29] The two *deotas* were drawn into a prolonged dispute in the mid nineteenth century. Such disputes often arose because of the close association between the structure of hill society and the hierarchy of *deotas* created, complemented, and reinforced each other. Contentions of the temporal world – within the village community and between peasants of different villages – could take the shape of hostile behaviour between *deotas*. The fact that most of these deities also had demarcated villages and people under their control effectively increased the number of people drawn into the dispute. There were instances when *deotas*, devotees, and the *rana* himself were embroiled in controversies pertaining to spheres of influence and honour.

The genesis of the dispute between Manan and Dum *deotas* lay in a fair that was traditionally held at Shamokhar, an open glade with a small pond in the centre, situated on the border of Upardes and Sihal *parganas* (the territories of the two contending parties). Both Manani

---

protected him from the evil eye to which, interestingly, even *deotas* were vulnerable.

[28] Rose 1970: I, 456.

[29] *SHSG* 1910, Kumharsain: 10. Both Rose 1970, I: 45 and *SHSG* 1910 refer to Mananeshwar (Manani) as Magneshwar (Mandni). Field work conducted in September 2004 suggests that the proper name is derived from the village of Manan where the temple is located.

and Dum used to attend the fair along with their devotees, and the two parties jointly conducted the activities.[30] Sometime around 1845, however, a disturbance at the fair gave birth to a prolonged feud between the two *deotas*. To prevent this confrontation from developing into a widespread unrest, Rana Pritam Singh, the ruler of Kumharsain, restrained Manan *deota* from going to Shamokhar. As compensation for this restriction, Manani could levy an annual fine (*chershi*) of a goat and one rupee and four annas in cash on the villages of Dakun, Rabog, and Jadun, where some followers of the Dum *deota* lived. Interestingly, this fine was realised personally by *deota* Manani, who toured these villages (once in three years) like a tax collector, accompanied by his palanquin bearers, musicians, and other servants. During the tax collection tour the peasants of the taxed villages had also to bear the unwelcome burden of feeding the followers accompanying Manani.

On account of the administrative incompetence of Rana Pritam Singh's successor, the state was brought under a council of regency between 1874–96.[31] Perhaps on account of representations made by followers of Dum *deota*, and the absence of a ruling *rana*, the earlier decision of Rana Pritam Singh was reconsidered. A new judgment – passed by Kot Ishwar Mahadev (obviously voicing the dominant view that may have emerged) – banned the holding of the Shamokhar fair altogether and disallowed both *deotas* from going there. Sometime after 1890, however, the *chershi* paid till then by some Dum villages to *deota* Manani was justifiably stopped. This prompted

---

[30] Cf. Beals 1964: 109, 110, 113. In his study of *jatras* in Karnataka, Beals observes that *jatras* are a social institution that "creates the only situation in which one village entertains other villages and in which competition between villages takes place." He further suggests that the *jatra* acts as a "kind of safety valve mechanism for regulating relationships between villages." Another perspective that Beals adds is that such institutions also help in diluting the internal social conflict of a village because "the requirements for total village cooperation evident in virtually every aspect of the *jatra* performance provide a mechanism for suppressing conflict and providing a superordinate goal which lessens the importance of the goals to be achieved through conflict."

[31] *SHSG* 1910, Kumharsain: 5.

the followers of Manani to argue that if *chershi* was disallowed, the fair at Shamokhar should be restored. It seems that members of the council of regency also took sides in this controversy. The council was, however, superseded in 1896 and the British government appointed an Indian administrator, Mangat Ram, as manager and *wazir* (minister) of the state. Finally, it was the new *wazir* who decided that the Dum villages would have to pay a *chershi* of thirty rupees every three years, but *deota* Manani would not be permitted to enter the Dum villages to collect it. It may be mentioned that the Shamokhar fair was never revived again.

Naturally, the confrontation over the relative power and territorial jurisdiction of the *deotas* was in reality a dispute between their followers.[32] Judging from the course of events, *deota* Manani seems to have been the more powerful of the two, almost certainly because of more influential supporters.[33] The powerful position of Manani is shown by the fact that, unlike other areas, the villages loyal to him do not on important festive occasions make a financial contribution to Kot Ishwar even today.[34] The considerable support mustered by both groups might also explain the prolonged and closely contested nature of the dispute and the need for the *rana* to play the role of mediator. Village or *pargana* loyalties played an important role in

[32] Peabody 1991b: 746; Herzfeld 1990: 370. In the context of the resolution of disputes pertaining to theft in Crete, Herzfield argues that there is a need to move "beyond the conventional dualities of theology and folk religion, or religiosity and instrumentality, or indeed structure and practice." He suggests that "some versions of structure are best seen as practice". Therefore, he contends that the use of religion in the resolution of disputes pertains to "strategic explorations of the tension between ideal order and daily experience."

[33] Rose 1970: I, 451; *SHSG* 1910, Kumharsain: 10. There were also instances of territorial conflict between Dum *deotas* of different places, such as between the Dum of Sharmala and the Dum of Gathan. Rose recounts that the Dum of Gathan forcibly seized the territory of three valleys from the Dum of Sharmala. The story, once again, clearly emphasises the importance of deities being derived from control over people and territory.

[34] Personal interview, 21 September 2004, with Surinder Shaunik, priest of Kot Ishwar temple (Mandholi).

the contest, and it needs to be remembered that different peasant clans usually dominated contiguous areas. It is likely, therefore, that assertive clans of the Kanet peasantry used the contest between *deotas* as an occasion to restructure relationships with the ruling group in the state capital. Despite his ritual dominance, the *rana's* might in reality have been confined to making a diplomatic choice between two or more equally powerful contenders.

IV

Some tentative suggestions made here try to interpret the relationship between nature, religion, and politics. To begin with, the topography of the region probably encouraged the emergence of small fragmented, socio-political entities. This was the world of scattered village communities and autochthonous belief systems often closely linked with their specific physical surroundings. Despite this fissiparous tendency, however, there existed forces that bound distantly situated people and places to each other. Significant among these tendencies was the superimposition of a broadly Sanskritic ideology that coalesced with monarchical authority and appropriated local myths to create an overarching hegemony. From its stronghold in the main river valleys of Himachal, Brahmanism sought to reach out to the semi-secluded, unorthodox world of the tributaries. In doing so it transformed both itself and the local cults that thrived there.

The interplay of nature, religion, and political organisation found expression in the continuous exchange between folk deities, peasant clans, and formal state structures. It was through the village god that the peasantry related to the world outside, and it was through the village god too that external forces sought to influence the peasants. Thus was created a cosmic vision that had to be rejuvenated through the periodic enactment of mythical events at *jatras* and fairs where the relationship between the hierarchy of gods and their followers was ritually elaborated. But even as this enactment pretended to reassert an unchanging past, hidden somewhere within its many rituals was probably a subtle reinterpretation that sought to make the enactment relevant to a changing society.

6

Myth, Legend, and Folklore in Himalayan Society

Making Histories

DESPITE THE REMARKABLE literary achievements of its classical age, pre-modern South Asia was also in large part a pre-literate society. The idea of popular literature, as understood by "literate" societies today, seems therefore not to have had a very long history in the region. It might even appear to be somewhat contradictory, for literate people represented the upper social echelons and there may have been nothing "popular" about what they wrote and read. This did not mean that the common people had neither the medium nor the means for public expression. An exceptionally rich oral tradition seems to have served the purpose that popular literature came to serve in some other societies. Indeed, it was probably the medium through which the elite and the popular communicated. For all practical purposes, then, South Asian societies had long nurtured an extensive and varied "literature": this was a literature that enjoyed immense popularity but was never written.

To historians this presents both a challenge and an opportunity. Practitioners of the craft are aware that the dominant viewpoint in a society is often expressed through inscriptions, scriptures, historical documents, and a wide range of literary works. These are materials that constitute the sources for formal history-writing. Oral traditions are, on the other hand, perceived as inherently egalitarian and also

Published earlier as C. Singh 2008.

as the ideological repositories of protest and rebellion. While the dominant viewpoint is more clearly structured, the "oral literature" of the subaltern seems rather fluid and malleable. The chronological authority of "official" historiography stands in contrast to the apparently ageless nonconformism of popular memory.

For some time now, scholars have argued that to ignore informal traditions as sources is to write one-sided and elitist history. In order to represent this counter-position of the people, therefore, the use of non-formal, unconventional sources has gained currency– though historians have been somewhat reluctant entrants in this field. Underlying this trend is the conviction that by this means an alternative "history from below" can be written. But is that true? Are oral traditions, for example, really the articulations of the underprivileged?

It goes without saying that history-writing is an immensely complex task. Apart from an existing body of knowledge formally recognised as history by scholars and institutions, there are ongoing processes whereby historical ideas and information are preserved and generated. This is what Bernard Lewis is evidently referring to when he speaks of histories that are "remembered, recovered and invented". While remembered history is represented by the historiography that enjoys formal social approval, recovered history, according to Lewis, is the reconstruction of a forgotten past through the recovery of new evidence. It is such reconstruction (or construction) of history that he appears to be rather wary of, for he sees it occasionally leading towards an "invented" history written "for a purpose".[1] Recovered and invented histories might well be by-products of political and social change, and the altered sensibilities that such change usually entails. History then comes to be told "not as it really was, but as we would wish it to have been."[2] Formal historiography, therefore, involves the prioritisation of contesting interpretations, and an acceptable history is evidently the dominant interpretation around which a consensus is temporarily achieved. If this struggle for acceptability occurs between conflicting histories based on documented or recorded evidence, it

[1] Lewis 1975: 12.
[2] Ibid.: 72.

is equally likely that oral narratives – so successfully passed down through generations – are the result of such contestation. In short, oral traditions are not necessarily counter-narratives to dominant ideology, nor are they invariably hidden undercurrents of resistance. They might, in fact, be victorious ideas emerging from this struggle for dominance.

Within the various forms that oral tradition can take, it is popular memory – taken as oral history – that seriously challenges the academic standards of scholarship which historians set for themselves. It is a field in which "the tension between competing historical and political aims is most apparent: between oral history as recreation (in both senses) and as politics, between canons of objectivity and an interest, precisely, in subjectivity and in cultural forms."[3] This is a tension that originates primarily from empirical questions regarding the nature of historical sources, and as to how and to what purpose these can be used. Criticism regarding the utilisation of oral sources usually questions their reliability for writing an objective history. Like most information concerning the past, even memories about it tend to take the form of time-determined, sedimented layers in which awareness of the present always exists. If we admit that elements of bias are to be found in all historical sources, oral history may be spared the opprobrium of being regarded as singularly unreliable. In fact, historians today no longer make serious claims to objectivity and empirical truth in the way they were once inclined to.

As for the study of popular memory, it is sometimes suggested that this is possible "only where empiricist and positivist norms break down".[4] Almost every surviving source of history incorporates the assumptions, values, and theoretical perspectives not only of the society that originally created it but also of those that successively accepted and perpetuated it. In this context, then, popular memory is no exception. Though it has some claims to being intrinsically democratic and to representing people whose subordination prevents them from recording their own histories, unwritten tradition should not be

[3] Popular Memory Group 1982: 216.
[4] Bommes and Wright 1982: 255.

construed as being independent of dominant historical interpretation. Even to the extent that it is a product of subaltern consciousness, popular memory remains a part of the larger domain within which the contest for domination occurs. In fact, "it exists in its relations to the dominant discourses and not apart from them or by itself."[5] The very fact that a particular kind of memory persists is perhaps because it has undergone the process of disputation, transformation, and inclusion into a narrative that a society (or social section) deems appropriate and worth preserving. Such a construction of tradition is a form of historical reasoning that can, and often does, function as a political force. This is also a situation in which many of the myths that constitute oral tradition begin to blend with politics.

One might reasonably suggest that the society in which a myth is narrated believes it to be a truthful description of events that occurred in the distant past. Since in this respect they are a matter of faith, myths acquire the status of authority in situations where no definite answer is available.[6] It is precisely because of this quality that people in power have tended to resort to stories of mythic antiquity of a foundational nature in order to justify their position.[7] Myths may assume various forms and be used for several different purposes, "as associated with gods and rituals, as affirmations or charters of lands, titles, institutions and beliefs, as explanations at various levels and as problem-exploiting and problem-palliating in various ways..."[8] Indeed, so diverse yet crucial has been the function of myths in pre-modern societies that one might agree with the argument that "what is called myth, not what is called history, has virtually monopolised all human reflection about former times."[9] To a great extent, therefore, myth was the means by which pre-modern societies sought to give

[5] Ibid.: 226.
[6] Bascom 1984: 9.
[7] Trompf 1989: 625.
[8] Kirk 1984: 58.
[9] Trompf 1989: 622 further points out that, apart from the content of myths being arranged as a sequence of events, "they have an almost universal tendency to locate the greater part of these in a primordiality" that gives to them a "pastness".

meaning to the world they lived in, and one wonders whether historical thinking, particularly at the popular level, became initially possible primarily because of myth.[10]

It might be useful here to try and make some general distinctions between myth, legend, and folklore. The overlap between the three is so great that an attempt to indicate the difference may seem trivial and superfluous. Without engaging in a detailed interrogation of this question, it suffices to point out briefly the relationship that these forms of narrative appear to have with each other and with history. Resting as they did upon faith, myths were also reservoirs of dogma and the sacred. The principal personae in a mythical narrative were usually deities, animals, or superhuman ancestors (but with all the predilections of human beings) who lived at a time when the world and its inhabitants were very different from what they are today. Legends, while being very similar to myths in most respects, existed in an age quite comparable with ours. Legendary figures were essentially human, and the stories they were part of were not always considered sacred. The folktale, on the other hand, seems to have had the freedom of the myth but not its sanctity. It carried the secular wisdom of the legend but seems to have lacked its rootedness. It is through very picturesque language that Jacob Grimm conveyed his understanding of the issue:

> The folktale (marchem) is with good reason distinguished from the legend, though by turns they play into one another. Looser, less fettered than legend, the folktale lacks that local habitation which hampers legend, but makes it more home-like. The folktale flies, the legend walks, knocks at your door; the one can draw freely out of the fullness of poetry, the other has almost the authority of history. As the folktale stands related to legend, so does legend to history, and (we may add) so does history to real life. In real existence, all the outlines are sharp, clear and certain, which on history's canvas are gradually shaded off and toned down. The ancient myth, however, combines to some extent the qualities of folktale and legend; untrammelled in its flight, it can yet settle down in a local home.[11]

[10] Ibid.: 648.
[11] Grimm 1883: III, xv.

Overlapping Realms: The Great and Little Traditions

To understand the functions of myth, legend, and folklore in Indian society, they need to be juxtaposed with its conceptions about the social and cosmic order. One of the most useful instruments for understanding these has been the concept of Sanskritisation, and the rather broad but relevant twofold division that is usually made between the great and little traditions.[12] Sanskritisation was a process that enabled certain sections of society to improve their position in the social order. The great and little traditions, on the other hand, seemed to represent the entire ideological and religious spectrum within which such improvements in status could take place. One needs to emphasise, however, that even though Brahmanical culture provided the framework for the process of Sanskritisation, it was not insulated from popular customs. It synthesised and incorporated diverse aspects of folk belief, and in doing so it established a cultural continuity between the great and little traditions. Local traditions interacted with an influential Brahmanical one that successfully accommodated many of their principal beliefs and also provided an intelligentsia that mediated between regional diversities. Yet it would be difficult to deny that there was also a tendency for the Brahmanical great tradition to superimpose some of its own thinking upon non-Brahmanical belief systems.[13] But this was not a confrontational position. There was what has been called in another context "a shared and contested universe of ideological discourse".[14] And the interaction between the two was a process by which there occurred "the dissemination of universal values and the universalization of parochial values."[15] In this context Marriott makes an interesting argument when he says that

> for understanding why Sanskritic rites are often added onto non-Sanskritic rites without replacing them, the concept of primary or indigenous process of civilization again offers useful guidance. By definition, an indigenous

[12] Cf. Chakrabarti 1992: 123–49.
[13] Srinivas 1965: 167.
[14] Herzfeld 1990: 320.
[15] Chakrabarti 1992: 148.

civilization is one whose great tradition originates by "universalization" or a carrying forward of materials which are already present in the little tradition which it encompasses. Such an indigenous great tradition has authority in so far as it contributes a more articulate and refined statement or systematization of what is already there.[16]

This did not, however, result in the undisputed dominance of Brahmanical ideology. Nor did it bring about the homogenisation of "Hinduism" or a drastic reduction in the number of folk cults that have flourished over most of South Asia. Numerous regional traditions, in fact, continued to remain popular over large areas. It has been suggested that the gods, rituals, and practitioners of the little and great traditions addressed two different yet overlapping and also complementary concerns. These were matters that have been broadly divided into the "transcendental" and the "pragmatic".[17] While one was associated with the cosmic order and the divine, the other pertained primarily to solving the mundane problems of daily life. Mandelbaum explains: "In India, the gods charged with the cosmic verities are not expected to attend to a baby's colic or a lost cow. Yet both baby and cow must be cared for, since they are part of the grand design. In India, the answer is through specialisation of function and hierarchical arrangement among supernaturals, as among men."[18]

The hierarchical positioning and wide range of functional specialisations did not mean that the numerous deities (to whom people resorted) were located at different levels of theological (or spiritual) development. All that this categorisation seems to indicate is a division of roles in a "community's religious universe".[19] Local gods, even though subordinate to Brahmanical deities, exercised considerable powers of their own.[20] Not surprisingly, therefore, Sanskritic and

---

[16] See Marriott 1955: 197, 200.

[17] Mandelbaum 1964: 10.

[18] Ibid.: 11; cf. Herzfeld 1990: 320. In the context of the mountain villages of Crete, Herzfeld sees the interaction between "doctrinal and local concepts of Orthodoxy" as being part of the larger relationship that exists between "structure and strategy".

[19] Klass 1995: 109.

[20] Mandelbaum 1964: 9.

non-Sanskritic practices have continued to coexist all over India.[21] Marriott has shown that even amongst Brahmans living in the area of ancient Brahman settlements, as many as 55 per cent of the deities worshipped could be non-Sanskritic. And only 15 to 19 per cent of deities worshipped by the lower castes were Sanskritic.[22] What probably made this coexistence possible was the ingenious method of identifying each subordinate god with one or the other of the great Brahmanical gods. This was further simplified, in a sense, by the argument that the confusing multiplicity of deities and their numerous forms "no matter how parochial or non-Sanskritic, are but manifestations of a single divine Oversoul (*Paramatma*)."[23]

The vast array of gods and beliefs encompassed by the little and great traditions was indeed remarkable. But the convictions and practices that they engendered were not restricted simply to the domain of religion. They were also contributory factors in the creation and sustenance of socio-political systems. What appears to have facilitated this overlapping of religion, social structure, and polity were the large number of myths and legends that were usually overarching phenomena influencing almost every sphere of a society's ideological existence. As articles of faith, as expressions of history, and as social and political prescriptions, these myths not only anchored a society to its immediate surroundings, they also created a larger worldview within which it organised and situated itself.

Polity, Legitimacy, and Primordial Myths

The most dominant myths in pre-modern societies were usually those associated with the legitimisation of authority. Scholars are agreed on the fact that in the Hindu kingdoms there existed an intimate ideological and ritualistic equation between the ruler and the presiding deity of the kingdom.[24] This was often a relationship rooted in a

[21] Atkinson 1976; Berreman 1964: 53–69.

[22] Marriott 1955: 209; Gonda 1976: 88. Marriott's study is with reference to the village of Kishan Garhi situated in present-day Haryana.

[23] Marriott 1955: 218; Gonda 1976: 95.

[24] Singhi and Joshi 1999; Richards 1998; see also Peabody 1991a: 29–56; Peabody 1991b: 726–54.

primordial past, or in a quasi-historical event that ostensibly changed a dynasty or the nature of its rule. By this means the importance of the king and the victory of good over evil were explicated.

While each principality of the western Himalaya explained its origin by means of some such myth, perhaps the most interesting ones are those associated with the kingdoms of Kulu and Bashahr.[25] The essence of a myth lies in its recounting and it would be relevant here to dwell at some length on their narration. As a qualification, we need to point out that there are as many versions of myths as there are narrators. The ones mentioned below are those upon which there has so far been a fair degree of agreement.

The Kingdom of Kulu

Two myths and one semi-historical legend are central to the manner in which religion and polity were perceived in pre-modern Kulu. The first myth was situated in a time when gods and demons struggled for domination, while the second (more earthly) sought to explain and describe the formation of the Kulu kingdom. Within historical time seems to be located the legend that recounts the establishment of the rule of the Brahmanical god Raghunath over Kulu.

(1) Myth A[26]

The demon (*asura*) Tandi, his sister Hidimba and other *asuras* lived in, and dominated, the area that lay to the south of the Rohtang pass [i.e. towards the Kulu Valley]. Upon Bhim – one of the Pandavas brothers – seems to have fallen the task of exterminating the demons that then controlled Kulu. This task Bhim accomplished successfully

---

[25] Rathore 2000. It may be important to mention that a great number of these myths are altered stories derived from the *Ramayana, Mahabharata, Puranas*, etc. Local poets and bards have changed many of the stories to suit their convenience. In some versions of the local *Ramayana* or *Ram Katha* we find the Pandavas battling Ravana. While in the local recounting of the *Mahabharata* the abduction of Sita is referred to.

[26] *Kangra DG* 1918, II, III & IV: 20; Harcourt 1972: 35. Harcourt's account was written around 1870.

and he even ran off with [took as his wife] Hidimba. Tandi, who resisted this liaison, was killed.

Bhim had a follower – Badar [Vidhur of the *Mahabharata*?] – who married a daughter of Tandi. Their sons were Bhot and Makar, who were brought up by the sage Bias Rishi. When Bhot grew up he married a Tibetan woman, named Sudangi. Makar, who seems to have been a Hindu, however, separated from them because they ate cow's flesh. He founded a town on the left bank of the Beas which he named after himself Makarsa. This name, written in various forms, was for long applied to the whole of Kulu. Makar's descendants are said to have ruled there for a time, but the dynasty ultimately died out.

(2) *Myth B*[27]

The dynasty that finally came to rule Kulu had been driven out of Hardwar by neighbouring chiefs. One of the cadets of this family, named Behangamani, found his way to Kulu. He was temporarily successful in asserting himself in the Parbati valley of Kulu, but subsequently was pushed into living the life of a fugitive in the village of Jagat Sukh. It was here that he met a Brahman who read in his face the signs of royalty and assured him of victory in his endeavours. Thereafter, when Behangamani was on his way to a local fair he carried on his back a frail old woman who too was heading the same way. The old woman ultimately turned out to be the goddess Hidimba. Having thus obtained the blessings of the goddess Hidimba, Behangamani was spontaneously accepted by the people of Kulu as their raja.

A variant of this myth refers to a tyrannical chief who ruled at a place called Bhanara.[28] It was for deposing this much-hated ruler that the goddess Hidimba approached the young adventurer at Jagat Sukh. After persuading him to join the cause, she grew to a gigantic size and carried Behangamani on her shoulders. With the support of a large following of local people, the chief of Bhanara was defeated and the descendants of Behangamani have ruled the country ever since with the support of Hidimba.

[27] *Kangra DG* 1918, II, III & IV: 21.
[28] Shabab 1999: 71.

(3) *The Legend of Raghunath*[29]

This legend pertains to the time of Raja Jagat Singh (1637–72), one of the most famous of the Kulu rulers. It is said that the raja learnt that in his kingdom there resided a Brahmin named Durga Datt who possessed a *patha* (about three pounds) of pearls. Goaded by avarice, Jagat Singh sought to appropriate these pearls forcibly. On being thus compelled to part with the pearls, the Brahmin along with his family committed suicide by setting fire to his house. This was perceived as Brahminicide, and the legend goes that each time food was set before Jagat Singh it turned into worms. To overcome this curse that the dead Brahmin had cast upon him, the raja was advised that an idol of Raghunathji should be brought from Ayodhya and installed in Kulu. It was through the efforts of another Brahmin, named Damodar Dass, that such an idol was finally brought to the kingdom. Lord Raghunath was placed on the throne of the raja who thereafter regarded himself only as the god's viceregent.

The Kingdom of Bashahr

In the state of Bashahr, too, primordial myths sought to explain the origins of the ruling family and legitimise its right to rule.

(1) *Myth A*[30]

According to this story the ruling family descended from Sri Krishna of Hindu mythology through his grandson Pradyumna. The latter came to Sarahan [in Bashahr state] with the purpose of marrying the daughter of the ruler of this area – Basava Deo (or Banasur). It is not clear whether the marriage took place, but Pradyumna is believed to have killed Banasur and taken over his kingdom. The capital that Pradyumna established was located at Kamru in the Tukpa *pargana* of Kinnaur.

---

[29] Rose 1970: I, 474; Hutchison and Vogel 1982: II, 458–9, Shabab 1999: 73–4.

[30] *SHSG* 1911, Bashahr: 5.

A variant of this myth has been preserved as a story in which the marriage is itself a central question.[31] According to this version:

Once it so happened, they say, that the Asura king Banasur's daughter Usha saw a handsome prince in her dream and began to pine for him. Her friend Chitralekha painted for her the portraits of all the young princes of India. When Usha saw the portrait of Pradyumna, the grandson of Krishna, she recognised him as the one she had seen in her dream. The Asuras were masters of witchcraft and with the help of Chitralekha they managed to transport the prince Pradyumna from Dwarka to their capital Shonitpur, in his sleep. Pradyumna's sudden disappearance caused a furore in Dwarka, and Krishna himself proceeded towards Shonitpur with his armies. In the ensuing battle between the Pandavas and the Asuras, the Pandavas won, and as a peace offering Banasur offered his daughter in marriage to Pradyumna and so the young couple got married. Shonitpur in Himachal is now known as Sarahan.

(2) *Myth B*[32]

This is a story that suggests that the Bashahr ruling family is of Brahmin origin. We can recount it here:

Two Brahmin brothers came from Kanchanpuri [Kanchipuram?] in the Deccan (South) to visit the temple of goddess Bhima Kali situated in Sarahan. Their visit coincided with the fact that the throne was vacant because the last raja descended from Pradyumna had just died. The goddess Bhima Kali had indicated to the state officials that whosoever entered the palace gate at a certain time should become the raja. The younger of the two brothers happened to wander in at the right moment and was promptly hailed by the people as their sovereign. His older brother had to be content with the office of priest to the royal family and the village of Ranwi near Sarahan, in *jagir*. The Brahmins of Ranwi are to this day spiritual advisers to the raja and his family.

[31] Vyathit 1984: 30.
[32] *SHSG* 1910, Bashahr: 5.

There are some interesting similarities in the content and structure of the myths of the two kingdoms. The apparently older myths (marked "A" above) trace the emergence of a moral polity to the defeat of the *asuras* (demons) in their conflict with the gods or their associates. The Pandavas evidently played a significant role in these battles. A marriage alliance between the two contending sides seems to have resulted from the contest. From this alliance sprang the original family that ruled over the kingdom conquered from the *asuras*. It is perhaps not without significance that in Kulu the progenitor of this ruling family was Makar (the Hindu) and not Bhot (the cow-flesh eater). For the moment, at least, ethical rule seems to have been thus established.

But the struggle between good and evil is a constant and unending one. In the subsequent myths (marked "B" above) the old ruling family was no longer at the helm of affairs, and the inhabitants of the kingdom were waiting for a righteous ruler to appear. A stamp of legitimacy was further provided by the role that the goddess played in the selection of the new ruler. In Kulu, Behangamani's struggle to defeat an unjust chieftain and return the kingdom to its earlier moral state appears to have further justified his right and need to rule. In Bashahr, the Brahmin lineage of the ruler was perhaps validation enough. That the elder of the two brothers came to serve as "spiritual adviser" to the kings (descendants of the younger brother) conforms with Sanskritic perceptions about the social position of Brahmins. At the time the Bashahr myths were documented by colonial officials (some time before 1910), the story about the descent of the family from Pradyumna was more popular than the one of Brahmin origin. The fact nevertheless remains that the latter myth has persisted, indicating thereby that it must have at some earlier time served a purpose and been acceptable to the people.

A new historical phase seems to be highlighted by the legend in which Lord Raghunath was made the ruler of Kulu. This transfer of power, interestingly, coincided with the assigning of the kingdom of Mandi to the god Madho Rai by Raja Suraj Sen in 1648.[33] It is also possible that the importance of Badri Narayan grew in Bashahr

---

[33] Hutchison and Vogel 1982: II, 385, 459.

during the same period. A detailed examination of the role these legends played in the polity of the western Himalayan states can form the subject of a separate study. Tentatively, however, one may suggest that stories about the installation of the new presiding deities mark a more explicit alliance between ruling dynasties and Brahmanical religion. The sanction of the dominant religious ideology was thus sought and obtained.

The purpose of the primordial myths appears to have been to create a political order in which monarchical rule was considered essential. It was also one that had to be legitimised by Brahmanical deities. It was only then, perhaps, that an ethical and moral world could come into existence.

Territory, Social Order, and Intermediate Legends

The establishment of a moral order also required that a continuous struggle be waged at all levels. If primordial myths told the story of how just monarchs came to create and rule kingdoms, other myths and legends were needed to explain the organising principles of the socio-political system at the lower level. It is not possible to recount all the large number of myths and equally numerous variants that seem to serve this purpose. By way of example, however, two of the most popular ones may be worth exploring. Retelling legends is always a tricky and contentious business and trying to interpret them even more so. But the extent to which the legends of Mahasu and Srigul have long gripped folk imagination in the hills of Shimla, Sirmur, and adjoining parts of Uttaranchal make the risk worth taking. The inevitable disputes and disagreements that arise while dealing with these legends indicate the factious wrangling that must often have preceded even those versions upon which a temporary consensus was achieved. Given below are rather brief and abridged renderings.

The Legend of Mahasu[34]

It is important to remember that the cult of Mahasu in the region is part of a vibrant living tradition. Several irreconcilable versions of the

---
[34] Rose 1970: I, 302–15, 404–17.

legend have always existed and it would not be very surprising if new ones are still slowly being created through a gradual and piecemeal process of reinterpretation.

(1) *Hanol Version*

Between the Tons and Pabbar rivers there lived a race of evil spirits who, led by their chief Kirmat, thrived on human sacrifice. A Brahmin couple [Una/Huna Rishi and his wife] of village Madrat above the Tons had lost six of their seven sons to the demons in this manner. It was the fear of losing their last surviving son that brought about a vision to the wife that "Mahasu of Kashmir" would save their child. Through miracles arising from the Brahmin's faith, he managed to travel to distant Kashmir and obtained a promise of support from Mahasu. The Brahmin was asked to return home and make a plough of silver with a share of pure gold, and to yoke it to a pair of bullocks that had never before been yoked. Every day he was to plough a portion of his land. On the sixth Sunday after his return, he discovered that he had only managed to make five furrows in the field that day. From four of these furrows sprang the four Mahasus (Bhotu, Pabasi, Bashik, and Chaldu) and from the fifth arose their mother. From the other parts of the ploughed land emerged countless warriors. In the battle that ensued, the evil spirits were massacred and Kirmat, too, was pursued and killed.

After this war, the four victorious Mahasu brothers parcelled out the conquered territories between themselves. Bhotu got Hanol, between Pabasi and Bashik was divided the territory of Garhwal, while Chaldu was free to exercise dominion wherever he could find a following. It was in the Shimla Hill States region that Chaldu became particularly powerful, and he moved around freely collecting his dues from the villages that he passed through.

(2) *Bashahr Version*

The Mahasus originally ruled in Kashmir and were engaged in a constant feud with a rival god named Chasralu. After one particular battle, a severely injured Chasralu fled and was pursued by Mahasu into the area that is now the domain of Mahasu. Chasralu saved himself by taking shelter in a cave, but the entire territory fell to Mahasu. The story of Mahasu has thereafter been a tale of the continuous appropriation of new areas from older deities. At the time that this version of the legend was recorded by H.A. Rose (in the early years of the twentieth century) the struggle between an aggrandising Mahasu and other gods whom he sought to displace from their territories was still continuing.

(3) *Version III*

A third, more detailed, and Sanskritic version has also been mentioned by Rose. It is quite similar to the legend preserved in Hanol.

The story begins at an earlier time when the Pandavas stayed at Hanol for nine days before proceeding to Badrinath and then disappearing. Thereafter, the Kali Yug began and demons like Kirmat made Maindrarath (on the Tons) their home and began to roam freely. It was Kirmat who devoured the seven sons of Huna Brahmin [Rishi], thereby compelling him to go first to the Devi at Hatkoti, and then to the mountains of Kashmir to seek the help of Lord Shiva. Impressed by the faith of Huna Rishi, Shiva assured him of help and asked him to return home. As Shiva had foretold, a Devi appeared at Maindrarath and from different parts of her body were born the four Mahasus. Then were created the other minor gods: Kiyalu, Banar, and Sher Kalia. From the Devi's hair arose a huge army of heroes.

In the battle that ensued, Chalda Mahasu killed the demon Kirmat at village Khandai. Another demon, Keshi (who usually lived at Hanol), was killed in the Masmor mountains, and the country thus freed from their oppression. The hill people rejoiced and offered to pay a share of their produce as revenue to Mahasu in return for protection against evil spirits and demons. Initially, the people did not know how to worship Mahasu, so Huna Rishi dictated Vedic hymns for this purpose.

The country that had just been conquered was then divided between the Mahasu brothers and other minor gods. Each god was assigned a territory and ordered to take charge of it. When all the gods had gone to their respective places all the land was regarded as the kingdom of Mahasu, and the capital was established at Hanol.

The hierarchies in Mahasu's kingdom having thus been established, it was believed that if any irregularity occurred in their territory, the gods in charge of it and the people would be called upon to explain the reason.

The Legend of Srigul

(1) Sirmur Version[35]

Bhakaru, a Rajput of Shaya, had no offspring. His desire for a son prompted him to journey to Kashmir and consult a knowledgeable pandit there. The pandit advised Bhakaru to marry a Brahmin girl by whom he would become the father of an incarnation. Bhakaru, accordingly, married a Bhat girl to whom were born two sons Srigul and Chandeshwar. Soon after their birth the parents died and the sons were sent to the care of their maternal uncle.

Unable to tolerate mistreatment at the hands of his aunt, Srigul fled to the forest and took up his abode on Chur Dhar. One day, from the top of Chur Dhar he saw Delhi and wished to visit it. So he left his home in the care of Churu, a Bhor Kanet by caste, collected a number of gifts, and set out for the city.

Reaching Delhi, Srigul went to a trader's shop. Through his miraculous powers, he made a skein of silk that he was carrying weigh more than all the possessions of the trader. The trader complained to the Mughal emperor and Srigul was arrested while cooking his food. In the struggle to arrest Srigul, the cooking vessel overturned and the food flowed out in a burning torrent which destroyed half the city.

Eventually Srigul was taken before the emperor who cast him into prison. But Srigul could not be fettered, so the emperor, in order to defile him, had a cow slaughtered and pinioned him with the thong of its hide. Upon this Srigul wrote a letter to Guga Pir of the Bagar in Bikaner and sent it to him by a crow. The Pir advanced with his army, defeated the emperor, and released Srigul, whose bonds he severed with his teeth. Srigul then returned to Chur Peak.

[35] Ibid.: 290–2.

During his absence, the demon Asura Danun had displaced Chur (Srigul's servant) and taken possession of half of Chur Dhar. Srigul, having failed to dislodge Danun, appealed to Indra who sent a bolt of lightning and expelled Asur Danun from Chur.

(2) *Jubbal Version*[36]

Srigul and Chandeshwar were the sons of Bhokru, the chief of Shadga. Upon their father's death, Srigul resolved to give his kingdom to Chandeshwar and to live in Chur Dhar. But ultimately, on the advice of his minister (Devi Ram) Srigul gave his brother only a part of the kingdom and made Devi Ram the regent at Shadga during his own absence.

Srigul then set out for Delhi and stayed at a Bhabra's shop. Once, when he went to bathe in the Jumna, a butcher passed by driving a cow to slaughter. Srigul remonstrated with the man but in vain. So he cut him in two. The emperor sent soldiers to arrest Srigul but they were all killed by him. So the emperor himself went to see such a daring man. When the emperor saw him, he kissed Srigul's feet and promised never again to kill a cow in the presence of a Hindu. So Srigul forgave him.

Srigul, however, had to return to Chur Chandni, which was in danger of being polluted by a demon. Upon his arrival, he killed the demon. Then Srigul sent for Devi Ram and his (the minister's) two sons from Shadga, and divided his kingdom among them. When the three new rulers had finished building their *rajdhanis*, Srigul sent for them and bade them govern their territories well, and he made the people swear allegiance to them.[37]

Unlike the primordial myths explaining the emergence of the states of Kulu and Bashahr, the legends of Mahasu and Srigul are not entwined with the legitimisation of a particular ruling family. But the

[36] Ibid.: 296–7.

[37] It may be mentioned here that the *bhandars* (granaries) of Srigul are located at the old capital at Jorna, Sarahan (in Jubbal), at Shadga (in Sirmur), and at Deona. At the beginning of the twentieth century a *patha* of grain was collected from every house over which Srigul held sway. Rose 1970: I, 298.

urgent need to restore righteous rule is quite apparent. For Mahasu, the rise of demonic forces after the arrival of the Kali Yuga seems to have provided the compelling reason to make an appearance. Srigul, on the other hand, had to contend with the threat of Muslim rule in distant Delhi apart from an aggressive *asura* nearer home. Whatever the original cause requiring godly intervention, the outcome of both legends was the establishment of a kingdom of victorious gods. In both cases, the kingdom was sub-assigned either to subordinate deities or to trusted and responsible associates. The association of the plough with the legend of Mahasu might possibly suggest the extension of agriculture and the settlement of new villages in an area that was also partly pastoral. It appears that a system of taxation was also brought into existence and the people were advised to obey their territorial rulers. Each territory thus assigned was to be properly governed because the people and the new ruler were ultimately answerable to the god himself.

Compared to myths connected with the legitimisation of ruling families, a much greater degree of popular participation in the establishment and maintenance of a socio-political system is evident here. Not kings and principalities, but delineated territories, villages, and ordinary people seem to be the major concern of these intermediate legends. Approval for local autonomy is also noticeable in these legends where clear territorial divisions were made between the gods. This autonomy is still treasured in western Himalayan society today. The continuous contestation for control over territory and villages was also, however, a part of how this autonomy could be exercised. The growing influence of Chalda Mahasu at the cost of other gods is a case in point.

Mahasu, of course, was not always victorious in these contests. The traditions of the Rawain region of Uttaranchal tell us of his defeat at the hands of Samsu (Duryodhana) and also Karna. In the latter case, it seems that the people of Devjani village (in Garugarh Patti) were tired of the heavy grain tax they had to pay to Mahasu at his temple in Hanol and also the enormous expense incurred by them every time the peripatetic Chalda Mahasu toured their village. The peasants appealed to Karna *deota* of Kandah to rid them of Mahasu.

The latter obliged and so the village of Devjani was lost to Mahasu.[38] Similarly, Srigul seems to have been vanquished by the god Biju at village Deothal in Kuthar state.[39]

How is one to explain the references to distant places and people in these legends? The mention of Kashmir in both legends, for instance, or the roles of the Muslim ruler of Delhi and Guga Pir in the legend of Srigul appear to be extraneous to their immediate environment. Perhaps these excursions into different areas are important for situating the legends, but not fundamental to the ultimate message they seem to convey. Till such time as a better answer can be given, we may argue along with Trompf that "When a people slowly discovers its cosmos is after all so tiny and its past only one small segment of the whole world's past, its members tend to clutch at the newly introduced events that appear more significant for placing their own achievements and human adventure in an adjusted, more appropriate context."[40] References to Kashmir and Delhi may perhaps be explained as a reaching out, or a widening of mental horizons. Essentially, however, the legends remain grounded in the polity and society of the region in which they arose.

Small Communities and Village Folklore

The narratives of Mahasu and Srigul were important sagas that bound fairly extensive areas and a large number of people to a common believed history. On the other hand, there were hundreds of small succinct stories that provided a sense of identity to little villages and tiny communities. Each village had its wealth of folklore through which it created a meaningful world for itself. Lovell argued that

> Locality is constructed through the intermediary of deities which are themselves extensions of natural and environmental features. By providing these deities with names, a place is created for humans to dwell in, and the gods are simultaneously provided with an identity and a place of

[38] Bijalwan 2003: 52–3.
[39] *SHSG* 1911, Kuthar: 4.
[40] Trompf 1989: 633.

their own ... The action of naming a deity therefore imbues a space with a sense of place, no longer an anonymous feature in the environment.[41]

The settlement of a new hamlet, an outbreak of pestilence, or the failure of a crop: around each such social experience could be woven an explanatory story that contributed to the formation of a collective memory. These minuscule histories of scattered peasant communities were told by innumerable tales that simultaneously stretched upward, through a series of mediating legends and myths, to the grand narrative of epic proportion approved by Brahmanical orthodoxy. Each of these was, therefore, an element that constituted the enormous body of folk memory that for long remained almost the only history that ordinary people of the western Himalaya knew.

For a peasant of Jataon village (Mahlog state), the powerful Srigul may have been a god to approach in times of serious trouble. But for the many small problems that cropped up all too frequently, it would have been wiser to appease *deota* Jit Danon in his own village. This *deota* had once been Jit Ram, a Kanet of Sherla village whose spiritual achievements caused him to be worshipped after his death.[42] It did not seem to matter whether he was called *deota* or *danon*. Madhor Deo, the god of village Mangu (Baghal state), was once a man who had died without male issue.[43] Dev Boindra of Kotkhai was, before he became a god, a prince of Nadaun who was fond of gambling,[44] while the Boindra of Devri (Sirmur) was a man who came from Nahan.[45] Biju, the deity of Kuthar (as distinct from the god Bijat), is believed to have been Bijai Pal the son of Ajai Pal, who was the raja of Kotguru,[46] and Devi Kundin of Dudan (*tehsil* Pachhad, Sirmur) was the blind daughter of Raja Sur Prakash of Sirmur. She became a goddess after she fell in battle against the forces of the Mughal emperor.[47] These are

---

[41] Lovell 1998: 54–5.
[42] Rose 1970: I, 465.
[43] Ibid.: 469.
[44] Chauhan 2000: 70–1.
[45] Rose 1970: I, 466.
[46] *SHSG* 1911: Kuthar, 4.
[47] *Sirmur SG* 1907: 47.

a few examples of how such stories illustrated the memory of hundreds of villages. It is perhaps possible that through this reservoir of folklore we may, slowly but surely, assemble an understanding that bridges the gap between folk memory and academic history – if indeed such a thing is desirable.

Postscript

In regions such as the western Himalaya, history as a cultural creation will always have to reckon with myths, legends, and folklore. Myths have been used to convert information accumulated over ages and obtained from diverse sources into an integrated narrative. Their purpose was not necessarily to deal with particular places and personalities, but to create a structure by which society and polity could be organised. It has been suggested that myths are inclined to repeat the same sequence because they seek to "render the structure of the myth apparent".[48] They are also a method of using analogy for describing a perceived reality. In doing so, myths and legends create a number of cause–effect relationships that are regarded as essential for maintaining order in the real world.

The most important characteristic of myths, however, is their timelessness. To quote Godelier: "Mythical thinking can only appear as temporal thought tracing the origins of things, unmasking original and still present origins – it is both analytic and synthetic, going back to a past but living history, back to the eliminated but eternally present genesis in order to explain the present world order."[49] Is it surprising then that though a myth invariably refers to an age long past, it still "explains the present and the past as well as the future"? Lévi-Strauss had suggested that myths had, in modern times, been replaced by politics. He elaborates this by explaining that "When the historian refers to the French Revolution, it is always as a sequence of past happenings, a non-reversible series of events, the consequences of which may still be felt at present. But to the French politician,

---

[48] Lévi-Strauss 1978: I, 229.
[49] Godelier 1978: 213.

as well as to his followers, the French Revolution is both a sequence belonging to the past – as to the historian – and a timeless pattern which can be detected in the contemporary French social structure and which provides a clue for its interpretation, a lead from which to infer future developments." [50] He may, indeed, have been correct.

During the Dushehra celebrations at Kulu in October 2004, a dispute between two *deotas*, which had been long festering, came to the fore. Shringa Rishi of Kothi Chehni and Balu Nag of Vakya Tandi contested for occupying the position to the right of Lord Raghunath at the parade of gods in Dhalpur Maidan. Their position in the hierarchy of *deotas* depended upon where they were located in relation to Raghunathji. Supporters of each contending side forwarded arguments based on the mythological relationship of these deities with Lord Raghunath. However, the actual political underpinnings of this dispute were not hidden. The territories dominated by these *deotas* overlapped with two different constituencies of the state legislature (Banjar and Ani constituencies) that were also strongholds of two different political parties: the Bharatiya Janata Party and the Congress. In this struggle, the two *deotas* were represented by the respective members of the state legislative assembly. Interestingly, the Kulu Dushehra Committee that was to resolve this dispute was headed by a third member of the legislature. The *pujari* of the Raghunath temple, on his part, was of the opinion that the quarrelsome gods could enjoy the privilege in alternative years![51]

To contemporary observers it is apparent that myths of various kinds are often the façade behind which politics is practised. And politics is, in considerable measure, the basis upon which histories are written. In this complex sequence of interconnections, it should not surprise us then if we do occasionally see myth and history walk hand in hand.

---

[50] Lévi-Strauss 1978: I, 209.
[51] *The Tribune*, 25 October 2004.

7

The *Dum*

Community Consciousness, Peasant Resistance, or Political Intrigue?

THE STATE OF Himachal Pradesh covers a considerable portion of the western Himalaya and the physiographic features that constitute it vary considerably. These geographical differences have in turn left an indelible imprint upon the manner in which society in the various (fairly distinguishable) parts of Himachal was organised. One such area has been broadly termed the mid-Himalayan zone. Here was located a peasantry often considered typical of the western Himalaya. Despite its far-flung hamlets, and widely scattered cottages and landholdings, the social life of peasants here was closely interwoven. Survival in the Himalayan countryside required a high degree of co-operation between peasant households. The wide range of activities that constituted the economic life of the villages and hamlets required them to come together to make the best possible use of the region's numerous but extensively dispersed natural resources. Social organisation appears to have been very closely related to physical surroundings. The resources that the mountain environment yielded were such as could only be made use of through either a pooling of manpower or a well-formulated division of labour. For example, a peasant household could not on its own extract and transport the large quantities of stones, slate, and timber needed for house construction. Similarly, the need in summer to pasture flocks in

First published as C. Singh 2002.

the alpine grasslands and simultaneously transplant paddy in low-lying terraces near the valley's bottom required a division of labour that an average peasant family could not always carry out. Community co-operation was essential.

Further reinforcing this environment-engendered co-operation was the emergence of a community "consciousness". This was bolstered partly by caste affinity and more so by the shared faith in a common folk *devta*. The hold that religious beliefs had upon the mind of the hill peasantry should not be underestimated. A combination of village-level co-operation (for economic reasons) and community consciousness (as a socio-political phenomenon) was probably the central organising principle of rural life in the mountains. This, interestingly, was also the factor that enabled the peasantry to resist unbridled exploitation by those in authority. Co-operation within the community and collective resistance to unwelcome external intervention were therefore not only inextricably linked but were, in a fairly strong sense, equally the product of the physical environment.

II

It can be justifiably suggested that the historiography of the western Himalaya has not overcome its obsessive preoccupation with political events. While the study of political history is far from being an undesirable pursuit, it needs to be rooted in an understanding of the society which generates a particular variety of politics. Political developments of historic significance are not the creations of whimsical individuals in authority. Nor would many scholars today hold a brief for the "great man" theory of history. On the other hand, one need not be an uncompromising proponent of "history from below" to suggest that that perspective complements the dominant traditional approach.

The available documentary information on the history of Himachal Pradesh seems quite explicit on matters pertaining to territorial disputes between the petty princely states, the administrative and socio-economic reform that the rajas carried out in their respective states under British supervision, and the manner in which a few political activists of the region were gradually drawn into India's struggle for independence. It seems that politics in Himachal was a triangular conflict between the princes, freedom fighters, and the British; that such people moulded society and economy – they "knew better" as it were – ruling and reforming an ignorant hill peasantry towards modernity. Documents by their very nature frequently reflect the interests of the dominant sections of society and enable them to ensure, through legal means, a continuity of their privilege. A historical narrative that unquestioningly accepts the standpoint of official records is quite likely to be an account of the public activities of a select and powerful few.

Who then speaks for the peasant? How is one to write a "popular" history focused on the populace and ordinary daily life? There appears to be at present an "imagined" paucity of source material for writing a history that goes beyond the rajas' courts and their surrounding officials and sycophants. I use the word 'imagined' because some of the existing archival sources, when subjected to proper questioning, might yield interesting information.

An attempt is made here to examine some instances of unrest that appear to have origins of a "popular" nature. Social and political protests were evidently expressed in forms rooted in local tradition and strongly supported by the social structure. Before elaborating on this, it is worth noting that documented information is not always the best material on which to base such a study. The exploration of such themes can be substantially enriched by adopting research methods that have until recently lain beyond the bounds of academic history-writing. Popular memory and oral traditions constitute a living culture. They confront the professional historian with a consciousness frequently in conflict with the historical understanding that emerges from literary and written evidence. The two are not, however, completely irreconcilable constructions of the historical past. Documented works, while pretending to be authentic and objective histories, are frequently a means by which the dominant understanding imposes itself. "Popular" memory, on the other hand, while articulating the counter-position of the underprivileged, is by definition and logic linked to the dominant understanding. Aspects of popular memory that are acceptable to those in power get assimilated over a period of time to the prevailing (i.e. dominant) historical reconstruction. On the other hand, subversive traditions are sought to be suppressed and likely to be found more often in the undercurrents of less-known symbols, stories, and myths of subordinated social groups.

III

The specific nature of socio-political protest is often linked to the character of the state. The manner in which disaffection was expressed by the aggrieved, as also the response to it of those in authority, depended upon the hierarchy of interests that existed (or emerged) in any given state system. Martin has shown the tensions caused in the English countryside by the transition from a feudal economy to agrarian capitalism within the political confines of an absolutist state. What is relevant from our point of view is the fact that the protest of the peasantry was often "reformist" and based upon the "legality of their actions".[1] The English peasants' understanding of their own position and the methods they adopted need to be considered briefly. Martin observes:

> In rioting, the peasants felt that they were putting the king's laws into execution. Such laws had been long neglected by local JPs who were doubly ill-thought of because they were often the very offenders against the enclosure statutes ... This "legalistic" attitude was reflected in the fact that rioters claimed to have held warrants from the King endorsing their actions.
>
> The limited and "reformist" goals of the revolts were evident in the fact that the rebels actually promised to cease their activities if the King would take action to reform enclosures within six days ... The riots were remarkably free from violence against persons, all feelings were directed against the offending hedges, fences and ditches.[2]

Further explaining this understanding of the peasantry is a perceptive observation by E.P. Thompson on subordinated communities and their relationship with superior social sections:

---

[1] Martin 1986: 115–16, 175.
[2] Ibid.: 175.

At points the culture and values of these communities may be antagonistic to the overarching system of domination and control. But over long periods this antagonism may be inarticulate and inhibited. There is often a kind of "cut-off": the villager is wise within his own village, but accepts the inevitable organisation of the outer world in the terms of the rulers' hegemony: he bitterly resents the exactions of the landowner and the moneylender but continues to believe in a just King or a righteous Tsar. Very often every protest is legitimised in terms of the dominant system, by taking over its rhetoric and turning it to a new account: the rulers are unjust or forgetful, they must be recalled to their duties, they must intervene to prevent their subordinates ... from exploiting the poor. Only in exceptional circumstances do the people reach out from their local experience, their (as opposed to assumed) values and offer a more general challenge.[3]

The explanations forwarded by Martin and Thompson are not as irrelevant to the study of western Himalayan society as might appear at first glance. Even the peasantry in Tehri and Garhwal organised the *dhandak*; a form of customary rebellion against exploitation that has been quite well explained by Ramachandra Guha.[4] He says the *dhandak* was an effective method by which the peasants utilised ambiguities in the dominant ideology to obtain redressal for their grievances. In Himachal, customary rebellion appears to have taken the form of the *dum*.

IV

On the origins of the *dum* in Himachal, an interesting argument was forwarded as early as 1920.[5] The undifferentiated and close-knit nature of the Kanet peasantry, it was implied, lay at the root of this form of customary rebellion. Despite the out-migration of sub-groups over a long period of time and the consequential expansion of the Kanets across a vast area, they retained a strong sense of community identity. Central to this identity was the family or ancestral god, to whom all

[3] Thompson 1977: 265.
[4] Guha 1989.
[5] Mandi SG 1920: 85.

members of the community were equally subject. Not only was the ancestral god the focal point of religious worship, he was also the authority to which disputes of a more worldly nature were frequently referred. Apart from being related to each other, the community deities exercised a remarkable influence over geographically delineated stretches of territory. Brahmanical dominance and orthodox forms of social segregation, though they had some ritual significance, were unable to make much headway in matters of daily life. Even the Thakurs and Ranas, whose socio-political superiority was accepted by the Kanet peasantry, were considered part of this overall structure and

> came to be regarded as the representatives of the territorial gods and carefully maintained the theocratic basis of Kanet institutions. Nor were they able to crush the democratic instincts of the people over whom they ruled. The communal form of worship lent itself to combination for political purposes and the development of the *dum* . . . enabled the Kanets to retain some measure of control over the actions of the rulers.[6]

It has been argued above that the physical environment in which the mid-Himalayan Kanet peasants were located required them to maintain a fairly close-knit social organisation. Agricultural and pastoral activity in the mountainous regions could be successful only where the community was bound by generally acceptable principles of division of labour. This also involved the establishment of methods of decision-making and social control by the "community". Translating the process of "community" decision-making into a protest movement was only one logical step forward. The manner in which customary peasant resistance was organised has been described in interesting detail in the *Mandi State Gazetteer*:

> When abuses transgressed their [rebels'] very liberal ideas of what was reasonable, they resorted to a *dum*, their almost infallible remedy for the redress of grievances. The *dum* is one manifestation of the democratic spirit found amongst the peasantry of the hills and in several respects, bears a resemblance to the modern forms of labour combination. Its

---

[6] Ibid.: 86.

effective weapon is the general strike, the malcontents attempting to achieve their objects by bringing the ordinary affairs of government to a standstill. A *dum* is not usually undertaken lightly, but when a decision has been reached its execution is prompt. A gathering is proclaimed by the beat of drum and the rebels, or reformers as they regard themselves, collect together at some appointed spot, which may be a temple, a hill or a forest.[7]

An important aspect of the *dum* was the manner in which the protesters were bound to each other by means of an oath, called *gatti* in the upper hills and *chawl* in the lower areas.[8] Religious symbolism seems to have been an integral part of peasant resistance in the hills. In form, at least, the customary rebellion was not projected as a violation of existing rules and conventions. On the contrary, it took on the appearance of being a reassertion of tradition. The oath to resist unjust oppression was further strengthened by the approval provided to it by the local deity, for we learn that the protesters would

> gather at a convenient temple and swear in the name of the god not to obey the chief or official, to whose methods they object. The oath is administered by the ringleader by distributing small stones or other trifling objects among the assemblage and the acceptance of one of these signifies the taking of the oath. Thenceforth those who have entered into the oath pay no revenue to and disregard the authority of the ruler or official in question, and the oath can only be cancelled by the latter meeting the malcontents at the temple and making up his differences with them. A goat is then sacrificed and both sides agree that the oath is at an end.[9]

It might be fruitful here to mention some instances when *dums* were organised in the princely states of Himachal. A few years before 1839, it seems that one such rebellion broke out in Kulu against Raja Ajit Singh and his guardian Tulsu Negi. Both the raja and Tulsu Negi were forced to flee in the face of this unrest, in which a significant part was apparently played by Kapur Singh, the *wazir* of Saraj.[10] During the course of this *dum*, however, the leaders of the rebellion

---

[7] Ibid.: 86.
[8] *SHSG* 1911, Bashahr: 85; Bilaspur: 12; Mandi SG 1920: 68.
[9] *SHSG* 1911, Bashahr: 85.
[10] Hutchison and Vogel 1982: II, 471.

violated certain established conventions when they dragged out the wife of Tulsu Negi from the temple of Jamlu where she had taken refuge. The series of droughts that ensued in the Saraj area were believed by the people to have been a consequence of the desecration of the temple. Subsequently, to get the curse removed the descendants of the *dumyas* were called upon to do penance.[11]

Alexis Soltykoff, a Russian traveller who passed through Nahan in 1842, gives a brief description of what appears to have been a *dum* in September that year. The mountain he describes may have been Chur Dhar, located at the borders of the Sirmur and Shimla districts – also the abode of the influential Srigul Deota, suggesting the religious sanction that protesters often claimed for their *dum*: "... a revolution broke out in this tiny kingdom and the peaceable villagers, driven to extremities, armed themselves with pikes and betook themselves to a high mountain which I can see from here and which is partially covered with snow. There ... they entrenched themselves, and declined to come down until they obtained what they considered their right."[12]

In 1859 similar unrest broke out in Bashahr state against the cash assessment of land revenue introduced there in 1854. Apparently, a scarcity of coins prompted the rebellion, and the fur stopped flying only with the restoration of the old system of paying revenue in kind. The other demand of the rebels – that an unpopular *vakil*, Paras Ram, be removed from office – was also acceded to and the old rule regarding the appointment of *wazirs* was reintroduced. In the entire episode it seems that Fateh Singh, an illegitimate brother of the raja, played an important role. Yet what is significant is the demand of the peasantry that the traditional system of revenue administration be restored.

Disturbances occurred again in 1893 in Mandi (Saraj) when the peasantry protested against an encroachment on their rights, as well as against the imposition on them of *begar* thrice a year. The immediate pretext that triggered the unrest was the introduction of a smallpox vaccine which included buffalo lymph. The disturbances were easily suppressed, though they did prompt the authorities to

[11] Rose 1970: III, 318.
[12] Garrett 1971: 121.

rectify some of their initial mistakes. Once again an official, the *wazir* Jawala Singh, was held responsible for "tactlessness" and reverted to his post in Panjab.

The earlier suggested association of the Kanet "community" – if one is permitted to stretch the meaning of the word – with this form of protest finds support in a state gazetteer observation, which says the trouble that broke out in Baghal state in 1905 had the support of the "entire Kanet community". In this case too, however, there was an element of court intrigue, and to improve the administration an additional official had to be appointed by the British for help to the regent ruling in place of the minor raja.

The clearest available description of a *dum* is of the 1909 unrest in Mandi state. Without getting into the details of this rebellion, suffice it to say that the issues involved included the question of land revenue assessment, *begar*, and official corruption. Jiwa Nand, the *wazir*, was perceived as the prime culprit because of his success in isolating the raja from the people. The rebels, led by one Sobha Ram of Gandhiani village in Sarkaghat, acted according to a plan of action that the rebels regarded as "constitutional". Gradually, increasing numbers of agitators marched to Mandi on various occasions to make collective representations to the raja. Despite the largeness of the crowds that gathered in Mandi town, "no excess of any sort was committed". The protesters were at pains to say they had no grievance against the raja, "their sole aim was to save him and the state from the *wazir* and his confederates." Ultimately, two companies of the 32nd Pioneers had to be requisitioned by the state administration in a show of force despite the rebels desisting from violence. Jiwa Nand was dismissed and the agitators dispersed peacefully after offering *nazar* to the raja. In keeping with the specific methods adopted by the peasantry to express disaffection, it explicitly adopted a strong ideological position. The *Mandi State Gazetteer* of 1920 is quite explicit about this:

> . . . the leader and his followers have a curious idea that they are helping the Raja and that it is the proper function of the people to step in when things are going wrong; they do not think they have done wrong and point to the absence of looting or molesting of women. Similarly, the

malcontents in their representations were careful to affirm, although various State officials had oppressed them, the Raja had not, and they declared the matter to be a private affair between themselves and their ruler. "The King can do no wrong", is a statement which the hill man accepts literally, for he believes his Raja to be as much god as man. The faults of administration are ascribed to the incompetence of his ministers, or dishonesty of his officials; and when they become so glaring as no longer to be tolerated in silence, the people decide on a change of administration in the interest of the Raja as well as of themselves.[13]

In order to arrive at some sort of generalisation it can be suggested that the *dum* was a form of peasant resistance that had much in common with similar protest movements in pre-modern societies. As a method of protest it was firmly rooted in a strong "community consciousness", its foundations embedded in a social system powerfully influenced by the ecological surroundings, and which had as a result evolved effective means of collective action. That this form of customary rebellion continued in Himachal even during British rule – when society had slowly begun to change – needs further explanation. Perhaps the essentials of peasant life continued broadly the same over the colonial period. Little research has been done on the nature of pre-modern Himachali society and the economic rationality that governed its daily life. The process by which colonialism tightened its grip over state and society in the western Himalaya, too, remains a question only half-answered. A fuller explanation of the *dum* will have to await the unravelling of these and other interconnecting threads.

---

[13] Mandi SG 1920: 68–9.

8

Between Two Worlds
The Trader Pastoralists of Kinnaur

NOMADIC PASTORALISM WAS for long the primary economic activity of societies in many parts of the world. There are, furthermore, numerous instances showing its successful combination with a tribal form of organisation which is also sometimes considered "the political dimension of pastoral nomadism".[1] Pastoralism, nomadism, and tribalism are, however, not inevitably interdependent socio-economic phenomena. It is now well understood that all tribal groups were not pastoralists or nomads, and sedentary agriculture was (and still is) practised by a large number of tribes. Conversely, it can be argued that all pastoralists were not tribesmen. The former could be, as I will endeavour to show, an integral part of a caste-oriented society supporting a fairly complex non-tribal state structure. Nomadism as a way of life, nevertheless, came to be more closely associated with pastoralism because it was "at least partially based upon movement of people in response to the needs of their herds and flocks."[2] But these seasonal movements with flocks could differ in nature from full-fledged nomadism and have been also classified as transhumance and semi-nomadism. The relationship between pastoralism, nomadism, and tribalism is therefore an extremely complicated one. Perhaps for that reason it has always been very difficult to make empirical generalisations based on these phenomena.

First published as C. Singh 2004.
[1] Tapper 1991: 54.
[2] Salzman 1967: 116.

If tribalism and pastoralism are frequently thought indistinguishable, it is not because they invariably share some fundamental empirical or theoretical similarities. More apparently, it is their *difference* from sedentary, non-tribal society that seems to mark them out. It is, at times, believed that the difficulty of establishing political and economic control over the nomads (due to their mobility) and tribals (because of tribal loyalties) prompted sedentary states to deal with them in a similar fashion.[3] The long-term objective of sedentary states is seen to be the conversion of pastoralists to settled agriculture. While this may be true in most cases, exceptions cannot be ruled out. Enforced sedentarisation would rarely be the policy in a state where settled agriculture, though crucial and predominant, was inadequate and pastoralism contributed substantially to revenue. Western Tibet was clearly one such region and the medieval Tibetan state was successful in harnessing the resources generated by pastoralists, and exercised control over them without forcing them to take to agriculture. A fifteenth-century source indicates that in addition to the cultivated area assigned as a grant to the monastery at Tholing, "the nomads of the land have to give, from their own resources, salt and the equivalent of [such] field crops to the monks, no one can avoid these duties, which have been assigned . . ."[4] Gellner has argued that even if they functioned as political units they were not closed, self-contained societies but, more likely, part of a larger cultural world. He points out that "tribes may or may not be cultural units, but they certainly are political ones," and further that the "tribe does not fill out the world, but it defines itself in terms borrowed from a wider civilization . . ."[5] Much the same might be said about pastoralism. It is worth considering whether pastoralism has for very long now been an independent, self-sustaining system; whether it has not been inevitably linked to, and even dependent upon, non-pastoral economies and societies. That pastoralism must necessarily take cognisance of a larger non-pastoral world (both socially and economically) in order to

[3] Tapper 1991: 54.
[4] Vitali 1996: 111.
[5] Gellner 1983: 536.

define itself is now recognised. Even culturally, as Talal Asad contends, "the point, surely, is to identify and analyse the nature of the total system within which nomads exists and reproduce themselves as a distinctive cultural, political and economic entity."[6] There is evidently a larger system within which pastoralism could be seen to be contained. In this context the significant question, raised by Asad, is not "What are the spatial/social boundaries of (nomadic) society?", but "What are the critical elements and limits of the system of reproduction of an ideologically defined social group?"[7]

Yet another question that has attracted the attention of scholars is the possibility of identifying characteristics that distinguish "tribe" from "state". Several distinctions can, perhaps, be made in this regard between the ideal conceptions of both "tribe" and "state". Such an exercise might even be useful for examining theoretical possibilities. But in understanding social realities it could create complications of its own. Tapper notes that "the 'pure' tribe is an empirical impossibility" and "the 'pure' state is similarly impossible".[8] Any empirical study of the relationship between "tribe" and "state" would, therefore, be dealing with societies placed within a wide range of deviations from their theoretically conceived "pure" state.

This is, perhaps, equally true of pastoral nomadism. Pastoral societies around the world have exhibited such diversity that the disagreement over what constitutes "pastoralism" persists. A rudimentary definition of it, as being the "exploitation of the primary

[6] Asad 1977: 422.

[7] Ibid.: 424.

[8] Tapper 1983: 66, 67. The difference between "tribe" and "state" that Tapper notes is useful: "As bases of identity and political allegiances and behaviour, 'tribe' gives primacy to ties of kinship and patrilineal descent, while 'state' insists on the loyalty of all persons dwelling within a defined territory, whatever else their relation to each other. 'Tribe' stresses personal, moral and ascriptive factors in status, while 'state' is impersonal and recognises contract transaction and achievement. The division of labour in the 'tribal' model is 'natural'; in the 'state' model it is complex. The 'tribal' mode is socially homogeneous, egalitarian and segmentary, the state is heterogeneous, egalitarian and hierarchical. 'Tribe' is within the individual, 'state' external to him."

produce (the herb layer) through the intermediary of gregarious migratory herbivorous flocks or herds", can be conveniently arrived at. Lefebvre has further suggested that "Nomadic pastoral societies that have settled and become agro-pastoral have preserved their initial productive organisation."[9] The truth and inadequacy of such a definition are both apparent. The cultural connotations that give meaning to, and represent the essentials of, pastoralism are not reflected in this bare description. The complexities, therefore, of attempting to provide a widely acceptable definition of pastoralism are immense. For the present purpose, it suits us to adopt the very general description of pastoralism being a "cultural economy" which was "dependent on extensive systems of livestock husbandry".[10] Rodgers' description is, however, quite complex. He mentions several categories such as nomadism, seasonal migrants, diurnal movement, stable pasture, and also adds that "a further set of agricultural activities could be superimposed on these simple categories."

This allows for considerable space within which a large number of diverse societies might possibly be accommodated. For example, Ratnagar has pointed out that the word *grama* included not only cultivated fields but also grazing ground, and further that cultural values were a very significant factor that needed serious consideration in any study of pastoralism.[11] Though a wide range of economic activities were often pursued by many such societies, an evaluation of "the amount of time spent on such activities and the degree of dependence upon livestock" would also be important when deciding whether they can be considered pastoralists.[12]

The adoption of particular occupational practices by pastoral people can be partly explained by the nature of their interaction with sedentary society. Equally important has been the role of religious beliefs and customary practices as a means of retaining both a pastoralist identity and an economic specialisation that distinguished them from non-pastoralists. It is ecological factors, however, that seem

[9] Lefebvre 1977: 2.
[10] Rodgers 1991: 201.
[11] Ratnagar 1991: 187, 192.
[12] Salzman 1967: 117.

to have normally been central to the emergence and sustenance of pastoralism and the multiple occupational strategies linked to it. A large number of studies of the phenomenon have quite convincingly shown it as a response to the ecological conditions in which a society is situated. Typical of the ecology-centred approach to the study of Himalayan society is the argument that "the mountain ecology of the Himalaya confronts its inhabitants with special problems and each of its different ecological zones reflects a concomitant local adaptation in the integration of subsistence production and ecological finality."[13] Even semi-arid conditions contribute towards making pastoralism a viable survival mechanism and one has to keep in mind the connected nature of resources as well as the fact that subsistence strategies frequently merge into one another rather than being sharply opposed.

The Kinnaur pastoralists can be best understood from this perspective and be more accurately described as agro-pastoralists. In both capacities – as agriculturists and pastoralists – they were closely associated with the emergence and administration of the state.

Kinnaur

The area called Kinnaur (today a district) occupied the upper or northeastern portion of what was formerly the princely state of Bashahr. It consists of the uppermost part of the Satlej river basin which is bound by immense mountains with peaks ranging from a height of 16,000 to a little over 21,000 feet above sea level. Because of its location in the midst of the Great Himalayan range, Kinnaur is made up of an enormous mass of rocky spurs thrown up by the main range. These spurs create steep and narrow valleys through which mountain streams flow rapidly to join the Satlej. The steepness of the entire countryside is revealed by the fact that the Satlej, during a passage of seventy-three miles through Bashahr's territory, descends from 7600 feet to 2800 feet. Like the valleys of most of its tributaries, the Satlej valley too is narrow and has hardly any open spaces suitable for agriculture near the river bank. Some open space is, however, available along the banks of the Baspa River, though most of the

---

[13] Brown 1987.

cultivable land and villages in Kinnaur are located much higher up along the slopes flanking the rivers. The state of Bashahr, according to tradition, was seen as consisting of broadly two territories: Kochi and Kinnaur. Kochi was the better cultivated and more open area lying southward in the lesser Himalaya, while Kinnaur was, as we have seen, the extremely mountainous and sparsely cultivated territory in the Greater Himalaya, and which was bordered at its north-eastern extremity by the Zanskar range.

In Kinnaur the area suitable for agriculture is very limited. All cultivated land has been laboriously developed into terraces over a long period of time and is therefore permanently settled, though it has also sometimes been suggested that shifting cultivation, involving the cutting and burning of forests, was once common practice.[14] At present, however, there is little evidence to support this contention. Lt. W. Murray, Superintendent of the Simla Hill States in the 1820s, wrote in a communication to his superior about Kinnaur that "The country . . . does not exhibit a single level spot equal to the dimensions of a field of two acres, square measurement," and that "The inhabited regions are confined to the dells and gorges which intersect them and drain off the streams, the cultivated parts forming so small a proportion as to appear as patches or steps of stairs up the slopes of the mountains."[15] Later, in 1932, Hamilton was to observe that "Culturable ground is so limited and the forces of nature are so hostile that the country is not self-supporting."[16] As early as 1818, Gerard had noted that the grain produced in the villages of Kinnaur was "insufficient for consumption".[17] Even today, the scope for the extension of agriculture remains almost as limited as before, though the encouragement to horticulture with the introduction of the apple has enabled the utilisation of new and larger areas. Despite the emergence of many new economic options, however, pastoralism – the traditional supplement to agriculture – has not yet been completely abandoned. Under the circumstances, it is extremely unlikely that

[14] Hamilton 1932: 22.
[15] Murray 1824: 288.
[16] Hamilton 1932: 32.
[17] Gerard 1993: 294.

there ever existed the possibility of a full-fledged agricultural economy emerging in the area, either in pre-colonial or colonial times.

It must also be pointed out that pastoralism could not, by itself, have ever been a viable alternative either. Large-scale sheep-rearing was impossible if the flocks were to remain within the territorial confines of Kinnaur throughout the year and depend entirely on its internal resources. Consequently, it was the adjoining lower areas to the south and south-west of Kinnaur that provided the necessary grain and summer pastures. Without access to these additional external resources, life in the area would likely have been impossible. This, in a sense, made Kinnaur quite similar to some of the other regions of the world where agro-pastoralism was practised.[18] Environmental factors and the combination of various occupations so essential for survival in Kinnaur were described by Murray thus in 1824:

> surrounded by rocks of difficult access, inimical to industry, offering little inducement to cultivation in a climate of protracted rigours, the inhabitants of Kunawar have followed the course which nature dictates, and we find them active, enterprising and industrious, occupied in extensive commercial intercourse and trade; rearing vast flocks which form their chief dependence and trafficking into remote countries under great hardship and privation to gain a comfortable subsistence for their families at home.[19]

An examination of the Forest Department report reveals that nothing really seems to have changed in this regard even more than a century later.[20] Hamilton wrote, "the people make up for the shortage of food by importing grain from the low hills and plains and a large proportion of the community is engaged in this as well as in other trade with Thibet; for which purpose sheep and goats are the chief means of transport. Sheep are also kept for the production of wool both for trading purposes and for the local manufacture of clothing. There can, therefore, be no question of the great importance of sheep and goats for the very existence of the Kanawaris . . ."

---

[18] Black-Michaud 1986; Molnar 1981: 33. Jacob Black-Michaud has studied the Selselah and Bairanwand pastoralists in Luristan in Iran.
[19] Murray 1824: 278–9, 282.
[20] Hamilton 1932: 32.

Whatever the mix of economic strategies adopted by the Kinnauras, it is evident that animal husbandry was central to both agriculture and trade in the rugged and inhospitable area in which they lived. The pivotal position that the Kinnauras assigned to sheep- and goat-rearing in their lives is reflected by a detailed though unsympathetic report completed in 1959:

> The local people have come to believe that their economy is based on the rearing of sheep and goats. The tract is extremely cold. They need warm garments which are made of the wool from the sheep. The flesh of these animals is an integral part of food for them. The cultivated holdings are steep and so situated that carriage of farm-yard manure is inconvenient and un-economical and that their manuring is only possible by penning sheep and goats there. The terrain is so difficult that transport of food-stuffs and other necessities of life is not possible by other means of transport and that trade with Tibet is only possible with the sheep and goats. They, therefore, want that no limitations on their number and no restriction, whatsoever, of their grazing in the forests should be imposed.[21]

While duly reporting these arguments put forward by the Kinnauras, the official who conducted this study was far from persuaded by their point of view. From the very beginning he was of the opinion that migratory flocks were "an evil", a "nuisance as they are allowed to enjoy unfettered freedom to graze" and that "their number has got to be brought down with a heavy hand."[22] In conformity with the view that seems to have then prevailed in bureaucratic thinking, he felt that the Kinnauras, by resorting to sheep farming, had chosen the easier, unsustainable path of over-exploiting forest resources. For purposes of "development" this was considered a less desirable option than the terracing of more fields for cultivation and the adoption of modern agricultural techniques. The Kinnauras, it was felt, needed "proper guidance" and in order to reduce their flocks which "they are not going to do voluntarily . . . it is again necessary to achieve this by taxation."[23]

[21] Parmar 1959: 58.
[22] Ibid.: 14.
[23] Ibid.: 59.

However, migratory shepherding in Kinnaur was not an isolated economic activity that could undergo changes or be deliberately modified without affecting other aspects of life in the area. Different sections of Kinnaura society while engaging in specific, traditionally assigned socio-economic functions were also – direct or indirect – participants in a network of production strategies. This makes it impossible to classify them into rigid categories. If we were to consider only the most important economic activity of each section of the Kinnauras as the sole determinant, a large number of them would fail to qualify as pastoralists. On the other hand, because of the considerable income obtained from migratory flocks tended by some members of the family, many Kinnauras would not be considered full-fledged agriculturists. An important portion of the population, apart from being agro-pastoralists, might even emerge as active traders! The complexity of the relationship between agriculture, pastoralism, and trade, and their interdependence makes it difficult to quantify their respective contributions to the total economy.

The task of enumerating migratory flocks has invariably been difficult and prevented officials from arriving at accurate figures of the number of sheep/goats. The general impression until relatively recent times, however, has been that flocks in Kinnaur have been increasing rapidly.[24] Flock-owners and shepherds were also accused by officials of falsifying numbers in order to avoid taxes. For example, in Pangi (Chini *tahsil*) a village of a hundred families, the sheep/goats were said to number ten thousand, though the estimate in revenue records was much less.[25] In the context of the area adjoining the south of

---

[24] Chatur Bhuj 1928: 20; Parmar 1959: 57. Parmar provides figures for some years, and the fluctuations in the figures further confirm the difficulty of a census of migratory animals. The figures noted below are of Chini *tahsil* that coincided roughly with the area of present-day Kinnaur.

Year	Sheep and Goats	Year	Sheep and Goats
1884–9	38,305	1916	99,282
1904	102,968	1926	105,634
1910	76,707	1950–1	89,983
1913	55,556		

[25] Parmar 1959: 57.

Kinnaur, Fraser observed in 1815 that "The villagers always showed an unwillingness to disclose the amount and the sources of their property; and it may be presumed that their sheep, as one of those, were concealed from the view of strangers; a conduct that might arise from a fear of betraying grounds for tax or tribute to be imposed on them . . ."[26] Fraser's argument was perhaps only partly correct, for he happened to visit the area at a time when the flocks were away at their summer pastures. Even the deliberately reduced number of livestock put forward by flock-owners would make it clear that pastoralism constituted an essential part of Kinnaura life. So much of the economy revolved around sheep-rearing that it was also the measure of a family's wealth and its capacity to pay taxes. Some rudimentary form of enumerating flocks must certainly have been followed by the pre-colonial state. This was essential to estimate the "grazing tax" and other levies on wool and wool products which were an important source of state income. In all the states of Himachal, and even in the British-administered districts, taxes on pastures and pastoral products were an important part of state revenue.[27]

In all Himalayan areas bordering the entire length of the Tibetan plateau, gelded sheep and goats have always been used as pack animals to transport essential goods and trade commodities.[28] Similarly, the treacherous mountain paths of many parts of Kinnaur could only be negotiated by these sure-footed smaller animals. This marked the point at which trade and pastoralism overlapped despite there being spheres in each of these occupations which were distinct and, therefore, required some element of specialisation. Goats and sheep are able to carry only small loads of merchandise. In difficult terrain, these loads become even smaller. Though many traders bought additional pack animals to transport their goods, it was probably important for a successful Kinnaura entrepreneur to keep a large flock of his own. But to maintain a large flock in arid, resource-starved Kinnaur required something more than a merely casual interest in shepherding. Only through skilful husbandry could the flocks grow large enough to

[26] Fraser 1982: 212.
[27] C. Singh 1998: 28.
[28] Furer-Haimendorf 1988; Fisher 1987.

yield an adequate number of pack animals, which were in turn the most important means of transport and trade. These pack animals, because they were saleable livestock, also however represented what can be considered a purely pastoral form of income. The rearing of sheep and goats was the full-time occupation of a large section of Kinnaur's population.

These flocks, apart from being a regular source of wool and meat were, as earlier mentioned, the usual "beasts of burden". In the Kinnaur villages near Tibet, yaks were also bred and these were especially useful for carrying the heavy loads of traders travelling to markets in the Tibetan plateau. Fraser noted that in Kinnaur yaks were widely bred and the peasants regarded yaks "their best riches next to corn".[29] It must, however, be pointed out that there were many narrow trails where even the yak was too large to manage the carrying of goods. It appears that despite this extensive involvement with the rearing of sheep and goats in Kinnaur, the requisite number of suitable pack animals was not always readily available. There was consequently a great demand for sheep of the adjacent Changthang area in Tibet, which were particularly appreciated both for their wool and their ability to carry large loads.[30] Few details regarding the number of sheep and goats imported into Kinnaur are available, but it could by no means have been negligible. Trebeck, who went to Spiti (which adjoins Kinnaur), observed of it that "The sheep are almost all imported from Chan-than, as well as the goats, the kids of which degenerate, both in size and quantity of wool."[31] The number of sheep/goats imported in 1914–15 is, however, recorded only as approximately 1000.[32]

The remarkable manner in which the transportation of goods and even survival in the cold desert depended upon sheep is described by Gerard, a British official who toured the area in the mid-nineteenth century. During the course of his journeys through desolate countryside, Gerard often ran short of food supplies. On the occasions that he was able to procure enough grain, he would – as was natural

[29] Fraser 1982: 263–4.
[30] Moorcroft and Trebeck 1970: 207, 316.
[31] Ibid.: 316.
[32] Mitchell 1915: 21.

in such a sparsely populated area – fail to muster the required number of porters to carry it. Over one such occasion he expressed his frustration to a resourceful Kinnaura who, he says, "soon afterwards, returned with a large flock of sheep and said, 'I'll make you a real Tartar: you have grain for ten of twelve days, and now you have no use for porters; load the sheep with the grain, finish it first, and then kill and eat the sheep: this is the way we travel on the inhabitable tracts; we never think of grain as long as we have plenty of sheep.'"[33]

To the Kinnauran his flock was not simply the means to livelihood; it was in times of desperation life itself.

Society and the Family

It is a reflection of the hegemonising influence of Brahmanism that the rulers of Bashahr chose to trace their ancestry to one of the principal characters in Brahmanical mythology. Their right to rule was claimed from a forebear who had forcibly dislodged a powerful *asura* that once ruled the territory and whose capital lay within present-day Kinnaur.[34] On the other hand it is equally indicative of the social proximity of Bashahr to non-Brahmanical Tibet that, according to local Buddhist belief in Kinnaur, "each Raja of Bashahr is at his death re-incarnated as the Guru Lama or Guru of the Lamas, who is understood to be the Dalai Lama of Tibet."[35] The Bashahr raja was sometimes considered semi-divine and worshipped by many of his subjects.[36] Like the rest

[33] Gerard 1993: 149 fn.

[34] *SHSG* 1911, Bashahr: 5. One story goes that the ruling family is descended from the celebrated Sri Krishna of Hindu mythology through his grandson Parduman, who came to Sarahan to marry the daughter of Raja Basava Deo (or Banasar). We are not told whether the marriage took place, but Parduman is said to have killed his prospective father-in-law and usurped his power. His capital was at Kamru in Tukpa *pargana* of Kanawar. Another, less popular, myth traces the origins of the ruling family to two Brahman bothers from the south (*dakkan*). In both stories the Brahmanical (non-indigenous) roots of the rulers and the non-Brahmanical nature of the territory and aboriginal population seem to be emphasised.

[35] Rose 1970: I, 98.

[36] *SHSG* 1911, Bashahr: 5.

of Himachal during medieval times, the state of Bashahr probably originated with the rise to monarchical power of a chieftain after he had suppressed several other Thakurs (feudal chiefs) who earlier dominated different parts of Bashahr. Kamru, a village in the Baspa valley of Kinnaur, was the original centre of the chiefship that seems to have expanded into the fairly extensive Bashahr state. However, the new state capital of Sarahan – with its temple of Goddess Bhima Kali (the state deity) – was situated in territory that lay outside and south of Kinnaur. It perhaps signified a recognition of the northern origins of the state for Kinnauras to continue exercising considerable influence in the affairs of the Bhima Kali temple.[37]

Conforming to the general pattern of community or "caste" distribution that prevailed in most princely states of Himachal, even in Kinnaur the Kanet agro-pastoralists constituted the largest and most powerful section of society. Below them were artisan groups such as the Domangs (smiths), Ores (carpenters), and Chamangs (weavers) who made up the lower castes. The general term "Koli" was also applied to these lower-caste groups that frequently worked as labourers in the fields of the richer Kanet landowners. Unlike more complex Brahmanised societies, there were in Kinnaur no intermediary castes. Not only was intermarriage between upper and lower castes socially prohibited, but considerations of untouchability restricted common dining and the entry of the lower castes into the houses of the Kanets.[38] Even between different clans of Kanets, however, there existed a differentiation based on a perceived hierarchical status. In a broad sense, as one progressed from the lower hills to the higher and more isolated mountains, the position of the Kanet clans *within* the overall Kanet hierarchy declined. The notion of superior and inferior Kanets, nevertheless, did not seriously affect the status of a clan in the area in which it was located. This was because Kanet clans usually occupied distinct territories or different villages and were rarely ever hierarchically placed in the same area. As a result, not only did the Kanets of Kinnaur have a social grading of their own, but the Kinnaura Kanet clans were not to be found in other parts of

---

[37] Chatur Bhuj 1928: 12.
[38] Rose 1970: II, 446; Sanan 1998: 54.

Bashahr state. As might be expected, even within Kinnaur these clans dominated different *parganas* or different villages within *parganas*.[39] These territory-based divisions, nevertheless, did not rule out the consciousness of differing caste status or the possibility of upward mobility in a larger and shared caste-oriented social structure.

Towards the end of the nineteenth century it was observed that the Kanets of Kinnaur "are called Jads or Zads and form a distinct sub-caste with which the Kanets of the lower ranges do not, as a rule, intermarry or eat, though they will smoke and drink with them."[40] This statement may not be entirely true, because the term Jad was more appropriately applied to the Kanet population of some villages located in the areas bordering western Tibet.[41] The "true" Kanets of the rest of Kinnaur considered themselves superior to the Jads. Though they were not subordinate to any substantial superior caste, the Kanets, it seems, were still not beyond the influence of a "Sanskritising" Brahmanism. While making a community-wise enumeration of the landowners in Kinnaur for the 1928 settlement, Chatur Bhuj, the settlement officer, clarified that proprietors who had been classified as Kanets during the previous settlement were now – with the permission of the raja – entered under the caste name "Rajput". In conformity with the hierarchy between clans, the Kanets of the border *parganas* of Sialkar and Pooh, however, continued to be mentioned under the head "Kanet". The change in the caste name from "Kanet" to "Rajput" was possibly prompted by the objective of making the caste status of the Kanets commensurate with their political influence. Before this, the term "Rajput" had not been applied to any social group of the area.[42] Despite its considerable geographical isolation, Kinnaura society could escape neither the impact of an

[39] Rose 1970: II, 446–7.
[40] Ibid.: 458.
[41] *SHSG* 1911, Bashahr: 22. The Gazetteer notes that "In Kanawar the *pargana* of Sialkar, seven villages in *pargana* Tukpa, and two or three villages in *pargana* Shua are inhabited by people of apparently pure Tibetan stock. These are called Nyams, or Jads or Zars, and are also alluded to as Kanets."
[42] Chatur Bhuj 1928: 23. There was no Brahman landowner in Kinnaur and of the others assessed for revenue by Chatur Bhuj in 1928 the numbers recorded are: Rajput (formerly Kanet) 4608; Kanet (Jad) 728; Lohar 168;

ever-expanding Brahmanical society nor the politics of upward-caste mobility.

In terms of political and administrative power the three hereditary *wazirs* of the state, who were all Kanets, stood next only to the raja. A fourth, *sarhadi wazir*, was non-hereditary and appointed from amongst the influential families of the border *parganas* adjoining Tibet. This in effect meant that the Kanets in general and Kinnauras in particular occupied not only most of the administrative positions in the state and but also exerted considerable influence in the raja's court. In 1928, it was recorded that "at the present moment most of the Raja's personal *entourage*, and the majority of the subordinate State officials are Kanawaris."[43] It appears that the interaction with and participation in the formal institutions of the state resulted in the emergence of an elite amongst the Kanets. With the establishment of British domination and their increasing intervention in the administrative affairs of Bashahr, it appears that the hereditary *wazirs* and other court functionaries were pushed into insignificance.

In the villages, however, Kanet control over the socio-administrative structure was far more tenacious. Fluctuating political fortunes at the higher level seem to have had little effect on the complete control exercised by hereditary village functionaries. Almost every large village in Kinnaur had its own local deity and it was by virtue of being its representatives that these Kanet functionaries asserted themselves.[44] Because of the absence of Brahmins in Kinnaur, even the hereditary temple priests (*pujaris*) were Kanets. Even in many temples outside Kinnaur where the Kanet peasantry was dominant, we learn that "The *pujaris* ordinarily belong to the first class of Kanets."[45]

Koli 1084; Baddi 157. The total population of *tehsil* Chini according to the 1921 census was 20,455.

[43] Chatur Bhuj 1928: 23.

[44] Rose 1970, III: 447. Among the officials at the village level are mentioned the (1) *Chares*: the hereditary headman of each village (2) *Grokch*: the hereditary *kardar* of the village deity, who speaks on his behalf (3) *Mathas*: the hereditary *kardar* of the deity. His duty is to petition the deity on behalf of the public (4) *Pujyares*: whose hereditary duty is to worship the deity.

[45] Rose 1970: II, 470.

This then was the broad socio-political system within which agro-pastoralism was practised in Kinnaur. It must, however, be remembered that agro-pastoralism was not a straightforward economic response to a physical environment. As a strategy of survival that balances different economic activities, it has been adopted by many societies. The relative share of agriculture and pastoralism in the total economy has always varied in each such society. Within the societies, furthermore, the dependence of separate social groups and families on these activities differed. There was also an array of corresponding cultural values and perspectives that contributed to, and sustained, the agro-pastoralist's world. The Luri tribesmen of Iran, for example, regarded the "patrilineal extended family" as being endowed with "almost infinite potential for economic expansion". They believed that ideally around such a family an invincible "agro-pastoral combine" could be most successfully organised.[46] To be at the head of such a combine was the mark of a successful individual.

In most of Tibet, both agriculture and pastoralism contributed equally to the economy of its constituent sub-regions. Tibetan state and society as a whole, too, seems to have been organised along lines that complemented such a combination. Muhammad Haidar Dughlat, who led a military expedition into western Tibet in the early-sixteenth century, observed that "the inhabitants of Tibet are divided into two sections. One is called the Yulpa – that is to say 'dwellers in villages' – and the other the Champa, meaning 'dwellers in the desert.'" These were not two separate social formations that Dughlat was talking of and this is shown by his clarification that the pastoralists were "always subject to one of the provinces

---

[46] Black-Michaud 1986: 57. Jacob Black-Michaud argues that "For an individual to achieve this ideal position three main conditions must be satisfied. The head of such a family must have several able-bodied sons or unmarried brothers to assist him, over 100 ewes and enough land to provide considerable grain surpluses, the cash profits from which may be reinvested in the purchase of male lambs and kermanshah ewes. For it is reckoned that once a man controls sufficient land and unsalaried agnatic labour, beside enough ewes to keep a nomadic household and its sedentary dependants liberally supplied with milk products, his potential for pastoral expansion is limited only by his skill at combining the management of these various resources."

of Tibet".[47] Judging from his description it seems that, while the sedentary agriculturists dominated, the population of the nomads too was considerable, and a single flock of load-carrying sheep engaged in "trade in Hindustan and in the mountains of Hindustan" could number ten thousand.[48] Muhammad Dughlat refers to the "Dolpa" as a tribe of the Khampa. He probably means the Dokpa. Most importantly, this tribe consisted of more than 50,000 families and was considered the only one among many such tribes.[49] Tibetan society, it appears, came to terms with its desolate landscape by encouraging entire tribes to continue with pastoralism while simultaneously enabling the population of certain areas to engage in settled agriculture. While the overall economy was the result of a combination of agriculture and pastoralism, there may not perhaps have been any significant social section that could be regarded as "agro-pastoralists" by occupation.

Agro-pastoralism as practised by Kinnauras was more akin to that of Luri tribesmen. The unit of production was the family, which appears to have been particularly suited for this purpose. While inter-caste relations in Kinnaur exhibited in some small way the ideological impact of "Sanskritisation", family organisation seems to have been influenced by economic compulsions rather than considerations of Brahmanical social propriety. Irrespective of the caste to which they belonged, most of the relatively prosperous, flock-owning families were usually divided into two: the *kim mee* and the *arung mee*. The *kim mee* members of the family resided permanently at their village home and tended the family's cultivated holding. The *arung mee* was the migratory pastoral branch of the Kinnaura family which usually consisted of men and teenage boys who travelled virtually the year round with the flocks. The latter visited their homes only for short periods in the year as they migrated with the flocks from the winter to the summer pastures and *vice versa*.

When the adult sons of a family were considered mature enough to manage its affairs, one amongst them was chosen as the householder

[47] Dughlat 1972: 407.
[48] Ibid.: 408.
[49] Ibid.: 409–10.

to look after the house and cultivate land. After retaining a small portion of the house for themselves, the parents retreated into a kind of semi-retirement. The new householder (*talang sa*) and his wife (*talang see*) now became the new heads of a joint family, while the other brothers (*zet sa*) were assigned the itinerant task of tending the family flocks. Appropriate maintenance of social relations and the fulfilment of family obligations *vis-à-vis* the village community was the specific responsibility of the *talang sa*. Family status depended on how the *talang sa* was placed in the hierarchy of his own village. In this regard, much depended on the support he received from the *zet sa* and how successfully they managed the flocks and trading activities in order to obtain additional income for the family.[50] Despite the precise division of economic functions between individual members, the pastoral and agricultural possessions of the family were regarded as a joint holding and constituted a single economic unit. Because of the prevalent system of polyandry, the *talang see* was deemed wife to all the brothers. This is often seen by scholars as a method of population control in an area of extremely limited resources.[51] Further research seems needed to establish the credibility of this notion. Polyandry did, nevertheless, lead to a larger number of girls remaining unmarried and becoming *zomos* or Buddhist nuns. The principal nunneries were at the villages of Kanam and Sonam.[52] According to the *Bashahr State Gazetteer*, "Polyandry was in former times directly encouraged by the state through penalties exacted on partitions. When a set of brothers divided movable property, one-half share of the whole was appropriated by the state, and divisions of immovable property were refused official recognition."[53] By the second decade of the nineteenth century an increasing number of joint families based on polyandry were breaking up to build new houses and form separate units. The administrative report of 1911–15 sees this "splitting up of holdings"

---

[50] For much of the information on this account I am indebted to Vidya Sagar Negi who allowed me to read the manuscript of the book on the Kinnaura pastoralists which he is jointly writing with R.S. Pirta.
[51] Chandra 1987: 210.
[52] Rose 1970: III, 453.
[53] *SHSG* 1911, Bashahr: 16.

as "a sign of increased prosperity owing to the gradual opening up of the country and the influx of money spent on the roads, buildings and [forest] exploitation works."[54] Cash payments made by timber contractors to Bashahr state revenues and labourers during the late-eighteenth and early-nineteenth centuries were certainly much more considerable than at any time earlier. Given the altered notions of propriety and progress that accompanied colonialism, the break-up of the joint family and construction of separate houses might well have been considered a mark of "increased prosperity".

Pastoral Practices

Equally interesting is the fact that even the animals owned by the family were divided into those kept permanently at the village (*kim zet*) and those seasonally shifted (*arung zet*) over long distances to pastures situated at varying elevations. Among the larger *kim zet* were cows and oxen necessary for cultivating the agricultural holding of the family. Usually a small number of sheep, rather than goats, were the other animals included amongst the *kim zet*. The number of *kim zet* was maintained at a bare minimum because these animals had to be stall-fed through the long and harsh winter. During this period, the surrounding countryside was under snow, or at any rate devoid of herbage suitable for them, and the *kim zet* survived only on hay that had been cut and stored before the onset of winter. The *arung zet*, on the other hand, consisted of the greater part of the animals owned by the family and included both sheep and goats but never cows and oxen.

To meet the requirements of winter fodder for animals housed permanently in the village, specified patches of land (*banjar ghasni*) in and around the village were set aside to grow fodder. It might be of interest to mention that in some areas even this land was irrigated.[55] Moreover, in some parts of Kinnaur grazing grounds called *panwis* were set aside as pastureland. By established tradition, *panwis* were

---

[54] Mitchell 1915: 28.
[55] Chatur Bhuj 1928: 23.

neither to be cultivated nor allowed to be re-afforested. We are told that "*Panwis* are burnt annually in the winter under the supervision of the local forest guard . . . The burning of the coarse dry grass on the slopes below the forest belt, in addition to stimulating the growth of the new grass, serves as a useful means of fire protection."[56]

Such pastures, it must be emphasised, were different from those that occurred naturally in the higher reaches above the tree-line. Grass in the *ghasnis* (hill slopes where animals were not permitted to graze) was allowed to dry naturally in autumn. It was then cut, further dried in the sun, and thereafter stored in the house as animal stall-feed over the winter. *Panwis*, on the other hand, were opened in spring to all the animals of the village once the snow had melted. Despite this systematic procurement of adequate fodder for the *kim zet*, there was a limit to the amount that could be stored and a shortage during winter almost inevitable. It was observed that the animals that stayed back in winter "have to exist on a *seer* or half a *seer* (*pakka*) of food a day and are nearly dead by the end of winter. When the snow begins to clear away they are taken out to graze on these hills and in a week or two are in better condition than if they had been stall-fed on grain all winter."[57] It is hardly surprising, therefore, that the extreme shortage of fodder meant that in winter almost all sheep and goats were taken down to the lower hills.

The migratory cycle of the Kinnaur flocks has been thus described:

> For grazing purposes the flocks belonging to the local people are sent to the Alpine pastures in Chini Tahsil in the main Sutlej Valley, in Baspa Valley and Bhaba Valley during summer i.e. from about the middle of May to the end of October. The flocks start coming down in the end of October on their way to the lower hills in Mandi, Bilaspur, Kulu, Suket, Sirmur, Simla and Solan, when they graze from about the middle of December to the end of April. During April and May again the flocks remain in transit on their way to the Alpine pastures. All the flocks do not move to lower hills during winter. About a quarter of them remain in Upper Bashahr. Those that remain are pastured in the Valleys, low down on sunny slopes where the snow does not often come, or when

[56] Hamilton 1932: 11.
[57] *SHSG* 1911, Bashahr: 53.

it does, thaws quickly. In May, these flocks are on their way up to the Alpine pastures; they linger, however, to graze the tender grass of the open slopes and then pass quickly through the forests to the higher grounds where they remain till October. In parts of the valley they are brought down in September in certain places in the forests to be sheared, and are taken back again. Sheep are shorn twice a year, in spring and autumn. When the time for leaving the high ground is near, the goats being more delicate than the sheep, return first. Their stay in the forest is short, and is confined to open glades where the scant sweet herbage is supplemented by oak loppings and besides these places the only parts of the forests that are regularly grazed by both sheep and goats are those near villages, *dogris*, fields and along paths.[58]

Shepherds from the different parts of Kinnaur took their flocks to specific pastures over which they had through the years probably acquired a strong customary claim. Each flock followed a migratory route that was established as a matter of tradition and which gave it access to different grazing grounds.[59] As they travelled to their winter pastures in lower areas, and even after reaching them, the Kinnauras engaged their flocks in transporting goods to and out of villages not easily accessible. Parmar recorded that while transiting the pastoralists "linger on" in the lower Bashahr area and "engage their flocks in the carriage of Potatoes and other food stuffs from the villages in the interior to the roadside depots."[60]

During the summer months, the extensive forests and pastures of Kinnaur became available to pastoralists. Apart from ensuring the return of the Kinnaura flocks, this also encouraged shepherds of the lower hills to migrate northwards with their sheep and goats. Despite the sudden influx of animals that this entailed, there seem to have

---

[58] Parmar 1959: 211.

[59] Migrating flocks from different parts of Kinnaur followed specific routes till very recently. It is difficult to agree with his statement that "Herds and flocks follow any route they like . . ." (Parmar 1959: 54.) Yet he explicitly mentions several routes used by the shepherds. The process of seasonal migration involved the prior establishment of a working relationship with people and villages en route and the right to use pastures along the road followed.

[60] Parmar 1959: 51.

been sufficient pastures available in Kinnaur, even though there arose occasional disputes for the best of them.[61] Shepherds raised temporary shelters (*dogris*) in the higher pastures where, as Gerard observed, they resided with their flocks for four or five months in the year.[62]

It was this entwining of pastoralism, transportation, and trade that prompted and enabled the Khampa traders from Spiti and Tibet to bring their ponies and flocks to lower Bashahr in winter.[63] Similarly, some of the Kinnaura shepherds moved with their flocks into Tibet in summer. It was never easy to distinguish between traders and pastoralists in Kinnaur. Given the nature of the terrain, almost every trader was probably a pastoralist first and not simply – as one might be tempted to believe – an owner of pack animals. Either he, or the shepherds he employed, spent a considerable amount of time tending sheep on a varied range of pastures. The sheep were in part the source of at least one very important item of trade – wool.

Migratory flocks (*arung zet*), further, consisted of two categories of animals: the *laadi* (or *ladoo*) were pack animals, and the *shai zet* were mainly female goats, ewes, lambs, and kids.[64] The *laadi* were invariably the male of the species (usually gelded). Rams and male goats kept as studs and she-goats required for procreation were never used as pack animals. While they were on their migratory route, the procedure for moving these two categories of animals between camps also differed. The *laadi* started at dawn and travelled rapidly with their loads straight to the next camp so as to reach by midday. They were thereafter, unloaded and allowed to graze for the remainder of the day. The *shai zet*, on the other hand, moved at a more leisurely pace. They were allowed to browse as they went along – even making minor detours off the main route – and reached the camp later in the evening. There were times, however, when during the course of the main summer or winter migration a flock of *laadi* (laden with

[61] Mitchell 1915: 5; Chatur Bhuj 1928: 2; Hamilton 1932: 9; Parmar 1959: 60.
[62] Gerard 1993: 220.
[63] Parmar 1959: 51.
[64] Ibid.: 211. As told to me by my friend and colleague Vidya Sagar Negi, who has spent many of his younger days tending migratory flocks in Kinnaur.

merchandise) was taken on a trading detour which could be fairly long and time-consuming.

Trade

It seems that the particularly advantageous position of the western Himalaya, especially Kinnaur, in the Indo–Tibet trade was not initially appreciated by the British. Their attempts to capitalise on the existing trans-Himalayan trade through Nepal and other parts of the eastern Himalaya did not meet with success. British failure to link up in the east with the Tibetan trade was largely because the bulk of the trade within Tibet moved in an east–west direction. Only minor trade routes entered India over the eastern Himalaya. It has also been suggested that not only political power but also the internal trade of North India was centred in its north-western region, especially Panjab and Rajasthan; that as a result this area became the meeting place of merchants from Tibet, Kandahar, and the seaports of Gujarat.[65] For wool and borax, Tibet was one of the most important sources and these commodities were brought to India through the Satlej valley. Rampur, the capital of Bashahr, was the most important place in the valley to which merchandise from Tibet, Ladakh, and the Panjab plains was brought.[66]

In this network of trade the Kinnaura pastoralists played a significant part. They participated not only in the main strands of commerce that stretched from the Tibetan plateau to the North Indian plains, but also created a fine web of exchange relationships throughout the mountainous region. The pastoralists migrated along with their flocks across a vast expanse of mountainous territory, utilising the resources of even the remotest pastures. They were therefore best suited to connect the far-flung villages with the main trade routes. It was their ability to transport goods in fairly large quantities over treacherous, almost impassable paths that was crucial to the economy of the region. In 1888, it was noted that the "hill paths by which the

[65] Pemble 1971: 61.
[66] *Simla DG* 1889: 72–3.

wool is brought down to Rampur are so precipitous that sheep, more sure-footed than larger beasts, are commonly used for the carriage of merchandise."[67] Apart from wool and borax, salt was an important commodity obtained from Tibet. Cotton piece-goods, wheat, and rice were the main items of export that passed through Kinnaur to western Tibet.[68] These were by no means the only articles of trade. *Pashm* was brought in from Tibet along with *charas* and finished wool products such as *numdahs* and carpets. Other wool products manufactured locally and traded in were *pattu* cloth and woollen blankets. Among the exports to Tibet were raisins, *neozas* (edible pine nuts), tobacco, horseshoes, saddles, agricultural implements, and firearms. The commodities that were sent down the Satlej valley to Panjab were *neoza, zira* (cummins), honey, *ghi, karru*, violets, *dhup*, apricots, grapes, and yak's tail.[69]

Almost all trade in Kinnaur eventually converged on the Satlej valley which acted as a natural channel for the flow of merchandise between western Tibet and Panjab. As it approached the Tibetan border, however, the main trade route split into three smaller ones which crossed into Tibet over several mountain passes. The three routes were (1) Sialkhar Chango; (2) Shipki; (3) Lingo Morang. Of these the first was the most frequently used. Each of these routes joined the road connecting Tibet with Ladakh and Central Asia at different points.[70] In western Tibet the town of Gartok was the most important market, and by the beginning of the twentieth century the British had appointed one Jai Chand, a nephew of the Thakur of Lahaul, as their agent in Gartok "to protect trade interests".[71]

Gerard's description of Gartok (also known as Garoo and by several other names) illustrates the fascinating link between pastoralism and trade. He writes that it

> is a collection of black tents inhabited by pastoral tribes for six months. In winter, the Tartars retire chiefly to Eegoong on the bank of the river,

[67] Ibid.: 72.
[68] Fraser 1982: 275; *SHSG* 1911, Bashahr: 61–2.
[69] Murray 1824: 289.
[70] Mitchell 1915: 17, 21.
[71] Sherring 1998: 310.

two stages down the stream, and the Chinese governors reside at the Fort of Tuzheegung, where they have houses. Garoo is the most famous mart for wool in Chinese Tartary, and there is a fair of 10,000 or 20,000 people in July, well attended by merchants from Yarkand. Wool, borax, and salt are the principal exports, and these articles are exchanged for the produce of the plains of India.[72]

Gartok, then, was evidently a summer market that attracted traders, pastoralists, and nomads in large numbers from Central Asia, Ladakh, Kinnaur, Lahaul, and other parts of Tibet. It is neither possible nor appropriate to differentiate the people who came to Gartok on the basis of their occupation: trading, pastoralism, and some element of nomadism were for them inseparable and essential parts of life. Both the location of the market at Gartok in an open pasture and its temporary nature mirror the importance of nomadic pastoralism as a facilitator of long-distance trade. Fraser, who travelled extensively through the western Himalaya around 1814 has provided an interesting, though probably exaggerated, account of the Kinnaura traders: "The Kunawar merchants carry on a trade not only with the plains and the neighbouring Chinese provinces, but as above remarked, they are also the chief carriers between Garha, Ludhak, and Cashmere, and even push their commercial enterprises as far as Lahassa on the south-east, exchanging commodities between that place and Nepal, and between the latter and the Chinese towns in Little Thibet, and to the northward, trading between Cashmere, Yarkund, Kashgar, Garha and the various cities and people of these quarters."[73] Even if the Kinnauras did not trade directly with many of the places mentioned by Fraser, they were certainly part of this larger trade network.

Of the five Kinnaur *parganas*, it was the three border ones of Tukpa, Shua, and Sialkar which developed the closest links with the Tibet–Central Asia trade routes. A combination of trade and pastoralism, rather than agriculture, was probably the primary source of livelihood here. This seems to be reflected in the large size of the upper Kinnaur villages, so unlike the areas further south where tiny

[72] Gerard 1993: 144–5.
[73] Fraser 1982: 274.

hamlets were scattered haphazardly near scarce cultivable land.[74] When Gerard reached one such border village, Nisung in upper Kinnaur, he discovered that "there were none but women and children in the village, all the grown up men having gone to Garoo [Gartok] for salt and wool."[75] The people of the village of Pilo in *pargana* Shua were known to be "very rich, due to their trade with the Tibetans."[76] In some villages of this *pargana* there were very successful traders who were popularly considered to be "*lakhpati shahukars*".[77] It was about one such prosperous trader of Thangi village that Gerard wrote: "I reached the village of Konoo without a single farthing, not even to pay the guides, owing to the money I expected having been sent up to the valley of the Satlej. An inhabitant of Thungee, whom I had only seen once, when he heard of this, advanced me twelve rupees, which he said I might repay when he visited Rampoor in November."[78] While the inhabitants of villages near the border survived and at times even prospered on Tibetan trade, there were some traders further down the Satlej trade route who also became "men of considerable wealth" as a result of this trade.[79]

As a matter of tradition, traders from each of the border *parganas* were compulsorily organised into a separate group. Each of these trader groups, further, had a Tibetan counterpart that also came to the Gartok trade fair in summer and with which all their commercial transactions were conducted.[80] Any disputes that arose were settled by a committee of traders from various places, including Tibet.[81]

---

[74] *SHSG* 1911, Bashahr: 48.

[75] Gerard 1993: 102.

[76] *SHSG* 1911, Bashahr: Appendix II, xx.

[77] Ibid.: xvii, xxiv. The appendix is based on a directory compiled by Pandit Tika Ram Joshi who was private secretary to the Raja of Bashahr. Sonam Guru Shyaltu of Lippa is mentioned as a "*Lakhpati Shahukar*" and so is Tapgya of village Pooh. The other "rich men" of Lippa were Barji and Karam Ram.

[78] Gerard 1993: 76, 77, 102. Elsewhere he wrote, "I was exactly in the same predicament when I left Soogum for Manes; and Putee Ram, the intelligent Koonawaree, mentioned by Mr. Fraser . . . gave me ten rupees, and told me I was welcome to a hundred if I required so much . . ."

[79] Mitchell 1915: 18.

[80] *SHSG* 1911, Bashahr: 62.

[81] Ibid.

Though money was certainly used, a substantial part of the commercial exchange between Kinnaur and western Tibet was also in the nature of barter. This was more so in relation to salt and rice. We learn that Kinnauras going to Tibet got "two *seers* of salt for one *seer* of husked rice. When selling it again in Garhwal, Rohru or Rampur, they get two or two-and-a-half *seers* of husked rice for a *seer* of salt. Thus, making a handsome profit."[82] But this "profit" may not really have been as large as it appears. The shopkeepers at Rampur, the largest market in Bashahr, had evolved a devious method to skim off at least some of the gains that would otherwise have gone to peasants and small-time traders who came to sell their produce and merchandise. All the business in Rampur *tahsil*, through which the trade of Kinnaur passed to North India, was controlled by outsiders. It is noted that "All the shopkeepers in the Rampur *tahsil* are natives of the Ambala, Hoshiarpur or Kangra districts, or of the Patiala State."[83]

According to the *Rampur Assessment Report*, "Every shopkeeper keeps two kinds of weights, one equal to 5 *seers* (*pukka*) and the other weighing 4 *seers*, which for the purpose of sale was considered a five-*seer* weight '*pachsera*'. Those articles which are given to the cultivators are weighed with the latter, while those things which are bought from them are weighed with the former. There is always a difference of 25 per cent, between both 'weights'".[84] Measures for purchasing and selling cloth at Rampur were similarly of two unequal kinds and used as unscrupulously by the shopkeepers for their own benefit.

Between Two Worlds

Geographically, it is obvious that Kinnaur either linked or separated – depending on one's perspective – the forested slopes and cultivated valleys of the Great Himalaya and the barren cold-desert plateau of Tibet. It lay not only between strikingly different terrains but also between equally diverse societies. Yet its inhabitants had learnt to use the resources of these terrains and societies most effectively. They

---

[82] Ibid.: 63.
[83] Ibid.: 60.
[84] As quoted in ibid.

moved adroitly between two physical and social worlds and successfully negotiated what appeared to be rather serious contradictions. In fact, however, their regular and periodic "crossing-over", both literally and metaphorically, may not have been so difficult for them; it may even never have been a "crossing-over" at all. Kinnaur society seems to have reflected several of the characteristics associated with the two large ecological and social systems that flanked it. It was not a place where "The symbol systems of two different great traditions [Hinduism and Buddhism] compete for commitment..."[85] Fisher's study of Tarangpur (Nepal) has argued that Hinduism and Buddhism in the Great and Trans Himalaya represented two poles that remained "unaffected by each other". He sees the traders of Tarangpur as "*brokers of goods*" on the one hand but also as "*blockers* of ideas" on the other (emphasis mine). The integration they brought about, he argues, was "distinctly economic" rather than ideological.[86]

Kinnauras, however, do not seem to have been unduly disturbed by their location on the fringes of two great traditions. Nor did they act as "blockers of ideas" between Hinduism and Buddhism. In fact, the transition from one ideological world to the other seems to have taken place in Kinnaur itself. This is mirrored in the shades of beliefs prevailing in different parts of the region: the physical dimensions, as it were, of mental arenas. North-western Kinnaur and the upper Baspa valley were Buddhist in a more definite sense. Most of the older Buddhist monasteries were situated here while Brahmanical deities and even local *deotas* were almost entirely absent. In central Kinnaur, Buddhist monasteries and temples of local folk *deotas* were given equal importance and the Kinnauras saw no contradiction in this.[87] Lower Kinnaur, further south, was the country of Brahmanical deities which held sway over the people through numerous local village *deotas*. A hierarchical relationship existed between the two kinds of deities, with the Brahmanical gods dominating. As in the "Hindu" area of the Simla Hill States, even in lower Kinnaur "The gods of the village-

---

[85] Fisher 1987: 189.
[86] Ibid.: 96.
[87] Chatur Bhuj 1928: 3.

temples are subordinate to the god of a Deo *mandir* a 'great temple', and they performed certain services for him e.g. at a *yag* and at fairs, in return for the fiefs (*jagirs*) granted by him."[88] Though the state of Bashahr had originated in Kinnaur, with its expansion into a full-fledged kingdom the centre of political authority had shifted out and southwards to Sarahan and Rampur. With the institutionalisation of monarchy, socio-political prescriptions of formal Brahmanism came to be followed by the raja and the ruling family in and around the capital towns. But Brahmanical injunctions did not destroy the legitimacy of folk tradition. They simply included it at a subordinate level. By this means a hierarchy amongst gods was created and maintained. For instance, the three sons and one daughter of the mythical Banasur – the deposed ruler of the region – who were believed to have been killed in battle with Krishna or one of his descendants, came to be accepted as important village gods of Kinnaur. These three sons of Banasur came to be known as the three Maheshras located in various villages of the area. According to a local account: "It is said that Banasur who was a demon and who ruled in Sarahan, at a very remote period, was slain, and so the first son became the Maheshra of Shungra, the second of Kathgaon, the third of Chugaon, and Ukha, their sister, became the goddess of Nachar."[89] At the same time, like all other village gods, they occupied a place that was inferior to Lord Badrinath's, the Brahmanical deity which "ruled" the region from its temple at Kamru in Kinnaur. The original home of the Bashahr rulers (notwithstanding their claim to be outsiders and descendants of Sri Krishna), as already mentioned, was also Kamru.

No discernible boundary appears to have existed between Brahmanical convictions and folk tradition in lower Kinnaur. As one moved northwards beyond the influence of the Brahmanical "great tradition", purely local beliefs remained important: but with Buddhism replacing the Brahmanical tradition as the institutionalised religion. They not only coexisted with Buddhism but also played a crucial role in the life of the Buddhist population. Flexibility in belief was possibly a

---

[88] Rose 1970: II, 470; see also Rose 1970: III, 454.
[89] *SHSG* 1911, Bashahr: Appendix II, xii.

necessity for Kinnaura society in a situation where religious orthodoxy could jeopardise survival itself. Dr J.G. Gerard, who submitted a report to Capt. C.P. Kennedy on the state of education in the Simla Hill States in 1824, remarked of Kinnaur that "civilisation, morality and knowledge have made the greatest progress in the remote and secluded regions of Koonawur." He added:

> Koonawur, in spite of the defects of the Bussahir government and its remoteness from the capital, ranks above every other State in point of intelligence, active industry and good feeling, but it is foreign to the purpose to detail the circumstances that have contributed to give it this superiority. I shall only remark that there are no Brahmins in that country and there is much less of blind devotion in religion, but more of superstition. Education is there less cultivated than the actual acquirement of knowledge, which their intercourse with Chinese, their commercial pursuits and habits of hardihood encourage and establish.[90]

Trade with Tibet stopped abruptly in the early 1960s and has been restored only partially in recent years. The construction of roads, the rapid growth of tourism, and the successful introduction of the apple has opened Kinnaur both physically and economically to the rest of the country. Alternative sources of livelihood have emerged and few Kinnauras are now traders. Polyandry has virtually died out except amongst the poorest locals. But the pastoralist of Kinnaur and his *arung zet* can still be found in the alpine pastures in summer and in the shrub forests of the Siwaliks in winter: both he and the flock representing, as it were, the remnants of an ancient but dying tradition.

---

[90] Gerard 1824: 315–16.

9

Strategy of Interdependence
Gaddi, Peasant, and State

At the outset it must be understood that the Gaddis, amongst the best-known transhumant pastoralists of the western Himalaya, were also agriculturists and lived for several months of the year in permanent villages. While the Brahmaur subdivision of modern Chamba district (formerly Chamba state) is traditionally regarded as their homeland, they have for long occupied the higher, south-facing slopes of the Dhauladhar range in the Kangra district at a height ranging from "3,500 or 4,000 feet up to 7,000 feet" above sea level.[1] In pre-colonial times, their villages and cultivated land would have fallen within two kingdoms: Chamba and Kangra. Interestingly, it was often the same group of Gaddi families that occupied plots of agricultural land on both sides of the Dhauladhar range. Lyall, the British official who carried out the second land revenue settlement of Kangra district, noted that not less than "three-fourths of those who live in Kangra have also shares in lands and houses in Chamba territory." Most of the Gaddis found in Nurpur (Kangra) were, however, subjects only of Chamba state.[2] The majority of them were therefore regarded as subjects of both states.[3] They cultivated wheat as a winter crop in

---

Published earlier as C. Singh 1997.
[1] *Kangra DG* 1926: 176.
[2] Lyall 1889: 38.
[3] Barnes 1889: 42.

Kangra; then crossed to the north of the snow ranges in summer to cultivate another crop in Brahmaur.[4] Evidently, then, their position as cultivating peasants – requiring them to meet tax and other legal obligations towards the state – was quite clear. If one were to take into consideration only their activities as agriculturists, the Gaddis would appear no different from ordinary settled peasants. Even the internal social divisions within Gaddi society made Gaddi villages quite similar to the caste-divided villages of the lower hills and the adjoining Panjab plains.

What set the Gaddis apart, however, was the shepherding activities that most of them pursued for much of the year. Their extensive seasonal movements as shepherds enabled them to exploit the natural resources of areas lying in the different climatic zones well beyond their permanent homes. Despite their internal social divisions, the Gaddis projected a strong tribal identity as herders. It was in this capacity that their interaction with the state and settled society assumed particular significance. Andre Gunder Frank has argued, "nomadic pastoral" and "settled agricultural" are "not so much hard and fast categories of people as they are temporary conditions, which different people(s) adopt according to changing circumstances."[5]

Even a quick glance at the extent of their seasonal wanderings reveals their essentially transhumant lifestyle. In winter the majority of the inhabitants of the Brahmaur *wazarat* of Chamba state migrated to the low-lying areas of the Ravi valley or to Kangra, leaving behind only a few families which were entrusted with the task of caring for the cattle. Those left in charge of the cattle and houses were called *hiundasis*. Even in every large Gaddi village, only one or two such families remained behind throughout the winter. When the transhumant shepherds returned home, they had much work to do: the *rabi* crop was ready for reaping and the *kharif* one was then to be sown.[6] Most of their large flocks of sheep and goats were, in fact, moved from place to place, as is apparent from this account of 1904:

[4] *Kangra DG* 1926: 177.
[5] Frank 1992: 93.
[6] *Chamba SG* 1910: 203, 228.

In the beginning of the cold weather – October and November – they are driven to the low hills of Kangra, Nurpur and Pathankot from which they are brought back in April to their villages to manure the fields, and in June they are entrusted to a *malundi* or shepherd, for the summer months. After a month in the *trakar* pastures some are led up to the *dhars* of Churah, Brahmaur and other parts; and others were taken over the passes of the Pangi range to the *gahars* of Pangi and Lahul, where they remain during July and August. In the beginning of September the flocks commence the return journey over the Pangi Range and are brought back to the *trakar* pastures. In October the flocks are again led to the jungle of Bhattiyat, Nurpur and Pathankot, where they remain till March.[7]

The extended migratory movements of the Gaddis required them to enter into an understanding with people and institutions of different kinds. Most common in this respect was their interaction with the ordinary peasantry of the villages or neighbourhoods to which they migrated. Not all Gaddis, it seems, were engaged in tending their flocks in winter, for there were some who during this time made a living "threshing rice" and "serving in other people's houses".[8] The majority, however, herded sheep in the lower areas during the cold season. Thereafter, as summer approached, they undertook a long journey with their flocks to the higher mountains and continued to tend their sheep in the alpine pastures throughout the summer as well.

The shepherds kept their sheep in folds on village lands for a fixed number of days so as to manure the fields. At times a sheep was given (as *bhagti*) to the village immediately below the pasture in order to propitiate the local deity. The settlement officer noted in his report that "such sheep are sacrificed and later eaten in a village feast which the shepherds attended."[9] A fee was sometimes charged by villagers located near the mountain passes most frequently crossed by the

---

[7] *Chamba SG* 1910: 279. *Trakar* are pastures to and from which village animals can go and return the same day. *Dhars* and *gahars* are the more distantly located alpine summer pastures where herders have to camp out for long periods.
[8] Ibid.: 203.
[9] Lyall 1889: 41; *Kangra DG* 1918: III, Lahul, 222.

shepherds, or those situated at regular river crossings. The pressure on the resources of the former kind of villages was immense, while the bridges at the latter were often made of locally produced rope and had to be kept in good repair, or frequently re-built. For example, in the area (*kothi*) of Jobrang in Lahul, below the Kukti Pass (between Chamba and Lahul), shepherds customarily paid "one sheep per *ban* or *dhar* under the name of *batkaru*".[10] A fee was also collected by the Mandi administration at the Ul bridge, and at the Empress bridge over the Beas in Mandi town.[11]

Of particular benefit to the cultivators were the droppings of sheep and goats, and this is explicit in the observations of Barnes who wrote that:

> When winter sets in, and the Chamba mountaineers descend with their flocks upon the valleys of Kangra, the people contest with each other who shall house the shepherd and his flock, and a cultivator will give two or three rupees a night for the advantage of having the sheep folded upon his land. Night after night the shepherd changes his ground and before the harvest is sown, reaps a little fortune without the smallest exertion or cost.[12]

The Kanet peasants of Bangahal area put a very high value on the sheep manure and fed the Mandi shepherds without charge when the latter penned their sheep in the village. In fact, they even sent food supplies when required to shepherds in the alpine pastures.

Because of the continuous grazing of the Gaddi flocks in the forests en route, however, the new forest rules of 1891 were introduced as a protective measure. These rules restricted the period for which the Gaddis could stop in the Kulu valley during their migrations to and from Lahul. This in turn reduced considerably the fertility of the maize and rice fields in several parts of Kulu.[13] The annual migratory movements of the Gaddis appear to have frequently synchronised with the agricultural cycle of the peasants, for it was after one crop had

[10] *Kangra DG* 1918, III, Lahul: 222.
[11] *Mandi SG* 1908: 48.
[12] Barnes 1889: 30; Lyall 1889: 39, 42.
[13] *Kangra DG* 1918: II, Kulu, 89.

been harvested and the soil for the second crop was being prepared that the flocks passed through.

The relationship between the Gaddis and the agriculturists whose areas they passed through was complex. A factor of considerable importance were the numerous forest and grazing laws that both the pre-colonial and colonial states imposed, with varying degrees of success. These laws created a network of rights and dues within which the state, the tribal-pastoralist Gaddis, and the peasants were enmeshed. The Gaddis claimed a *warisi* in the grazing rights of certain pastures and forest areas. Many of these were situated in their home state of Chamba, while some others were claimed in Kangra, Lahul, and other places to which they went during the course of their pastoral migrations. The strongest of these claims, however, were in Chamba and Kangra – the two areas with which the Gaddis had the closest association.

A Gaddi's *warisi* was, in effect, a hereditary right that he or his family enjoyed in a well-defined grazing area (*ban* or *dhar*) of certain forests at particular times of the year. In earlier times when the pressure on land was limited, a *patta* for grazing sheep was quite easily obtained from the raja by some of the Gaddis,[14] and this ultimately led to the creation of an inheritance termed *warisi*. However, there was some uncertainty about its true nature and it was observed that: "What this *warisi* in a *ban* amounts to is a question which has never been decided and to which the parties interested cannot give a clear answer."[15] Lyall compared it to a *muqaddami* (managership), or the *watan* of southern India.[16]

In some of the *dhars* of Lahul it seems that *warisis* were gifted or sold among Gaddis. The original family to which it was granted by the raja of Kulu or the Thakurs of Lahul did not use the *dhars* any more. The new user, however, had to halt a day or so on his way back in the fields of the original owner.[17] The person who was originally granted

---

[14] Lyall 1889: 39.
[15] *Kangra DG* 1926: 269.
[16] Lyall 1889: 39.
[17] *Kangra DG* 1918: III, Lahul, 221.

the *patta* or his *waris* (inheritor) was expected to muster a group of shepherds along with their flocks for grazing the *ban*. By virtue of his being the *waris* the former was normally recognised as the *mahlundi* or *malik kandah* (master of the flock). His initial obligation was to "fill the *ban*" and his failure to do so could result in his displacement. It was the *mahlundi* who dealt with tax collectors, officials, and frequently even the representatives of the settled village community on behalf of the common Gaddi shepherds.[18] The *mahlundi* was also defined as "a man who possesses a large number of sheep and goats and also grazes those of others at a fixed rate of remuneration."[19] For these efforts he was adequately compensated in several ways; a large part of the compensation came in the form of *mailani*, or payment made by cultivators for sheep droppings.

A *warisi* could be claimed in a *ban* (normally a winter grazing area in the low hills) and in a *dhar* (alpine pasture). A large number of Gaddis held their *dhars* directly from the raja of Chamba and for this they paid fixed cash rent.[20] There were also *dhars* for which the *warisi* was claimed by the peasants of an entire village, such as those located in the outer Himalayan Bangahal area of Kangra proper, or by particular families such as those living in villages situated much lower down the mountain slope.[21] In the latter kind of claims, however, the entitlement to sheep manure appears to have been of greater significance. The Gaddi herders who normally utilised these pastures were, therefore, expected to pen their flocks in the fields of the *waris* for a certain period.

A *ban*, on the other hand, was generally to be found in the low hills and most of the Gaddi families claimed the *warisi* of *bans* in Kangra district.[22] These claims continued into the early decades of the twentieth century and the *Kangra District Gazetteer* noted that "In the greater part of Kangra every *ban* is claimed by some Gaddi family as its *warisi* or inheritance; the exception is in *tahsil* Nurpur

[18] Lyall 1889: 39.
[19] *Chamba SG* 1910: 279, note.
[20] Lyall 1889: 41; *Kangra DG* 1926: 274.
[21] *Kangra DG* 1926: 274–5.
[22] Lyall 1889: 38–9.

of which country the Gaddis commonly say that the *bans* there are open or free and that there is no *warisi* in them."²³ Such a claim did not necessarily lie over a consolidated stretch of land. It could lie across several scattered areas which, because they were part of a single *warisi*, came to be regarded as one *ban*.

Even while the British proceeded to establish complete governmental ownership and control over forests and extensive wastes or surrendered it in places to the village community, the claim of the pastoralists to their pastures remained undisturbed. With regard to the *warisis* of Gaddis and Gujars, Barnes noted that "extensive wastes and forests are usually considered the undivided property of Government; but even here there are subordinate tenures which cannot be overlooked."²⁴ Subsequent records reiterate this position by noting that "The State while transferring the property in the soil of the waste to the owners of the fields, necessarily reserved the existing rights of third parties; the rights of the Gujars to their *sowanas* or cattle walks, and of the Gaddi shepherds to their sheep runs, remained unaffected by the change . . ."²⁵ However, an element of confusion does exist regarding what constituted the basis of these grazing rights. On the one hand, the ownership of land was not considered essential for a Gaddi to claim a right to graze his sheep in an area. On the other, however, we also learn that many Chamba-based Gaddis were beginning to buy small patches of land in Kangra at inflated prices so as to lay claim to grazing rights in the area.²⁶ Quite possibly, the increased demand for pastures necessitated this.

The strength of the pastoralist claim was emphasised in numerous government records, where partly at least its legitimacy was derived from the important role that it played in the life of the peasants and in the larger economic system of the pre-colonial state. It was partly through sheep and goats that the apparently useless but extensive forest resources of the Himalayan states were converted into tangible and taxable commodities. *Banwaziri*, of which grazing dues

---

²³ *Kangra DG* 1926: 269.
²⁴ Barnes 1889: 19.
²⁵ *Kangra DG* 1926: 379.
²⁶ Ibid.: 262.

were an important part, was therefore an important source of revenue for the state.

The grazing tax (*trini* or *tirni*) was levied on virtually all pastures though the professional shepherds were taxed at a higher rate than were peasants who owned sheep.[27] In pre-colonial Chamba it seems that most peasants paid a substantial part of their *trini* in the form of wool or sheep and goats. An important change occurred when *trini* was first auctioned in 1863–4. The arrival of an increasing number of pastoral Gujjars probably made this newly adopted system a more profitable venture for the state.[28] As the pressure on pastures increased their monetary value, the state may have been prompted to grant a greater share of the grazing rights to professional shepherds and cowherds.

The corresponding escalation in the number and value of sheep seems to have encouraged some Gaddis to assert their position in stronger and clearer terms. Numerous Gaddi families had customarily grazed their sheep in the Nurpur *bans* of the lower Kangra hills without claiming their *warisi*, and the privileges of the latter position were enjoyed by the contractor of the raja of Chamba.[29] The raja's contractor was invariably a Gaddi who, in practical terms, was also a sort of headman of the shepherds. By the 1870s, however, several new claimants to the *warisi* of different *bans* had begun collecting a fee from other shepherds whose sheep constituted part of their (the claimant's) flock.[30]

The growing demand of pastureland may not initially have affected the peasants adversely. Not all of them kept flocks enough to require the use of extensive pastureland that lay beyond the vicinity of their villages. For their relatively smaller number of sheep the village pastures were generally adequate. The latter category of pastures were taxed at a much lower rate, and they were sometimes free.[31] On the other hand, in some of these pastures the claims of the

[27] Lyall 1889: 24; *Mandi SG* 1908: 47–8.
[28] *Chamba SG* 1910: 278.
[29] Lyall 1889: 41.
[30] Ibid.: 39.
[31] *Chamba SG* 1910: 278, 279. The people of Pangi *wazarat* of Chamba

village community, though originally obtained from the raja, were exceptionally strong. A case in point was the village of Kukti at one end of the Brahmaur valley. The residents of Kukti claimed control of all the neighbouring *dhars* along with the right to allow their use by whomsoever they chose. Interestingly, they also held the view that even the raja could not now "lawfully alter this arrangement".[32]

During the forest settlement of 1874–5 in Dehra *tahsil* of Kangra, the British sought to create reserved forests by freeing some forests from all rights of users. This was acceptable to the peasants of the area only in return for some special concessions from the government. Among the most important of these were "the promise never to close any more of the waste or forest land, and in an assignment of a share of the grazing revenue collected from the Gaddis and of the general revenue from the sale of trees."[33] The importance that the Gaddi herders had for the village-level economies over a large stretch of territory is, therefore, quite apparent. What is also quite significant is that its claim to a share in the grazing dues was firmly asserted by the village community while negotiating for land rights with the new colonial rulers.

Despite its assertion of a tribal identity, Gaddi society was by no means an egalitarian and undifferentiated one. The association of the Gaddis with permanent villages and settled agriculture has already been referred to. Added to this was the interesting fact that the internal divisions amongst them appeared to replicate the caste system of the neighbouring societies. Some of the fairly intricate Brahmanical *gotra* divisions and migration myths are also a part of the surviving Gaddi oral tradition.[34]

---

were exempted from paying *trini* on grazing land near their villages. Animals which were grazed in the "near pastures" and taken neither to high *dhars* nor the low winter grazing areas were called *ghareri*, and the dues paid for their grazing were called *trini-ghareri*. Even though the references regarding *ghareri* are to Gaddi villages, in this latter case it is their position as peasants that is under consideration.

[32] Lyall 1889: 42.

[33] *Kangra DG* 1926: 296.

[34] *Chamba SG* 1910: 138–9.

At the bottom of the social ladder were the village menials and artisans who normally performed the more laborious tasks within the settled villages. These were the Kolis, Riharas, Lohars, Badhis, Sipis, and Halis, and in most cases their "caste" names are derived from their occupational position.[35] Groups with pretensions to true Gaddis status did not, however, acknowledge the lower social groups as belonging to the Gaddi community.

Those who claimed the superior Gaddis' position were divided into three "classes". These were first, the Brahmins, secondly the Khatris and Rajputs, and finally the Thakurs and Rathis.[36] The sacred thread (*janeo*) was worn by the Brahmin, Khatri, and Rajput "castes" among the Gaddis, though it need not necessarily have signified an abandonment of their tribal identity or an integration into a larger regional social structure ordered by Brahmanical caste orthodoxy. A well-to-do member of the non-*janeo*-wearing superior Gaddi category could be permitted by the raja to wear the sacred thread in return for a "present or services". Though a very vague sense of socio-religious superiority may have emerged from such an exercise, it failed to create any social segregation between Gaddis who wore the *janeo* and those who did not. Intermarriage between the higher class of Gaddis irrespective of the sacred thread or "caste" was common and acceptable.[37] Moreover, the Brahmin or Rajput "caste" status of a Gaddi was not translated into matrimonial relations with corresponding castes in non-Gaddi society. It is, however, possible that the usefulness of exploiting internal "caste" divisions to relate to non-Gaddi society was, nonetheless, being realised by some Gaddi groups by the beginning of the twentieth century. While the Khatris within the tribe returned themselves as Gaddis during the 1901 census, the Brahmins and Rajputs preferred to be enumerated under their respective caste names.[38]

G.C. Barnes who carried out the land revenue settlement of Kangra in the 1850s wrote about the Gaddis that they "are the most

---

[35] Rose 1970: II, 256.
[36] *Chamba SG* 1910: 137.
[37] Ibbetson 1970: 205; Rose 1970: II, 256.
[38] *Chamba SG* 1910: 137.

remarkable race in the hills. In features, manners, dress and dialect, they differ essentially from all the rest of the population."[39] This distinct identity has been retained by the Gaddis over the centuries and in this they continued until very recent times. Neither the regular monetary transactions with the clearly caste-oriented neighbouring agriculturists nor the existence of a broad notion of "caste" within their own tribe seems to have diluted this consciousness of separateness and difference. On the contrary, it seems possible that the very nature of their interactions with the state and settled agrarian villages prompted them to reaffirm their transhumant pattern of life and social organisation.

The Gaddis were an integral part of the economic system of the state in the pre-colonial period. As cultivators, they paid land revenue to the state. But it was in their role as pastoralists that their importance lay. For the state, the Gaddis provided the means of obtaining revenue from its extensive natural resources. To the peasantry, the seasonal migrations of the pastoralists brought much needed manure, apart from several other benefits. While the herders were, in a way, virtually indispensable for both state and peasantry, they (Gaddis) on their part could hardly have survived without constant migratory movements over a large area. It was the transhumant herding activities of the Gaddis that bound the three to each other. It was from this relationship, too, that the Gaddis possibly discovered the benefits of retaining a distinct social identity. They had to negotiate skilfully between the increasing revenue demands of the state on the one hand and the expectations of the peasantry on the other. This was no easy task, and James Lyall noted this in his report: "I have heard old shepherds say that down to British rule it was like running the gauntlet to convey a flock across the low country to the *ban*. Every petty official or influential landholder tried to exact something as the flock passed him; a mild man easily daunted, had no chance, and the Gaddis picked out their ugliest customers for the work."[40]

This is not to suggest that things were very different under colonial rule either in the territories directly administered by the British or

---

[39] Barnes 1889: 42.
[40] Lyall 1889: 39, fn.

within the princely states. As the price of sheep and wool rose, the grazing tax was periodically increased. With the implementation of new forest policies and the closure of reserved forests both by the British and the native rulers, the pressure on the traditional grazing areas of the Gaddi flock increased.[41] As the search and struggle for newer and scarcer pastures intensified, the Gaddis probably found it necessary to close ranks to negotiate more effectively with the government and the peasant communities they interacted with.[42] Even under the changed circumstances, the shrewdness and the business acumen of the Gaddi were not to be underestimated. He invariably lived up to this well-known saying in the hills:

Gaddi mitr bhola
Denda top te mangda chola[43]

The Gaddi is a simple friend
He offers you his cap and asks for your coat.

---

[41] *Kangra DG* 1926: 277–8. There was considerable increase in the demand for Kangra wool and its price rose during World War I.

[42] Ibid.: 277, 438–8. *Kangra DG* 1918: 223. The Gaddis were, incorrectly, regarded by government officials as the prime culprits in the degeneration of forests.

[43] Rose 1970: II, 260. It might be worth mentioning here that the Gaddis were referred to as "the most prosperous agricultural class in the State".

10

Migration and Trade in Mountain Societies

AN ATTEMPT IS MADE here at a comparative study of migratory practices and economic entrepreneurship in two socio-economically diverse areas situated in very different mountain systems of the world. It is grounded in the expertise of the authors on their respective regions.[1] The fact that certain shared paradigms and common issues dominate social science research on mountain societies across the world enables us to explore substantive points of comparison and discussion. The broad sectional divisions indicate the main issues involved. Certainly, there are other equally important dimensions of research on mountain societies that fail to find place here on account of the constraint of space.

Migratory Practices

An assumption shared by social scientists studying the Alps or the Himalaya is the existence of a kind of "law of transhumance". At one

Coauthored with Laurence Fontaine, this was first published as "Migration and Trade in Mountain Societies: A Comparative Study of Historical Processes in Upper Dauphine (Alps) and Kulu–Kinnaur (Himalaya)". Work on it was initiated at the conference of the International Association of Economic History, Buenos Aires, 2002, at a session on "Mountains in Urban Development" organised by the Istituto di Storia delle Alpi, Lugano. Its proceedings were published in *Historie des Alpes*, 2003/8. It was further supported by the Franco-Indian programme of the Maison des Sciences de l'Homme, Paris, in 2007. Both authors would like to thank Jon Mathieu for his helpful comments on an earlier version.

[1] Fontaine 1996, 1998, 2003, 2005; C. Singh 1995, 1997, 1998, 2004.

level, this involved the seasonal movement of men and cattle over varying distances on a regular and traditionally determined basis. At another, it was an explicit act of migrating out from the mountains to pursue new and diverse economic opportunities. There appears to be a broad agreement with Braudel's famous description of mountains as the "factory of men for the use of others".[2]

Most notably, descriptions of mountain migrations are usually grounded in ecological premises. These emphasise ecosystem imperatives as being primarily responsible for surplus manpower and limited foodgrain availability. Ecological arguments are founded on the idea that long winters in mountains make this terrain unsuitable for agricultural production. Many other issues, too, have been explained through an emphasis on environmental factors.

Knowledge of Mountain Migrations

Several preconceptions underlie the present understanding of mountain societies. These are derived from the assumption that agro-pastoralism was the predominant way of utilising alpine resources. This system persisted in the French Alps till the nineteenth century and remains a fairly common practice in the Himalaya even today. Undeniably, agro-pastoralism was a traditional pre-industrial method of exploiting the alpine environment. But it was not the sole determinant of migratory practices. It needs to be recognised that agro-pastoralism was embedded in a larger socio-economic context. The differences in the context, therefore, bring to the fore variations in the two areas of study.

Till the twelfth century, the higher alpine valleys of the Alps were economically unimportant. The prosperous and densely populated low countries possessed the most fertile wheat fields. From the twelfth century onwards, and particularly in the thirteenth century, the economic growth of Europe became apparent. There was a rapid growth of towns and the sea offered more opportunities than challenges. Increasing prosperity manifested itself in new ways of

[2] Braudel 1966: I, 46.

dressing and nourishing oneself. These developments brought mountain regions into the mainstream. The building and ship industries required a large and constant supply of wood. The expanding clothing industry demanded greater quantities of leather and wool, and social status was indicated by a diet that required meat. These new commodities were the products of uncultivated regions, especially the mountains.

As a result, highland society responded to socio-economic changes in the lowlands. Livestock breeding became more advanced. A system of irrigating grassland was developed in the driest mountains. Simultaneously, large-scale transhumance farming came increasingly to be practised. Sheep descended to low-lying meadows as the higher pastures were unable to sustain large flocks over the winter.[3]

With this shift in the economy, the mountains became regions of high population. For instance, La Grave, situated 1400 metres above sea level, close to the Lautaret Pass, was the most populated village in the Upper Dauphine – more even than Bourg d'Oisans which commanded access to the valleys and had fertile land. Trade fairs were frequently held on the fringes of mountains. Even as the value of their produce increased, mountain areas became important because of their trade routes. This was true till the opening decades of the eighteenth century. A division in trade was established. Heavy commodities were transported by sea while luxury goods were carried overland, often through Alpine routes. Mule trains weighed down by silks, precious dyes, indigo, gold and silver thread, travelled over mountain passes. Trade irrigated the mountains in a multitude of thin trickles, winter and summer alike, because experienced guides guaranteed safe passage all year round.

The movement of men to higher altitudes was not, therefore, a result of overpopulation. It was an integral part of man taking possession of the mountains. This is essential for understanding the origin of migrations and explaining the development of densely populated areas close to the mountain passes, along the trade routes, during this period. From the Middle Ages onwards, the population here

---

[3] Duby 1984; Allix 1929: 110, 145–53.

continually alternated between the high valleys and the main trade axes (North–South, joining the Netherlands and Italy by way of the Rhine Valley; and East–West linking Italy to Spain through the south of France).

It is important to situate developments in the Alps within the different geographic scales in which it makes sense. Similarly, a clearer understanding of the role of peddlers in Europe emerges when one searches for their sedentary roots. This approach is contrary to the prevailing discourse in which peddlers are classed as rootless and itinerant. One needs to look beyond individual figures and concentrate on the structure of the society of which they were a product and part.[4] The first point of difference is precisely the structure of the two societies discussed here. In the Himachal Himalaya, north of Delhi, though the caste system was not rigidly established, the mental categories of caste were clearly present. This influenced the way people viewed migration.

Therefore, two realities need to be identified in the Himalaya: the colonial and the autochthonous. Suspicion for the itinerant and apparently "rootless" peddler – or migrant – so common in Europe, has a parallel in South Asian history. This was the distrust that government, especially the colonial state in India, had for nomadic people. In the second half of the eighteenth century, British administrators had begun regulating itinerant tribal populations more rigorously than settled peasants and declared migratory tribes were "criminal". They were subjected to special police regulation and their movements were controlled and restricted by the state.[5] While the British legally classified none of the migratory groups in Himachal as "criminal" tribes, the attitude of suspicion persisted. The itinerant practices of migratory communities were regulated and they were encouraged to become sedentary. This was in contrast to the approach of pre-colonial states in India that recognised tribes and itinerant people as an essential element of the socio-economic and political landscape.[6] The

---

[4] Fontaine 1996.
[5] Radhakrishna 1989; Baker 1991.
[6] C. Singh 1988.

interdependence of settled and migratory peoples was grounded in complex notions of caste, community, or tribe. While social categorisation of this kind was fluid and varied from region to region, the overlap of certain castes and communities with specific professional skills had created easily recognisable groups within society. The demarcation of migratory from settled people was by no means the most important social division.

Present-day migratory practices of Kinnaura and Lahaula pastoralists in the western Himalaya are very similar to the system of mountain transhumance that was once common in Europe. Seasonal migration of this kind was not purely an individual or family decision. It was the time-tested practice of an entire community or society. Were the mountain environment and society both inherently suitable for the adoption of transhumance as a socio-economic system?

A study of the alpine system reveals that inhabitants owned very little land, and this may have prevented them from developing a self-sufficient economy.[7] As earlier mentioned, the society and economy of the Alps responded to changes in the lowlands. They were integrated with the larger commercial routes from very early times. Village revenues had always come from the complementarity of the high and low countries, and from the numerous commercial routes that crossed the Alps. One may, therefore, argue that mountain people have always worked for others, either within or outside the village. One or two very wealthy families dominated the village. Members of these families were to be found in the big cities of Europe. This connection meant that the few well-placed village families had access to external markets. On the other hand, influential families from the Alps, but residing in cities, were able to attract the village population – either towards migration or towards the putting-out system in spinning or weaving – depending on the needs of the market.

A certain degree of inequality was also to be found in the Himalayan villages of Kulu and Kinnaur. Unlike the Alpine villages of Dauphine, however, inequality in these villages was moderated by the powerful influence of the community over crucial economic and

---

[7] Mathieu 2009.

social matters. The collective control of the Himalayan village community over water, forest and other natural resources is a case in point. In the Alps, on the other hand, the increasing demand for mules and horses for transportation and war divided village society. The wealthiest attempted to use the common pastures exclusively to maintain more of these remunerative animals, while the others tried to retain the older communal rules for the benefit of the whole village.

The meagre income that the average west Himalayan peasant derived from his small patch of land was supplemented by sheep and goats. Apart from the produce their flocks provided them, the people of Lahaul and Kinnaur used them as pack animals to trade between India and Tibet. In the higher Himalaya, successful families derived considerable wealth from this combination of pastoralism and trade. As traders and participants in the money economy, the pastoral traders of the Himalaya are particularly relevant here. By way of comparison, it seems worth mentioning that in the Alps few people were rich enough to possess large flocks. Community rules permitted each person to send only a limited number of animals to the common pastures. The richest members of the community entered into contracts with the poorest. The latter undertook to take the animals of the richer villagers to the pastures. In return, the owners of the animals were given a share of the products (milk, cheese, etc.). Behind these pasture contracts one may find concealed a certain degree of equality.

Kinnaur: High Mountain Economy of the Peasant-Pastoralist-Trader

Kinnaur was part of the princely state of Bashahr bordering Tibet. It occupied the higher reaches of the Satlej River basin which is bound by immense mountains. Very little area was suited to agriculture. All cultivated land was in the form of permanently settled terraces, though it has also been suggested that shifting cultivation involving the cutting and burning of forests might have once been practised here.[8]

---

[8] Hamilton 1932: 22.

Lt W. Murray, Superintendent of the Simla Hill States in the 1820s, wrote about Kinnaur that "The inhabited regions are confined to the dells and gorges which intersect them and drain off the streams, the cultivated parts forming so small a proportion as to appear as patches or steps of stairs up the slopes of the mountains."[9] As early as 1818, Gerard had noted that the grain produced in the villages of Kinnaur was "insufficient for consumption".[10] Even today, the scope for the extension of agriculture remains extremely limited and pastoralism has not been completely abandoned.

Conversely, pastoralism was not a viable alternative by itself either. The paucity of local natural resources meant that large-scale sheep or goat rearing was possible only through seasonal migration. Adequate grain and summer pastures had to be found in the adjoining lower areas. Without access to these additional external resources, life in Kinnaur would have been impoverished and extremely tenuous. This made Kinnaur quite similar to other agro-pastoral regions of the world.[11]

A combination of activities was essential for survival in Kinnaur. According to Murray, the people of Kinnaur were "occupied in extensive commercial intercourse and trade; rearing vast flocks which form their chief dependence and trafficking into remote countries under great hardship and privation to gain a comfortable subsistence for their families at home."[12] The situation remained strikingly similar even a century later.[13] The significance that Kinnauras attached to sheep and goat rearing is mentioned thus in an unsympathetic government report of 1959:

> The local people have come to believe that their economy is based on the rearing of sheep and goats ... The terrain is so difficult that transport of foodstuffs and other necessities of life is not possible by other means of transport ... trade with Tibet is only possible with the sheep and

[9] Murray 1824: 288; Hamilton 1932: 32.
[10] Gerard 1993: 294.
[11] Cf. Black-Michaud 1986; Molnar 1981: 33.
[12] Murray 1824: 278–9, 282.
[13] Hamilton 1932.

goats. They, therefore, want that no limitations on their number and no restriction, whatsoever, of their grazing in the forests should be imposed.[14]

The forest official who prepared this report regarded the migratory flocks as "an evil" and felt that "their number has got to be brought down with a heavy hand."[15] Colonial policies had successfully entrenched suspicion and hostility towards migratory people.

However, migratory shepherding was not the only economic activity in Kinnaur. Certainly, the primary association of Kinnauras with agriculture and migratory flocks allows us to regard them as agro-pastoralists. But they were also agro-pastoralists actively engaged in trade. The share of each activity – agriculture, pastoralism, and trade – in the total economy of the area varied according to circumstances and is difficult to quantify.

In all Himalayan areas bordering the entire length of the Tibetan plateau, sheep and goats have long been used as pack animals to transport essential goods and trade commodities.[16] Only sure-footed smaller animals could negotiate many of the treacherous mountain paths of Kinnaur. This marked the point at which trade and pastoralism overlapped. Goats and sheep are capable of carrying only small loads of merchandise, and in difficult terrain the loads have to be made even smaller. Though many traders bought additional pack animals to transport their goods, it was probably important for a successful Kinnaura entrepreneur to build up a large flock of his own. Only a large flock could yield an adequate number of pack animals to transport merchandise. However, skilful husbandry was a prerequisite for nurturing a large flock in semi-arid and resource-starved Kinnaur. Specialised herders probably bred and sold pack animals to agro-pastoralists who were also traders. This could be considered a purely pastoral form of income. Thus, the rearing of sheep and goats was a full-time occupation of certain sections of the Kinnaur population, but it was to some extent dependent on the success of trading activities.

[14] Parmar 1959: 58.
[15] Ibid.: 14, note 15.
[16] Furer-Haimendorf 1988; Fisher 1987.

The economic links of the Kinnauras with the lowlands to the south and the Tibetan plateau to the north-east were extended and sometimes indirect. Migratory practices here entailed not only the simpler economic activity of animal husbandry but also the complicated business of commercial and monetary transaction. Unlike the permanently settled peasant of the lower hill areas, the migratory agro-pastoralist trader of the higher regions was compelled to be a shrewd businessman.

Trade and Entrepreneurship

Current explanations of migration assume the existence of a liberal economy in which supply and demand were the only decisive factors. The complex nature of economic institutions in mountain regions is rarely examined. Such institutions have a crucial bearing on the functioning of the labour market and the flow of economic information. They influence the migration of different categories of manpower, especially in areas of large-scale employment such as construction work. There is a need to reconsider the dominant land-centred paradigm presently central to the analysis of migration in mountain societies.

While the significance of land is undeniable, the structure of power in mountain villages is equally important. The first detailed analysis of the Alps enables us to draw up a diversified picture of mountain villages and of the intricate and extensive pattern of migration that they developed. To migrations caused by poverty – and these are not specific to the mountains – can be added migrations controlled by elites acting as labour contractors. These elites were organised as merchant diasporas.[17]

The organised form of Alpine migration raises the important question of its specificity. Such a pattern of migration was not common in the Himachal Himalaya. Limited migration of this nature probably occurred in the nineteenth century from the mountains to the towns of Punjab. The present trend of migration is quite the opposite and

---

[17] Fontaine 2003: ch. 10.

includes immigration to the mountains from the plains and from other mountain regions. Perhaps the explanation for this difference can be found in the nature of urbanisation and economic development in the lowlands adjoining Alpine societies. Alpine migrants successfully developed functional linkages with lowland villages, towns and cities. They established business interests in distant places in Europe and sometimes specialised in activities such as book-selling and construction. Evidently, the wider socio-economic milieu of the two different mountain societies determined the options available to them. The milieu in Europe was apparently more conducive to migration from the mountains. There was a close social relationship between merchants trafficking throughout Europe and the elites of the Alpine villages. Such familial connections of migrants settled in the Indian lowlands with their Himalayan villages did not develop until the late twentieth century. Nevertheless, long-distance trade in the western Himalaya did extend to the northern fringe of the Indian plains.

The Structure of Trans-Himalayan Trade

Trade in the mountainous region of the western Himalaya was conducted in two stages. The first stage was dominated by migratory trans-Himalayan traders who came from the north, i.e. Ladakh, Yarkand, and Tibet over the Himalayan passes. Yarkandi and Ladakhi traders were usually engaged in transporting *charas* (a cannabis extract) from Leh to Kulu.[18] The upper reaches of the Beas (in Kulu) and the Satlej (in Rampur-Bashahr) valleys were usually the southernmost point to which traders from the trans-Himalaya came. In the category of trans-Himalayan traders may perhaps be included the people of the Lahaul and Kinnaur areas of Himachal Pradesh.

Kinnauras, however, frequently extended their migrations to the lower hills of Himachal, though they did not go into the plains. Trade was the most important non-agricultural economic activity in the areas bordering Tibet. Buddhist monasteries in Kinnaur were usually rich institutions because Buddhist lamas were also active

---

[18] Barnes 1889: 61; *SHSG* 1911, Bashahr: 62.

traders. The entire population of a village could be found engaged in trade.[19] Gerard, who travelled through Nisung village of Kinnaur, bordering Tibet, in the early nineteenth century discovered that "there were none but women and children in the village, all the grown-up men having gone to Garoo [Gartok in Tibet] for salt and wool."[20] The people of the village of Pilo in *pargana* Shua were known to be "very rich, due to their trade with the Tibetans."[21] In some villages of this *pargana* were successful traders locally popular as "*lakhpati shahukars*" (millionaire moneylenders).

For the inhabitants of the northern Kinnaur villages, trade with Tibet was crucial. Many of those who traded along the Satlej route became "men of considerable wealth" as a result.[22] Geographically, Kinnaur occupied an intermediate space between the cultivated valleys of the Himalaya and the barren plateau of Tibet. It lay between rather diverse societies. This made Kinnauras adept at negotiating with both sides. They adopted social norms that enabled them to successfully connect with the two large ecological and social systems that flanked them.

The arid mountainous region to the north of the Kulu valley was the territory of the Lahaulis. They paid a large portion of their taxes to the state in cash earned through trade.[23] British revenue officials observed that, unlike the Kulu peasants, the Lahaulis possessed "longheaded business instincts". Interestingly, many cultivators in Lahaul were prosperous enough to pay their taxes in cash.[24] Borrowing money for investment in trade was a common practice in Lahaul. Most of the creditors were themselves agriculturists and not professional moneylenders. The wool trade, in particular, required considerable financial support.[25] The familiarity of the Lahaulis with money and markets is illustrated by a British administrator's statement that

[19] *SHSG* 1911, Bashahr: 61; Gerard 1993: 79, 181–5.
[20] Gerard 1993: 102.
[21] *SHSG* 1911, Bashahr: Appendix II, xx.
[22] Mitchell 1915: 18.
[23] Diack 1898: 18.
[24] *Kangra DG* 1918: 59, 248.
[25] Ibid.: 219.

the "Lahulas are born traders and make much money by trade every year."[26]

The Low Hills: Merchants and Moneylenders

Traders from the Punjab plains and the low hills controlled the second stage of long-distance trade in Himachal. One trade route started from the plains and went up the Beas River valley all the way to Kulu. Punjabi traders purchased substantial quantities of rice from the low, well-cultivated hills of Kangra. Considerable profit was obtained by this enterprise, and some of the Sikh *kardars* (chief revenue officials of the district) had themselves speculated in the business in pre-colonial times.[27] The second important route followed the Satlej river up to the town of Rampur-Bashahr and perhaps a little beyond. Here the traders from the lowlands negotiated with the Kinnauras.

For certain articles, the Kulu valley was only a conduit to the plains. *Charas* was one of these.[28] An exceedingly large portion of the Kulu imports from Ladakh during the second decade of the nineteenth century consisted of *charas*. In 1913–14, for example, it amounted to more than three-fourths.[29] As intermediaries in this lucrative trade, the hill traders naturally stood to gain even though little of this commodity was locally consumed. Peculiarly, however, Chamba was an importer of *charas*, that too from Amritsar and Hoshiarpur.[30]

Though a large part of the trans-Himalayan long-distance trade was extraneous to the local economy, it did have a local impact. Local middlemen made some profit through transactions and long-distance trade connected local entrepreneurs of Kulu to the outside world. Moreover, there were lowland traders like the Gosains who developed strong business links with the interior villages of the Himalaya through their agents. They specialised in the opium trade. Gosain merchants

[26] Ibid.: 229.
[27] Barnes 1889: 27, 44.
[28] *Kangra DG* 1918: 173.
[29] Ibid., 1918: 129.
[30] *Chamba SG* 1910: 284.

from Jwalamukhi (in Kangra) advanced large loans at high interest rates to the peasants of Saraj (in Kulu); these were almost impossible to repay and made the peasantry dependent on the Gosains.[31] The Gosains belonged to a religious denomination that was entrepreneurial and actively engaged in money-lending and the purchase of opium from Saraj.[32] In the Rupi territory of Kulu, too, moneylenders were involved in the opium trade. In Shimla district Gosain traders aggressively advanced money to agriculturists producing opium.[33]

Areas that produced opium gradually became deficient in foodgrains. Money for importing foodgrains had partly to be obtained through the sale of opium. There were, in fact, some people (Sarajis: known as *basaju*) of the Inner Saraj area of Kulu who specialised in the annual import of foodgrains and made a profit in the process.[34] Little, however, is known about them, or even about other local-level traders. Written records of trading transactions are almost non-existent. Oral traditions regarding such activities testify to a vibrant local trade in various commodities.

Even though Himachal society was broadly structured along the caste system, it did not possess the complex Brahmanical hierarchies of lowland societies. The lack of social complexity enabled local entrepreneurs to emerge from the dominant peasantry, as was the case in the Alps. Unlike in the North Indian lowlands, no specific caste monopolised trade and business in the higher Himalaya. The dynamics of society in the mountain areas of Kulu and Kinnaur were, therefore, quite similar to those of the French Alps.

A network of relationships connected peddlers from the alpine region of France. Family connections were emphasised and the extending of credit occupied a central position at all levels of the mercantile structure. The limited information available on the Himalaya suggests a comparable scenario. Though many families participated in trade, a small number of rich families in Kinnaur and Lahaul were particularly successful in transacting business on a large scale. They

[31] *Kangra DG* 1918: 55–6.
[32] Ibid.: 55.
[33] Anderson 1917: 8–9; Thomas 1846: 22.
[34] *Kangra DG* 1918: 77.

wielded considerable influence in their home area. The availability of credit was an essential component of trade, and small traders were more dependent on credit than the bigger ones.

In the lower hills and adjoining plains entire communities specialised in commerce. Here the connection between family linkages and the availability of credit was explicit. It has already been noticed above that the Gosains in Himachal used credit as an instrument of economic control. The extension of credit to peasants and small traders in remote villages enabled the Gosains to develop new connections and monopolise the opium trade. It is possible that the Gosains converted the offerings and presents they received from followers of the faith into capital for investment in business.

Migration and the Chronological Gap

It is with respect to the second level of migration – migration out of the mountains in search of new economic possibilities – that we notice an interesting divergence in the two regions: a chronological gap is clearly noticeable in the development of migrations when we compare the mountain societies of the Alps and the Himalaya. In Europe, migrants from mountain regions were already a vivid part of descriptions of the Alps by the Middle Ages. On the other hand, only limited information is available about the Himachal Himalaya for the corresponding period, and in this the phenomenon of migration finds little mention. But migration from the Himalaya became more visible from the early nineteenth century onwards. Some explanation for this difference in the time of migration needs to be provided.

The migration of peddlers from the Alps was quite different from the migration that occurred at a later date from the Himalaya. This was because of the divergent historical experience of the two regions. Different long-term economic trends – the nature of commercial organisation, the emergence of industry, and most importantly the pattern of urbanisation – had a significant bearing on the pattern of migration.

While examining migration in France, two assumptions need to be reconsidered. The first is the inbuilt assumption in current explanations that a person is either a migrant or a sedentary person. Studies on migration perceive two geographic poles: one of *departure* and the other of *arrival*. As a result, there seem to be two primary "moments" in the life of the migrant: before and after migration. Till very recently, multipolarity, as the framework within which migrations functioned, was not regarded as a viable explanation. The second assumption is of explanatory models that atomise the social body. The "departure" (or the act of initial migration) is thought of as an individual choice, even though it is made possible by the family and the group of origin. "Chain migration" has been regarded as an independent, unrelated response or method for dealing with a particular situation. The larger social issue of "power" which might link migrants to each other in multiple ways is never seriously considered. Nor is the role of "political regimes" in mountain communities properly recognised. There is an urgent need to acknowledge that the social body is entirely, and only, a product of its constituents.[35]

Migration of the kind found in the French Alps developed much later in the western Himalaya. This was made possible by the emergence in the early nineteenth century of the kingdom of Punjab with its court and capital at Lahore. The appearance of a powerful regional political economy in north-west India engendered a shift of power and patronage away from imperial Delhi and closer to the mountains. The Lahore kingdom brought about greater concentration of wealth and employment opportunities in the region. The once-autonomous principalities of the western Himalaya were subjugated. The closer ties of the hill rulers and their subjects with the government at Lahore created greater possibilities for migration. Sikh rule over the mountain states was more systematic, and a heavier land-revenue demand was imposed. Its collection in cash probably encouraged local produce to be sold in the market, thereby bringing more money into the mountain economy.

The economic rise of Lahore from a provincial city to the capital of a prosperous kingdom attracted immigrants in search of livelihoods. Amritsar emerged as an important religious and production

---

[35] Fontaine 1998: 25–35.

centre. In the Kangra foothills, Hoshiarpur grew as a market town closely linked to the mountain economy. Similar developments in other urban centres of Punjab attracted migrants from the hills towards market, production, and labour. Migration in the region has therefore to be seen in the context of the larger political economy of Punjab and the opportunities it offered for new businesses and employment.

Irrespective of the different kinds of migrations witnessed in the two regions, it is evident that mobility was not a transitory rite of passage. Like the more "respectable" sedentary way of life, migration too could be regarded as a way of existing and appropriating territory. There is moreover a need to look beyond the argument that mobility was caused by a "push" or "pull" factor. Through these two binary points scholars have attempted to focus upon the reasons for migration and mobility. To this are applied two separate geographical and time points: the point of *departure* and the point of *arrival,* or before and after. While this approach has served a useful purpose, it does not take into account many other complex social processes that influenced long-term migratory trends.

Importantly, in both regions the act of migration or emigration did not necessarily mean an economic and cultural break with the home area. The retention of links with the home territory was integral to survival and success. Therefore, migration was not a one-time act but a continuing process requiring a renewal of connections with the mountain home. It was a "process" sustained by continuous links and return to the place of origin. In fact, the home region and the territories of migration were equal and interdependent components of the migrant's world. In such a situation, the bipolar perspective emphasising "push" and "pull", "departure" and "arrival" combined with "before" and "after", loses its primacy as an explanatory scheme. Despite the apparent but attractive correspondence of these bipolar terms with the concept of "mobility", the explicit break they create is illusory and simplistic.

Because of its exploratory nature, our study raises more questions than it provides answers to. Its objective is to open a dialogue between scholars engaged in the study of diverse mountain societies and deepen the understanding of such societies by a comparative approach. It is hoped also that this comparison will encourage more intense reflection on the subject. At a personal level, this exercise has certainly helped enrich our work in our respective specialisations by pointing out many of our own implicit assumptions and in revealing certain specificities that we tend to take for granted as being normal.

11

Pastoralism and the Making of Colonial Modernity in Kulu, 1850–1952

A DISCUSSION OF PASTORALISM in South Asia must recognise, first, that pastoralism involves some degree of movement; and second, that pastoral societies of the region have rarely been self-sufficient in economic and political terms.[1] Historically, pastoral people in the north-west of the subcontinent have for long functioned within larger politico-economic systems.[2] The study of pastoralism therefore involves an exploration of its interconnections with agriculture, trade, legal systems, the polity, and a host of other forms of social organisation.[3] Pastoralism has usually been "a particular activity within regions where more diverse economic activities are pursued." It seeks to make use of areas within such a region that are not suited to agriculture.[4] It has even been suggested that the growth of specialised nomadic pastoralism amongst a large population had a direct connection with the development of canal irrigation. As opposed to mixed farming systems, highly specialised irrigated agriculture required a larger amount of labour, and this consequently encouraged even the pastoral sector of the economy (and people connected to it) to become more specialised.[5] Pastoral people

---

A shorter version of this article was published as C. Singh 2009.
[1] Salzman 2002: 245.
[2] C. Singh 1988: 319–40.
[3] Glatzer and Casimir 1983: 308; Fortier 2001: 207.
[4] Galaty and Johnson 1990: 20; Salzman 2002: 260.
[5] Bates and Bates 1974: 186–93.

have constantly engaged with other sections of society and lived in a multifaceted world that scholars have only reluctantly recognised. Pastoralism is not simply a social response to ecological circumstances. It encompasses a wide range of complicated economic considerations and equally diverse social sensitivities.[6]

Agro-Pastoralism: The Complexities of Making a Balance

Mountainous conditions – limited cultivable land, the lack of irrigation, and easily accessible pastures and forests – encouraged an agro-pastoral economy in Himachal. There were, however, variations within the region in relation to the proportion of agriculture or pastoralism. As late as the 1950s, a forest official complained that the mountain peasantry, instead of trying to improve agriculture, "have taken to keeping large flocks of sheep and goats."[7] This, of course, was because labour invested in pastoralism tended to show higher productivity than efforts devoted to intensive traditional agriculture. Kulu, in particular, always accorded greater importance to pastoralism than many neighbouring territories. But this was a changing and dynamic relationship.

Most pastoralists in the Himachal Himalaya herded flocks of sheep and goats. A few, such as the Gujjars, kept cattle – buffaloes. The cattle owned by peasants were either stall-fed or grazed near their respective villages. Among them were oxen used for traction. Therefore, by comparing the number and kinds of animals kept by peasants in various parts of Himachal, a broad idea can be formed about the relationship between agriculture and pastoralism in specific areas. Nonetheless, the relative importance of the two sectors of the economy would have changed over the long term.

G.C. Barnes' revenue settlement of Kangra District (of which Kulu was a subdivision) in 1850 provides the earliest statistical information. This report enables us to make a rough comparison of different parts of the district.

[6] Galaty and Johnson 1990: 3.
[7] Parmar 1959: 1, para. 5.

Clearly, the number of cattle per peasant household (*asami*) in Kulu was below the average number of cattle kept by the Kangra peasant (Table 1). In Kangra valley proper, the average number of cattle owned by the peasant household was invariably more than the number of sheep and goats. In Kulu the reverse was true. The number of sheep maintained by the Kulu agro-pastoralist was more than the number of cattle, and almost twice that of the district average. Agriculture was therefore less important in Kulu than it was in the low-lying *taluqas* of the main Kangra valley, and shepherding was of greater importance in Kulu.[8] However, the agro-pastoral nature of the

Table 1

Average Number of Cattle/Sheep in Kangra District 1850
(per assessed peasant holding)

Pargana	Taluqa	Average no. of cattle to each asami	Average no. of sheep/goats to each asami
Kangra	6 taluqas	7.59	6.71
	Taluqa Bir Banghal	8.80	30.71
	a mountainous area known for an economy inclining towards pastoralism		
Nadaun	7 taluqas	10.52	6.73
Hamirpur	9 taluqas	6.32	3.14
Nurpur	16 taluqas	7.70	3.80
Kulu	**7 taluqas** (excluding taluqa Rupi)	5.90	10.48
Average for Kangra District		7.64	5.99

Source: G.C. Barnes 1889: 74–6.

[8] Galaty and Johnson 1990: 17. At a more general level it has been observed in connection with the extent of animals owned per capita in an area that: "Per capita holdings usually indicate the degree of pastoral specialization, with relatively low holdings signalling the need for economic diversification, medium-level holdings indicating greater pastoral self-reliance in subsistence,

economy meant that agricultural holdings were given primacy by the state and became the basis of revenue assessment. In most cases, they also became the basis for estimating the number of animals owned by the agro-pastoralists.

Agro-Pastoral System in Kulu

As early as the late nineteenth century British officials noted the high density of population on each "acre of cultivation". Hamilton, senior secretary to the financial commissioner, Punjab, in his letter to the revenue secretary of Punjab, explained that "the real reason for the high density is not scarcity of land, but the fact that the people are chiefly dependent for their livelihood on occupations other than agriculture."[9] He also noted that an increase in land revenue was possible not because of increased cultivation or higher prices, but because the people obtained additional income from service, grazing, and profits from selling the wool of their flocks. This money was used to pay the revenue, while agriculture provided them "little more than their food".[10] In 1872, Lyall had earlier observed that the elevated mountain villages of Kangra district enjoyed easy accessibility to considerable "wasteland". Peasants in such places made additional money by breeding and selling cattle, sheep, goats, and making ghee. For this reason, landowners in these mountain villages were better off.[11] All who maintained flocks were also closely associated with agricultural land. Montgomery pointed out that "even the graziers with large flocks of sheep and goats" were landowners "in a small way".[12] Apart from the essential food obtained from the small patch of land cultivated by the peasant family, it was "the produce of the flocks and herds in the shape of wool and *ghi*" that provided cash for market purchases and the payment of a part of the land revenue.[13]

---

large per capita holdings indicating the potential for or practice of semi-commercialised husbandry..."

[9] Diack 1898: 1, para. 2.
[10] Ibid.: 2, para. 4.
[11] Lyall 1889: 61.
[12] Diack 1898: 1, para. 2.
[13] *Kangra DG* 1918: 155.

Traditional Grazing Practices in Kulu

Moorcroft, who passed through Kulu and Lahaul in 1820, was among the early European travellers to notice the large-scale seasonal migration of sheep and goats between Kangra and Chamba on the one hand, and the Lahaul *waziri* of Kulu subdivision on the other.[14] After the area came under direct British rule, it became increasingly apparent to land revenue settlement officers that transhumant pastoralism was a crucial part of the economy of Kulu. It enabled the pastoralists of Kulu to use a range of ecological areas at different times of the year. Detailed descriptions by revenue officials reveal that the method of shifting flocks from one place to another was quite similar to that in many parts of the world. A detailed description makes interesting reading:

> The rams are kept at home till February, when they are all brought down to the lower pastures, and let loose among the flocks. In the following month, all the sheep and goats are driven home to pass the spring lambing season in the neighbourhood of the villages of their proprietors, and they remain there till the middle of June, manuring the rice and Indian-corn fields. They are then taken further up the hillsides to the *gahrs*, pastures in the forests at about 8 to 11 thousand feet elevations. The pastures, large open glades among the trees, are more properly called *thach*, which word is also applied to the level space in which a flock is penned for the night. In July when the rains have set in or are about to commence, the flocks are driven still higher up to the *nigahrs*, the sheep-runs on the grassy slopes above the limits of forest growth . . . The flocks remain in the *nigahrs* till the end of the rainy season, about the middle of September, and are driven back to the *gahrs* where they graze till the cold becomes severe and drives them down first to the villages of their owners and thence to their winter quarters. In this interval, they manure the fields which are being prepared for wheat and barley. The *gahrs* are generally deserted about the beginning of November.[15]

The traditional rights of the pastoralists to specific alpine pastures were recognised by the community and by the raja. British revenue

---

[14] Moorcroft 1970: 124.
[15] *Kangra DG* 1918: 107; Diack 1898: 36, paras 63, 41, Appendix II.

officials later recorded them in the register of "customary practices" (*wajib-ul-arz*) of Kulu subdivision. H.A. Rose had earlier noted that "the sheep graze in the *nigahars* and in *Asoj* in the *gahars*, where the grazing is not open to all, and the rights in the *gahar* and *nigahar* have been recorded." He also noted that "Each shepherd has his own *ban* [grazing area], but if it is not occupied by him, others may do so for a night when on their way to the pasture."[16]

Migrating sheep moved quite easily across the boundaries of princely states. This would have been true also in pre-colonial times. Lyall mentions the large-scale migration of Kulu sheep in his report of the early 1870s. He noticed that large flocks from Kulu were "sent into Mandi where a '*ban*' or run is leased from the Mandi Raja."[17] Large flocks had therefore necessarily to be moved to lower pastures outside Kulu if they were to survive the winter.

Conversely, Diack observed that in the higher Shanshar and Kanawar areas of Rupi *waziri* "certain alpine pastures are recorded as open to foreign grazing subject to the provision that sufficient must remain for local sheep."[18] This use of alpine summer pastures of Rupi by outsider pastoralists enabled Rupi herders to establish complementary relationships with agro-pastoralists of lower areas in adjoining native states. The large-scale migration of sheep from Rupi to winter pastures in other states indicates this (Table 2). The system of renting pastures in distant areas was not peculiar to Kulu. It was a practice followed also by the Afghan herders of the Hindu Kush. From our point of view the significance of this is that it reveals how "the nature of land rights shapes the structure and role of mobility in the pastoral system."[19]

Many shepherds of Kulu proper migrated to low-lying adjoining states. On the other hand, the pastoralists of Saraj *waziri* had access to sufficient winter pastures in the lower areas within Saraj. Only a small number of them left Saraj in search of pastures during the cold season.

Access to the summer pastures of Lahaul and Spiti was a matter of survival for the shepherds, not only those of Kulu but also of other

[16] As quoted in Diack 1898: 41, Appendix II.
[17] Lyall 1889: 86, para. 96.
[18] Diack 1898: 41.
[19] Galaty and Johnson 1990: 21–2.

Table 2

Pattern of Pastoralist Transhumance
Migratory Pattern of Kulu Flocks in Winter 1891

Sheep Belonging to	Grazing in Native States	Grazing in Kulu	Total	Per cent grazing outside Kulu	Remarks
Kulu Proper	18,948	76,617	95,565	19.82	
Rupi	21,897	22,750	44,647	49.07	Almost half the sheep grazing outside
Saraj	5,588	76,337	81,925	6.82	Very few sheep grazing outside
Total	46,433	175,704	222,137	20.90	Large majority of sheep (79.09 per cent) remained within Kulu area
Per cent of total	20.90	79.09			

Source: Diack 1898: 36, para. 63.

parts of Himachal. The rain-free trans-Himalayan weather of Lahaul provided the best sheep runs. Most of the Chandra valley in Lahaul was too dry for cultivation, and in summer only grass could grow in many of its higher uninhabited reaches. It was here that flocks of sheep and goats were to be found grazing.[20] In Spiti, the Pin valley provided the richest summer pastures, though the main Spiti valley too had some good "rolling downs covered with herbage on which the yaks, ponies and flocks of the people wax fat in the summer."[21] In the early decades of the twentieth century as many as six flocks of Gaddi shepherds (from Chamba/ Kangra), and one flock from Jagatsukh in Kulu, had the right to graze in Spiti.[22] Diack calculated (Table 3) that in addition to the Gaddi flocks that came from Kangra

---

[20] *Kangra DG* 1918: 183, 221; Harcourt 1972: 7.
[21] *Kangra DG* 1918: 255.
[22] Ibid.: 287.

Table 3
Migratory Pattern of Kulu Flocks in Summer 1891

Sheep belonging to	Grazing in Lahaul/Spiti	Grazing in Rupi nighars	Grazing in home nighars	Grazing in Inner Saraj nighars	Total	Per cent grazing outside Kulu	Remarks
Kulu Proper	49,795	—	45,770	—	95,565	52.10	More than half the sheep migrated
Rupi	683	3,938	40,026	—	44,647	1.52	
Saraj	3,801	19,426	42,241	16,457	81,925	4.63	
Total	54,279	23,364	128,037	16,457	222,137	24.43	
Per cent of total	24.43	10.51	57.63	7.40	100		

Source: Diack 1898: 36, para. 63.

through Kulu, "more than half the sheep and goats of the Kulu *tahsil* were driven to Lahaul-Spiti."²³

In summer, therefore, it was the Kulu herders who migrated in large numbers to the higher pastures of Lahaul and Spiti (Tables 3). Statistics reveal that transhumant pastoralism constituted an important part of the economy of Kulu proper. It had more sheep/goats than any other *waziri* but did not have adequate pastures either in winter or in summer. Kulu's shepherds were thus propelled into almost continuous long-range migratory movements.

What were the social and economic implications of this extended migratory system of Kulu proper? Did it open up greater possibilities for trade and exchange combined with pastoralism? Kulu lay on an important trade route to Ladakh and Yarkand.²⁴ While we have limited information on the Kulu shepherds' involvement in trade, many Lahaulas certainly profited from the Leh trade that passed through Kulu to the Punjab plains, at least till 1891.²⁵ Thereafter the goods began to be redirected through Kashmir and the trade through Kulu declined. Despite this the Lahaulas remained engaged in their time-tested business with Ladakh and Tibet. It was "the custom for one son in a family to leave the home and devote himself to trade."²⁶ This interaction with Tibet continued till much later. Walter Asboe argued in 1937 that "Were it not for the wool trade carried on between the highlands of Tibet and Lahoul, by way of supplementing the slender harvest he reaps, the Lahouli would be far worse off economically."²⁷ The wool trade therefore remained an important source of income for Lahaulas. Wool had long been an important item of trade between the pastoralists of the Tibetan plateau and the inhabitants of the Himalaya across the entire range. In Nepal, especially, the wool trade was "always monetised". Humphrey argues that "In the early twentieth century, the volume of the wool trade was so great that it determined the value of Tibetan

---

²³ Diack 1898: 36, para. 63.
²⁴ Harcourt 1871: 336–43.
²⁵ Coldstream 1913: 4, para. 10.
²⁶ Ibid.: 6, para. 19.
²⁷ Asboe 1937: 77; Rizvi 2001: 73, 74, 116, 117.

Table 4

The Importance of Lahaul as a Summer Pasture:
Flocks Grazing in Lahaul, 1890 and 1912

Year	Kulu Flocks	Chamba Flocks	Kangra Flocks	Total Foreign	Lahaul Flocks
1890	51,665	53,043	63.205	167,913	16,561
1912	44,665	25,409	58,778	128,903	29,536
Remarks				Decrease of 23.23 per cent	Increase esp. in goats

Source: Diack 1998: 38, para. 67; Coldstream 1913.

currency."[28] Lahaul was no different. In 1950 or so, about a hundred Lahaula families traded in Tibetan and Ladakh wool, and as a result the number of ponies "tremendously increased".[29]

Unlike the shepherds of Kulu proper, those of Rupi and Saraj did not migrate in summer. There were sufficient alpine pastures, especially in Rupi, for both local sheep and those from outside.[30] Within Kulu, therefore, the best summer pastures were in the higher reaches of the Parbati, Sainj, and Tirthan river valleys located in Rupi and Inner Saraj (central Kulu). Thus, while Saraj had a comparatively low level of long-range pastoral transhumance in both seasons (i.e. summer and winter), the Rupi sheep moved out from Rupi only in winter. In both *waziris* the summer was spent within or near the home district.

Pastoralism and the State

Shepherding was a crucial component of the Kulu economy. It was also an important source of state revenue. The sheep and goats of the peasantry were taxed by the raja and the British continued this practice in the revenue settlements of 1851 and 1871. This tax – levied at the rate of one anna per head per annum – allowed local flocks

[28] Humphrey 1985: 54.
[29] Singh 1952: 39, para. 54.
[30] Diack 1898: 36, para. 63, 41, Appendix II.

to graze in all pastures, including the *nigahars* (high alpine pastures). More importantly, because peasant cultivators owned the flocks, the tax was regarded as a part of land revenue. By 1891, however, the government decided to look more closely at the "profits derived from sheep farming". It estimated that while the sale of wool amounted to as much as "Rs. 50 per 100 full grown sheep", flock owners also earned additional income from the sale of woollen rugs, blankets, and meat in the market.[31] The administration therefore felt it was appropriate to levy an additional charge on the flocks. A distinction was now made between the pastures of the different *kothis* (revenue districts) of Kulu. While a single tax was fixed for the home flocks of a single *kothi* irrespective of where they grazed, flocks grazing outside the owner's *kothis* – in the high summer pastures of Lahaul, Rupi, and Saraj – had to pay an additional due of an equivalent amount.[32] The distinction made between local flocks and those of "foreign" shepherds resulted in the latter paying a higher tax.

Varying levels of taxation on pastoral livestock were not entirely new. Extensive seasonal migration occurred across boundaries of all kinds – of the village, the *phati, waziri*, and even of the princely state. The idea of "foreign" shepherds and the possibility of imposing a tax on outsider flocks had existed earlier. Kulu shepherds paid high rates for grazing rights in the winter pastures of Mandi in the early years of the twentieth century, and this was probably the continuation of an earlier practice. While referring to the shifting of the flocks of the higher *kothis* of Kulu to Mandi, it was seen that "Annual leases are usually taken of defined grazing grounds, otherwise fees are paid at the rate of Rs. 9-6-0- per hundred for both sheep and goats."[33] Conversely, outsider flocks (such as those of the Gaddis) that grazed in Lahaul during summer were taxed. Those from Kulu were exempt from this payment, as they had already been taxed by the raja of Kulu in their home territories at one anna per head per annum.[34] With the establishment of British rule in both Kangra and Kulu the definition

[31] Ibid.: 37, para. 64.
[32] Ibid.
[33] *Kangra DG* 1918: 105.
[34] Diack 1898: 38.

of "foreign" underwent a change. Regarding the Kangra shepherds (most probably Gaddis) who took their flocks to Lahaul in summer, Barnes now argued that while revenue derived from tax on grazing was "legitimate enough", "the graziers were residents of *our own* [emphasis mine] territory, who during the winter months had already paid a grazing tax of Rs. 2-0-0 per hundred head in the valleys of Kangra. It would not be fair to make these flocks pay double rates." For this reason, he chose to remit the tax.[35] But the force of custom overrode Barnes' recommendation. At the 1871 revision of the settlement, it was discovered that while Kulu's shepherds remained exempt from paying a tax in Lahaul, the Gaddis continued to pay the old customary tax to the raja in Rupi and to the colonial administration in areas under its control. Eventually, the government decided to continue the imposition of Re 1-9-0 per hundred on the Gaddi flocks.[36]

Trends in Pastoralism and Agriculture under Colonialism

A comparison of the number of sheep/goats owned by agro-pastoralists in Kulu may reveal some broad trends about the economy of the area. While earlier statistics are rather unreliable, the surveys between 1891 and 1912 appear to be more trustworthy. They enable us to draw some justifiable conclusions. By 1912, Kulu proper witnessed the largest increase in the number of sheep/goats (24 per cent over 1891) in the subdivision. On the other hand, the percentage increase of oxen in Kulu proper was the smallest (Table 5). Pastoralism was therefore of increasing importance in the area, and agriculture did not enjoy undisputed primacy. Moreover, not all cattle maintained by the peasantry were used directly in agricultural operations. While all cattle provided manure for the fields, many of them were milch animals thriving on easily accessible fodder in the forests and in grass preserves adjoining the village. Nonetheless, cattle – more than sheep and goats – were more closely associated with settled agriculture and the permanent agricultural homestead.

[35] Barnes 1889: 63, para. 401.
[36] Diack 1898: 38.

Table 5
Number of Oxen/Sheep in Kulu Proper, Saraj and Rupi 1891–1912

Waziri	1891	1909	1912	1912	1912	1912	1912
	Oxen (As mentioned in Coldstream's)	Sheep/goats	Oxen (Figure available only for 1909)	Per cent change in no. of oxen	Sheep/goats	Per cent change in no. of sheep/goats	Remarks
KULU PROPER Waziri Parol Waziri Lag Maharaja Waziri Lag Sari	34,392	95,565	35,823	+4.16	1,18,554	+24	
SARAJ Inner Saraj Outer Saraj	—	81,925	41,599	+25.81	75,744	-7.5	Epidemic has taken heavy toll on sheep and goats
Waziri Rupi	14,156	44,647 222,137	15,069 92,491	+6.44	45,245 239,543	+1.3 +7.83	Good trade in sheep and goats

Source: Diack 1898: 36, para. 63; Coldstream 1913: 2, 3, 6.

The *waziri* of Saraj had the largest amount of agricultural area in the subdivision. Its economy was inclined more towards agriculture. Correspondingly, we find a marked increase (25.81 per cent) in the number of oxen (Table 5). This does not deny, however, that pastoralism remained an important component of its economy. In *waziri* Rupi, too, the increase in oxen was greater than the increase in sheep/goats, thereby indicating some shift from pastoralism to agriculture.

These developments in different areas conform to the pattern of expansion in cultivated land in Kulu subdivision as a whole.

Information pertaining to a 34-year period (1911–45) reveals some broad trends. To begin with, we work on the assumption that a decline in the number of sheep indicates a decline in the dependence of local society on transhumant pastoralism. The drop in the population of cows suggests that it was becoming difficult to sustain large numbers of non-productive cattle in the peasant household and that (for various reasons) access to green fodder from the community forest was becoming increasingly difficult. The number of bullocks has to be seen in the context of the extent of area under cultivation. It appears that even as the area under cultivation was increasing, the number of bullocks was decreasing, albeit at a slower rate. This decrease in the number of bullocks may represent an overall reduction only in the number of extra animals that the average peasant household maintained simply to obtain manure. Severe restrictions in the new colonial laws upon the use of forest resources made the upkeep of numerous unproductive animals increasingly uneconomical.

Table 6 reveals that there was a rapid decline in the number of sheep/goats and cows, but the decline in the number of oxen was relatively much smaller. It can be argued that this trend indicates the increasing importance of agriculture *vis-à-vis* pastoralism.

A *waziri*-wise comparison of the cultivated area over different revenue settlement years provides a good idea about trends in cultivation and its links with pastoralism. Saraj (primarily Outer Saraj) had the largest part (almost half) of the cultivated area of Kulu subdivision, followed by Kulu proper. The share of the *waziris* of Saraj and Rupi in the total cultivated area of Kulu subdivision increased a

Table 6
Long-term Comparison of Agricultural Livestock in Kulu Subdivision 1911 and 1945

Waziri	Year	Sheep	Goats	Per cent change	Cows	Per cent change	Bullocks	Per cent change
Kulu Proper	1911	77,369	41,186		33,868		16,843	
	1945	77,284	31,874	−7.92	18,254	−46.10	15,702	−6.77
Rupi	1911	25,563	19,682		14,010		6,695	
	1945	16,295	9,661	−42.63	6,770	−51.67	6,090	−9.02
Inner Saraj	1911	15,658	10,766		7,557		5,452	
	1945	11,592	8,821	−22.74	6,808	−9.91	5,127	−5.92
Outer Saraj	1911	29,848	19,472		16,000		12,018	
	1945	23,411	14,195	−23.75	13,781	−13.86	10,048	−16.39
Lahaul	1911	22,313	6,385		1,731		479	
	1945	20,549	5,830	−8.09	1,520	−12.18	419	−12.52
Spiti	1911	2,237	2,536		–		–	
	1945	2,076	1,990	−14.81	–		–	
Per cent decline of agricultural stock in Kulu Proper, Saraj and Rupi (excluding Lahaul-Spiti)				−19.37		−36.14		−9.85

Source: C. Singh 1952: 16, paras 22, 17–18.

little (in terms of percentage) between 1891 and 1911, while that of Kulu proper declined (Table 7). This decline in its total percentage share, combined with the fact that acreage under cultivation increased the least in Kulu proper during this period, suggests that the Kulu peasantry had other sources of income (i.e. trade, carriage of goods, shepherding) and the benefits of extending cultivation were not attractive enough.

Moreover, in terms of percentage the greatest increase in cultivation took place in Waziri Rupi (13.72 per cent). Rupi was, however, the least cultivated area and had 18,821 acres of forest classified as reserved.[37] Probably for that reason it had a larger amount of land still available for cultivation. The cultivated area in Saraj increased by 8.10 per cent between 1891 and 1911, with the Inner Saraj area growing at the second fastest rate (after Rupi) of 11.17 per cent. Inner Saraj, too, was a less cultivated area. While it represented more than half the total area of Saraj *waziri*, it had only 32.47 per cent of its cultivated area in 1911.

Of considerable significance is the fact that the two most important areas for summer grazing in Kulu – Rupi and Inner Saraj – also witnessed the fastest expansion of area under cultivation in the late nineteenth and early twentieth centuries. The period between 1911 and 1945 saw a slower rate of agricultural expansion than the much shorter period between 1891 and 1911. Even in absolute terms the increase in acreage during this period of thirty-four years was less than it was in the earlier eleven-year period (compare Tables 7 and 8).

While the percentage increase in cultivated land was still the most rapid in Rupi, the expansion of agriculture in Saraj seems to have slowed down considerably (from 8.10 per cent to 2.87 per cent). Nonetheless, cultivation in Inner Saraj grew faster (5.52 per cent) than in Outer Saraj (1.60 per cent). It seems that Saraj (especially Outer Saraj) now had little scope for further agricultural expansion. The reasons for this probably had more to do with forest regulations than geography. Inner Saraj had more extensive forests and 11,357

---

[37] *Kangra DG* 1918: 120.

Table 7

Changes in the Cultivated Area in Different Areas of Kulu Subdivision Waziri-wise Comparison of Cultivated Area (in acres), 1891 and 1911

Waziri	Year	Irrigated	Unirrigated	Total Cultivated	Acres increase	Per cent increase	Per cent of cultivated area of sub-division
Kulu Proper	1891	3,910	23,875	27,785			37.83
	1911	4,029	25,121	29,150	+1,365	+4.91	36.86
Saraj	1891	1,194	34,321	35,515			48.36
	1911	1,308	37,086	38,394	+2,879	+8.10	48.55
Rupi	1891	—	—	10,135			13.80
	1911	—	—	11,526	+1,391	+13.72	14.57
Total	1891			73,435			
	1911			79,070	+5,635	+7.67	

Source: Coldstream 1913: 3, 4, 7. Compare figures also in Diack 1898: 4, which show minor variations.

Table 8

Waziri-wise Comparison of Cultivated Area (in acres), 1911 and 1945

Waziri	Year	Cultivated area	Acres increase	Per cent increase	Per cent of cultivated area of sub-division
Kulu Proper	1911	29,150			36.86
	1945	30,954	+1,804	+6.18	37.23
Saraj	1911	38,394			48.55
	1945	39,499	+1,105	+2.87	47.51
Rupi	1911	11,526			14.57
	1945	12,685	+1,159	+10.05	15.25
Total	1911	79,070			
	1945	83,138	+4,068	+5.14	

Source: C. Singh 1952: 68, 71, 73, 75, 79, 83, 94, 98.

acres of these were classified as "reserved", as compared to 5009 acres in Outer Saraj.[38] It was observed that livestock in Inner Saraj had decreased due to the "limited availability of grazing and strict forest conservancy".[39] Outer Saraj was a fairly well-cultivated area. Unlike in Inner Saraj, the peasants had relatively easy access to forest resources and a larger amount of pasturage. They kept "plenty of cattle and make *Ghee* for sale in Shimla".[40]

An interesting development during this period was the accelerated increase of cultivated area in Kulu proper both in absolute (1804 acres in comparison to 1365 acres earlier) and percentage terms (6.18 per cent compared to the earlier 4.91 per cent). This was in contrast to the impression conveyed by the statistics of the earlier period. Increasingly strict forest laws and fewer and more closely regulated pastures were beginning to take their toll on the migratory Kulu agro-pastoralists. They now considered agriculture more important.

[38] *Kangra DG* 1918: 120.
[39] C. Singh 1952: 38, para. 52.
[40] Ibid.: 38, para. 53.

Colonial "Modernity": The Implications of New Revenue and Forest Regulations

The question of "modernity" and its relationship with the nation-state in Europe on the one hand, and the growth of global colonial connections on the other has been a contentious and much-debated issue.[41] One facet of "modernity" in South Asia could be taken to be its early association with colonial rule, and the second phase thereafter linked to the emergence in the subcontinent of an understanding centred primarily on the nation-state. Our present concern does not require us to enter the larger theoretical discussion on modernity. But the introduction of new notions of property, ownership, and state regulation of natural resources under British rule marks a distinct break from the pre-colonial past. It offers us a point of entry into the field. Government regulations based on these new conceptions ushered in unprecedented changes. They transformed "traditional" social and economic organisations and created institutions that implemented and followed norms considered "modern" in a distinctly European sense.

Claims to the ownership of the forest and strict regulation of access to forest resources were asserted by the colonial administration after the Forest Act of 1865.[42] The Forest Act of 1878 further increased this regulatory control, and the traditional grazing practices of herders and shepherds came to be perceived as particularly destructive of valuable timber forests.[43] Central to the entire question was the "ownership" of common property resources. The colonial state viewed itself as owner of the "larger wastes", i.e. the forest and uncultivated land that lay beyond the confines of village boundaries. In Kulu about

[41] Washbrook 1997, 1998, 1999; van der Veer 1998, 1999.
[42] Rangarajan 1996: 27, 30.
[43] Rangarajan 1991: 65, 69; cf. Brower 2000: 127. This can be compared with Brower's observation that almost at the same time (1880s and 1890s) in the Wind River mountains of south-western Wyoming (later part of Yellowstone Timber Reserve) of the United States, the newly constituted Forest Service was working in close relationship with the "livestock industry" and "Established stockmen were invited to share in decision-making about forest grazing."

60 per cent of the total forest area was classified as demarcated or reserved forest.[44]

We need, nevertheless, to recognise that notions which restrict the concept of property rights to either private or state property may not be very useful in societies where the community regulated access to natural resources. While community control over resources represented a kind of common property, we need to recognise that "Common property is not one kind of property-rights arrangement but a whole complex of diverse and shifting relationship."[45] To regard property as being explicitly private or state-owned may also not be very fruitful in societies where definite claims to the use of different kinds of land and its resources were historically enjoyed by individuals and communities and duly recognised by the pre-colonial state.

The difficulty of this issue became apparent to Lyall in 1870 when he attempted to delineate peasant proprietorships of different categories of land in Kangra. The hay fields (*kharetar*) are a case in point. The question here was whether a peasant's claim to the hay field originally amounted to "a property in the soil, or to a right to three-months of the grass only".[46] The problem arose from the colonial need to overcome the fluid nature of claims on the produce of the land. An explicit legal division was sought between different kinds of property – something that the hill peasant neither felt the need for nor understood.[47] George Barnes, the first settlement officer of Kangra district, had earlier encouraged the partition and individual ownership of commonly held cultivated land. About wasteland Barnes was ambivalent and did not support individual ownership. Lyall, for his part, concluded that hay fields near the house (*gharu-kharetar*) or amidst cultivated fields were wholly owned by the peasant. Regarding hay fields situated in the forest (*ban-kharetar*), or on mountain slopes, he was of the opinion that the farmer could claim only its grass for a few months in the year. The latter land was therefore to be classified as "common property of the *mauza* (village)."

[44] *Kangra DG* 1918: 120.
[45] Berkes, Davidson-Hunt, and Davidson-Hunt 1998: 20.
[46] Lyall 1889: 143.
[47] Barnes 1889: 67.

With regard to Kulu (as different from the Kangra valley), however, Lyall concluded that village communities were clear neither about village boundaries nor about the implications that these had for communal proprietorship. For this reason Lyall argued, specifically in the context of Kulu, "that in the interest of the State and the people it was better that for the present, at any rate, the old theory of property should be adhered to by which waste lands are assumed to belong to the State."[48] The government's claim apparently rested on the belief that the "backward" Kulu peasantry was unlikely to appreciate the value of land as community property or manage it responsibly!

In making the revenue assessment in Kulu, hay fields were not separately assessed while calculating the revenue demand. This was because "Without free grazing for plough cattle, fallen leaves for manure, free firewood and, so far as necessary, free timber for building purposes a cultivator could not in this mountainous country pay so high a rate of rent as he does, and the Government revenue, which is calculated on the rent, would be lower than it is."[49] This certainly benefited the peasant and reduced the amount he had to pay as revenue, but it also weakened his full proprietary claim to the "wasteland" *vis-à-vis* the government. His right to "use" the hay field did not translate, in the long run, into his "ownership" of it.

However, Lyall did not intend to permanently close the door to community or individual ownership of wastes. He felt that it might, at a later date, become necessary to alter this arrangement and permit landholders to exercise full proprietary rights over the wastes. His purpose was to delineate, classify, and conserve the forest before permitting ownership of wasteland to the peasantry.[50] Later, when he was lieutenant governor of the Punjab, Lyall reasserted that in recording unoccupied land as government property he hoped "to obtain a position facilitating forest conservancy arrangements, and it was meant that except for this purpose the Government ownership of the soil should remain a theory of property, not a reason for treating

[48] Lyall 1889: 88, para. 100.
[49] Diack 1898: 21, para. 36.
[50] Lyall 1889: 90, para. 102.

the Kulu people differently from their neighbours in Kangra and elsewhere."[51] He viewed state ownership of land as "a trust on behalf of the people of Kulu", and felt that if "the genius of the people had been more democratic as in the case of the frontier Pathans, it would not exist."[52]

Another factor complicated matters further. A large number of pastoralists – both of Kulu and from outside – had traditional claims to the extensive alpine pastures of Kulu, Lahaul, and Spiti. Lyall was aware of these claims, but because of their "loose fluid sort of state" he was reluctant to "petrify them by bringing them to book". He observed that while the village records indeed mentioned the names of persons claiming the right to graze their flocks in the summer pastures (*nigahrs*), "these entries must not be accepted too implicitly, as it must have been difficult for the Superintendents to attest them thoroughly."[53] The colonial state was clearly reluctant to lose control over these pastures. By becoming the owner of the wastes and by edging out the village communities from any form of ownership or control, it made the pastoralists direct "tenants" of the government.

However, even in pre-colonial times the shepherds' claim to grazing rights in the distant alpine pastures would have been derived from the state or the raja. These rights and the territorial limits of the concerned pastures were well established when the British appeared on the scene. Similar rights were enjoyed even in the trans-Himalayan pastures of Lahaul by pastoralists who brought large flocks of sheep and goats to the area in summer. This claim to graze in the Lahaul summer pastures was enjoyed collectively by certain hamlets and *phatis* of Kulu. Apart from Kulu shepherds, the Gaddi pastoralists also brought their sheep to Lahaul and claimed their *warisi* or title to the pastures as arising from a grant by the Kulu raja. Interestingly, however, many of the best pastures in the Chandra valley of Lahaul were rarely used before the establishment of British rule.[54] A possible reason for the increased utilisation of the Lahaul pastures by the sheep of Kulu and

[51] As quoted in Diack 1898: 21, para. 36.
[52] Lyall 1889: 90, para. 102.
[53] Ibid.: 143.
[54] *Kangra DG* 1918: 221–2.

Chamba is that restricted access to the best forests and pastures in their home territory under new forest regulations compelled shepherds to search for alternative pastures in more distant places.[55] Lahaul, with hardly any forest, was best suited in summer for such grazing and it was decided not to increase the grazing dues for Gaddi shepherds there because its pastures were occupied only for a short duration and not good for any other purpose anyway.[56]

Post-Independence Situation

In post-Independence India, too, the state continued to ignore the relevance of local communities. The dominant role of government in both development and conservation remained unchanged.[57] There is an almost celebratory tone in Bachittar Singh's assertion that Lyall had secured "full proprietary rights in the forests and the wastes to Government."[58] Though Lyall had visualised the subsequent handing over of proprietary control over wastes to the village communities, officials in Independent India were unwilling even to consider the possibility!

Most of the contested wastes were grass preserves (*phats* or *ghasnis*) situated on steep slopes from which peasants obtained fodder grass. A detailed record of their extent, boundaries, and right-holders (for grazing and grass-cutting) was made in 1888–92. This information was, with great difficulty, revised in 1911. Some of the right-holders had died and passed on their claim to their descendants. In some cases these had been partitioned or passed on to unrelated people. After Independence, the revised information (and also the earlier first list) was treated as a mere recording of local knowledge and remained "without any legal sanction". It was not incorporated into the "record of rights", as was required under the Punjab Land Revenue Act.[59] Thereafter, a proposal was made to amend the Punjab Land

[55] Ibid.: 115–16, 223.
[56] Ibid.: 223.
[57] Chakravarty-Kaul 1998: 14.
[58] C. Singh 1952: 5, para. 10.
[59] Ibid.: 26, para. 34.

Revenue Act so as to make it compulsory for right-holders to inform the *patwari* (village revenue official) about any changes in claims on grass preserves.

But the matter turned out to be far more complicated. Under the British dispensation, *phats* and *ghasnis* had been included in the protected forests. Therefore, it was the Indian Forest Act and not the Revenue Act that now applied to them. While lower-level officials recommended (in November 1951) that the lists of right-holders be included in the "record of rights", the financial commissioner declined to approve of their inclusion.[60] Instead, he "ordered that these lists will form a part of the record informally and no presumption of truth will be attached to them as required by Section 44 of the Land Revenue Act."[61] For all practical purposes the government refused to recognise the legality of the right-holders' claim to graze their flocks and to cut grass from the grass preserves.

While revenue officers were sympathetic, forest officials were clearly reluctant to allow even restricted rights. The latter regarded the pastoralists as virtual intruders into the forest and the peasant as a "ruthless exploiter" of timber. While new forest laws could be introduced summarily by the state, the economic and social world of the mountain pastoralist was far more difficult to alter. The shepherd failed to comprehend the powerful extraneous interests that had begun to claim his pastures and forests. Like the colonial rulers, the officials of Independent India too regarded the hill peasant as an obstacle to their grand design of nature conservation. A forest official saw the mountain peasant-pastoralist as

> poor, diseased and apathetic. He is bereft of the desire of anything better... He has come to keep a large number of lean cattle to graze on the hillside without realizing what effect the un-restricted grazing produces on the slopes. He has come to believe that forests are the gift of nature and he has the absolute right to avail of the gift as he lives near or in the forests. He has little fore-sight that the absolute right is the misuse or abuse of the nature's gift and is bound to spell ruination.[62]

[60] Ensminger and Rutten 1991: 687.
[61] C. Singh 1952: 26, para. 34.
[62] Parmar 1959: 1, para. 7.

Not surprisingly, an unsubstantiated escalation in the number of cattle was perceived as the cause of soil erosion. Foresters argued that large numbers of cattle provided a good income with minimum labour, and therefore the peasants' numerous cattle roamed "about the grazing grounds in charge of children, old men and women or congenital idiots"![63] There was no recognition of the fact that forest restrictions dispossessed the agro-pastoralists of their traditional pastures and resources and confined them primarily to rapidly degrading Class III forests.[64] It was overgrazing in this category of forests that became illustrative of increased erosion.[65]

Significantly, the official rationale for restricting the access of shepherds and peasants to the resources of forests changed over time.[66] During the nineteenth century, primacy was accorded to timber extraction. It was argued that people in the Punjab plains depended on the Kulu forest for their timber supply, and it was therefore important to reserve a "very considerable area of deodar-producing forests so as to ensure a continuous supply of deodar."[67] By the 1930s or 1940s the reason for restricting access to forests was the perceived need to prevent environmental degradation.[68] Thereafter, the urgency of maintaining

[63] Ibid.: 3, para. 17.

[64] Ibid.: 2, para. 11. The reality of this, however, inadvertently appears in Parmar's report itself, albeit in a manner that still holds the peasants primarily responsible. In the section titled "Present Condition of the Forests and Causes for their Deterioration" he writes: "Even a century ago the forests in the Himalayas were so dense as to provide ample safeguards against erosion and floods. At that time large, mature trees were plentiful. But no proper control was exercised on them. During the last century, however, forests properly demarcated and reserved were alone worked under proper Plan and they are to this day well preserved. In others, the people thought themselves at liberty to cut down the forests and start cultivation. They were ruthlessly exploited by the owners and the right holders for timber and fuel or heavily lopped for fodder or grazed by cattle and browsers. This was a period of uncontrolled exploitation of un-reserved forests."

[65] C. Singh 1952: 8, para. 5.

[66] Saberwal 1999: 91, 93, 95, 106.

[67] Ibid.: 95.

[68] Ensminger and Rutten 1991: 683. These restrictions may, however, actually have been the cause for it. Ensminger and Rutten suggest that

"a proper balance between forests, pastures and agricultural lands" became a central question.[69]

Over the last couple of decades or so the question of sustainability has moved centrestage. This is particularly true where pastoral societies were seen as exploiting natural resources excessively. It has often been argued that overgrazing has been "an established phenomenon for decades", and that this was further aggravated by "increasing enclosures, the extension of cultivation and possibly an increase in the number of herd animals belonging to the settled population."[70] Such an argument assumes that pastoralists use cattle and sheep as merely a means of earning a livelihood or acquiring wealth by exploiting natural resources. While this is indeed true, more needs to be considered. For pastoralists, livestock has also been a "means of social communication" – something of far greater significance than its material worth might indicate. Livestock, therefore, had both economic and socio-cultural value and in this scheme of things economic considerations were by no means overriding. It is being increasingly realised that even amidst large herds and flocks, and despite the "tragedy of the commons" picture portrayed by older arguments, "pastoral (and other traditional) societies have evolved effective systems to manage common resources in the common long-term interests."[71]

Two interconnected processes provide perspectives into the relationship between pastoralism and modernity. At a local level, the process by which colonial rule permeated into peripheral areas and impacted marginalised peoples enables us to arrive at a comprehensive understanding of how pastoral societies in India changed over the

---

sedentarisation brought about by economic growth results in common grazing systems being over-grazed: that "sedentarization has increased the costs of maintaining common grazing." Using this argument, we might argue that the reservation and closure of forests compelled many agro-pastoralists to reduce their migratory flock and rely increasingly on agriculture and agricultural livestock, thereby putting pressure on village commons.

[69] Parmar 1959: 2, para. 13.
[70] Phillimore 1981.
[71] Warren 1995: 196.

last two or three centuries. At a larger level, however, the impact of British rule had on India as a whole provides the fundamental context. To quote Washbrook, British rule in nineteenth-century India was "attended by processes of 'peasantisation' and 'sedentarisation'; of de-industrialisation and de-urbanisation; of 'castefication' and religious 'communalisation'. However, the character of these did not become fully apparent until well into the new century and they were, perhaps, largely the function of economic, cultural, and political changes taking place only then."[72] Despite their apparent physical distance from the centres of colonial authority, mountain pastoralists were part and parcel of processes that had global dimensions. Their introduction to a colonial "modernity" and its life-altering conditions were a consequence of these processes.

---

[72] Washbrook 1997: 425.

12

Diverse Forms of Polyandry, Customary Rights of Inheritance, and Landownership in the Western Himalaya

> It is remarkable, that a people so degraded in morals, and many of whose customs are so revolting in nature, should in other respects evince a much higher advancement in civilisation, than we discover among other nations, whose manners are more engaging, and whose moral character ranks infinitely higher. Their persons are better clad, and more decent; their approach more polite and unembarrassed; and their address is better than that of most of the inhabitants of the remote highlands of Scotland . . . and their homes, in point of construction, comfort and internal cleanliness, are beyond comparison superior to Scottish highland dwellings.
>
> — James Baillie Fraser, 1815[1]

Introduction

EXCLUSIVE RIGHTS OVER property, as we understand these today in a market-oriented world, emerged rather late in human history. Claims to property may have first been made more clearly in commercial and trade transactions. Within urban centres, too, the greater value of land probably encouraged

---

Published previously as C. Singh 2011b.
[1] Fraser 1982: 208.

such assertions. This did not necessarily mean that an individual-centred notion of property became the norm even in the agricultural countryside. The idea of individually owned property was probably quite unknown, especially in peasant societies, where money did not mediate social relationships and where the individual had not yet acquired a status independent of his family and community.

In rural South Asia, too, individually owned and controlled landed property may not have become the norm until the unrelenting expansion of colonialism and capitalism gradually overtook simpler tradition-based societies. Pre-capitalist ideas of property were rooted in social relations. Claims of ownership were not attributed in entirety to any single person, institution, or collectivity.[2] Neither the individual nor the community could, therefore, be justifiably seen as the undisputed proprietor of the land and other assets upon which economic production was based. Colonial administrators in India failed to recognise this fact and persisted with their attempts to identify a legal owner – individual or community – upon whom an absolute right could then be conferred. In doing so they either destroyed or distorted the complex network of socially recognised claims and relationships that, in a sense, constituted pre-capitalist notions of property.

Ownership of property in the pre-modern world was clearly inextricable from social relationships. Negotiations between family, kin groups, and the community collectively defined what could be considered as property. This definition, therefore, was not an act but a process. It grew out of the practice of how worldly possessions were actually used, preserved, and transmitted to each succeeding generation. In so far as the individual was concerned, his significance was derived from his being a *member* of a particular social group. Nisbet suggests that in medieval society the position of the "autonomous individual" was rather indistinct.[3] Emphasising the pre-eminence of the "small social group" he argues that "The centrality of the community was much more than a philosophical principle

[2] Cf. Hann 1993: 299–320.
[3] Nisbet 1962: 80.

however. Whether we are dealing with the family, the village, or the gild, we are in the presence of systems of authority and allegiance which were widely held to precede the individual in both origin and right . . ."[4] If that were the case (and it appears to be so) then property – particularly landed property – would also be linked, in varying ways, to the different social groups to which the individual belonged. So it is to the group, rather than to the individual, that the study of pre-capitalist landownership must necessarily resort. For it was the group as a unit that secured a meaningful place for the individual.

An attempt is made here to present the polyandrous family as one such group. Though the practice was uncommon in much of the world, polyandry has been widely practised in parts of the Himalayan region. Himachal Pradesh, situated in the western Himalaya, had several areas where polyandry was a familiar custom until fairly recent times. These included large parts of the districts of Sirmur, Shimla, Kinnaur, Kulu, and Lahaul. In most of these areas, however, diverse forms of family organisation were to be found. Polyandry was one of the arrangements frequently followed; it was not a compulsory social prescription. I explore below how the polyandrous family and the community that supported it perceived the question of landownership in such areas. Needless, to say the structure of the family and the nature of rights and obligations assigned to each of its members (including women) has a bearing on this question. Customs pertaining to the partition and inheritance of land, too, are crucial factors for consideration. Also pertinent is the question: Which classes of society found polyandry an appropriate social practice?

Describing Polyandry

Families and households were invariably placed within a community. The community, in turn, nurtured explanatory legends (of origin, settlement, and social hierarchy) that contributed to the creation of a collective identity. This has been shown by Levine with regard to a polyandrous Nyinba village of the Nepal Himalaya, and the origin myths and legends in the folklore of the villages of Himachal Pradesh

---

[4] Ibid.: 81.

too are numerous.⁵ These legends also sustained numerous other institutions and customs that were crucial to its functioning and helped the community to contextualise its position within a larger history and geography.

The myths and folklore that underlie the mental world of local communities in the western Himalaya show a remarkable richness which, however, lies beyond my present concern. What is relevant for the moment is the manner in which households and families were linked to the community. A common lineage, real or perceived, often functioned as the primary social connection between different families. It was also a rudimentary form of political association.⁶ Wherever a village community consisted of a single dominant lineage, there was an explicit overlap of authority between community and family. This made the process of decision-making simpler and less contentious. Levine notes that the Nyinba village community also seems to have regulated the number of households that the village should sustain.⁷ But such was not always the case. Some villages included more than one lineage, and within such villages each lineage occupied a mutually acknowledged physical and political space of its own. It has been pointed out in the context of Jaunsar-Bawar (an area adjoining Himachal) that the village area was broadly divided on the basis of lineage – i.e. the lineages (*aals*) and sub-lineages (*bheras*) occupied distinguishable spaces.⁸ The morphology of villages, therefore, reflected these internal divisions. In Kinnaur, the *khel* and the *khandan* would be comparable expressions for lineage and sub-lineage respectively.⁹ Most villages in my area of study were, however, dominated by a single subcaste or clan.

More importantly, the pivotal units around which the economy and social organisation primarily revolved were the household and the family. Scholars have adopted divergent positions on what constitutes a family, and differences of opinion persist. The two viewpoints

⁵ Levine 1988: 21; Rose 1970: I.
⁶ Levine 1988: 43.
⁷ Ibid.: 248.
⁸ Majumdar 1962.
⁹ Raha and Kumar 1987: 64–5.

that have dominated thinking on the family have been termed by Claude Lévi-Strauss as the "verticals" and the "horizontals". The first viewpoint emphasises descent and continuity, while the second stresses the biological foundations of a basic family consisting of man, woman, and their children.[10] Even in India the household had, for administrative and legal purposes, to be repeatedly redefined during the colonial period.[11] Because of the importance attached to lineage and the powerful bonds of kinship manifest in pre-capitalist societies, British administrators were compelled to adopt a broad definition. This often included not only the "joint" family but also the larger kinship group. The diversity of family organisation in the Indian subcontinent would hardly have permitted a single explicit definition. Within the Himalayan region, the situation was equally complex.

Among the many factors influencing the structuring of society, perhaps the most important is the manner in which it organizes its economy and labour resources. Agro-pastoralists may often, though not invariably, choose to organise households in a manner quite different from a society dependent almost entirely on agricultural production. Among the agro-pastoral Luri tribesmen of western Iran, the head of a patrilineal extended family would aspire to have in his family "several able-bodied sons or unmarried brothers to assist him."[12] In Himachal, as we shall see, the agro-pastoralists of Kinnaur opted for a polyandrous family with a jointly organised system of production. The Gaddi herders, on the other hand, seem to have preferred partition into smaller nuclear families, even though they often worked collaboratively.[13] The agro-pastoral trading Nyinba, who are predominantly polyandrous and live near the Nepal–Tibet border, adopted a system derived from Tibet. At the top of the social hierarchy was the "corporate" landholding household known as *trongba*. To the *trongba* was attached a dependent "small household" of landless freed slaves. Associated permanently with the *trongba* could be an "adjunct household" that sustained divorced women. To quote Nancy Levine:

[10] Lévi-Strauss 1996: 1–7.
[11] Kasturi 2002: 99–100.
[12] Black-Michaud 1986: 57.
[13] Saberwal 1999.

Nyinba households are made up of families or, as anthropologists have it, groups concerned with reproduction and socialisation of children, where kinship is the criterion for membership. Fully developed *trongba* comprise extended families, overlapping sets of consanguineally related married brothers, their wives, and offspring. Nyinba differentiate these families as *paral*.[14]

It is important to note that each generation of brothers almost always had one common wife, and rarely was a second wife brought into the family.

Very similar to the Nyinba system were the customs of the Kinnaura agro-pastoralists of Himachal. The comments of Gerard, who travelled through the Kinnaur area bordering Tibet in 1817, are disappointingly brief. He notes only that in this area "polyandry or a plurality of husbands prevails."[15] Only much later, in the 1880s, did another traveller, Andrew Wilson, provide a slightly clearer description:

> Instances of three and five husbands are quite common; but without having gone rigidly into the matter, I should say that the most instances of polyandry were those of two husbands, and not because there was any objection to five or six, but simply because no greater number of brothers was usually to be found in a family, as might have been expected from such a system, and as also one of the great ends which the system is designed to effect.[16]

In adjoining Lahaul it appears that polyandry was practised in the same manner, though monogamous marriages were also fairly common.[17] In an apparent modification made to this practice, in the adjacent Chamba–Lahaul part of the princely state of Chamba the number of fraternal husbands was restricted to two.[18]

The custom was rather different in the lower Himalaya. D.N. Majumdar's detailed study illustrates this point very clearly.[19] His

[14] Levine 1988: 100–1.
[15] Gerard 1993: 2–3.
[16] Wilson 1979: 187–8.
[17] *Kangra DG* 1918: III, 194.
[18] *Chamba SG* 1910: 161.
[19] Majumdar 1962.

description of the joint family in Jaunsar-Bawar is at variance with that of the Nyinba described by Levine. But it is equally applicable to another kind of polyandrous system found in parts of Sirmur, Shimla, and Kulu in Himachal. In Jaunsar:

> All brothers marry together, and have *one or more wives in common*, instead of having separate wives. In fact, the Jaunsari family system is not only polyandrous but a combination of paternal polyandry and polygyny. All men of each generation who are brothers marry together with one or, as is usually the case, more than one wife.
>
> In principle and in practice, all the brothers form an inseparable group as 'fraternal husbands' in the name of the eldest brother. The wives, on the other hand, join the union individually, one after another, in the same way as is usually found in the polygynous system, except that the single husband is substituted by the polyandrous group of husbands.[20]

As was the case in the polyandry of Tibet and bordering areas, in this system too the oldest brother usually occupied a position of greater importance than his younger male siblings. But it was also apparently quite different from the simpler Tibetan polyandrous system where there was only one common wife. For purposes of differentiation, the lower Himalayan kind of family organisation has sometimes been categorised as polygynandrous.

In practice, therefore, the diversity in Himalayan polyandry was far more complex than was previously imagined. J.B. Lyall, the British official who prepared the revenue settlement report for Kangra district in 1872, was more inclined to regard the latter kind of polyandry as "a mere custom of community of wives among brothers." He noted that "In one house you may find three brothers with one wife, in the next three brothers with four wives, all alike in common; in the next there may be an only son with three wives to himself."[21] A closer examination of polygynandry suggests that there is some truth in Lyall's observation. Because of the fluidity that the polyandrous family organisation exhibited, it might be difficult to regard it as a distinct "family type". In Jaunsar-Bawar, "due to frequency of divorce and

[20] Ibid.: 72. My emphasis.
[21] Lyall 1889: 99.

of taking multiple wives," there was a likelihood that "every monogamous family may change to one or other of the forms . . . and even a polyandrous and polygynous family may be reduced to monogamous unions."[22] This point was once again emphasised by Gerald Berreman, who wrote that "an individual may experience in his or her life a single spouse, a multiplicity of spouses, a co-spouse or a multiplicity of co-spouses."[23] Evidently, then, polyandry, polygyny, polygynandry, and even monogamy in Jaunsar-Bawar were mere variations of a single form.[24] They were therefore not distinct forms of family or organisation. The same would be true of those parts of Sirmur, Kulu, and Shimla areas where marriage and family systems were similar.

How should then the diverse polyandrous practices found in Himachal be viewed? In the polygynandrous areas of Sirmur, Shimla, and Kulu there was no socially prescribed limit to the number of wives that fraternal brothers could take collectively. It was primarily the limited economic resources available for this purpose that acted as a constraint.[25] For each new wife who joined the family, a considerable bride-price probably had to be paid to the father of the bride. In fact, the necessity of paying a bride-price often meant that poorer families could afford only one wife. For the more prosperous households, on the other hand, it was a matter of prestige to have the largest affordable number of wives. This was quite obviously very different from the polyandrous practices of Kinnaur and Lahaul that were largely akin to those of Tibet and the Nepal Himalaya. It appears that unlike the lower Himalayan polygynandrous system, the custom in Kinnaur and Lahaul was more explicitly an attempt to conserve family wealth. The custom of there being only one wife limited the number of inheritors. However, the rule of there being only one common wife was not absolutely rigid. Brothers who were much younger than the oldest too could take an additional common wife if they so wished.[26] It was possible, however, that brothers falling

[22] Majumdar 1962: 80.
[23] Berreman 1987: 194.
[24] Ibid.: 186.
[25] Parmar 1975; Majumdar 1962; Chandra 1987a.
[26] Goldstein 1987: 212.

within a similar age group might not have found it necessary to do so.²⁷ Goldstein has argued that "the two polyandrous societies have different deep structures with the same surface structure, whereas the Tibetan and the non-polyandrous wealth conserving societies have different surface structures with the same deep structure."²⁸

But is this true? Despite the term "polyandry" being often used for both systems, were even their "surface structures" really what Goldstein suggests? Moreover, is wealth conservation not an important consideration in a polygynandrous system? Conversely, was Tibetan polyandry entirely inspired by wealth conservation?

Explaining Polyandry

It is not necessary that similar institutions should arise from the same causes, or for that matter serve identical purposes. Nevertheless, it might be worthwhile to examine whether institutional similarity, in this particular case, extends beyond appearances. It is highly unlikely that a single factor can credibly explain the emergence of polyandry in a society, notwithstanding its own explanations in this regard. Apart from their frequent claims to adopting it as a time-honoured social tradition, such societies successfully point to the numerous appreciable benefits that polyandry provides.²⁹ Cultural factors, though subtle and significant, may not tell the entire story.

Nor, for that matter, can we regard polyandry simply as a social institution for population control, as did Andrew Wilson. He wondered "what desperate means are had recourse to in order to get rid of the pressures caused by the acknowledged law of population."³⁰ Parmar used census data to emphasise that gender imbalance in the population was one reason for the adoption of this custom. He also sees the need to avoid the partition of scarce land as a cause for polyandry. Peculiarly, however, the areas he refers to were also those where more than one wife could customarily be kept by polyandrous

---

[27] Peter 1963: 313.
[28] Goldstein 1987: 215.
[29] Levine 1988: 9.
[30] Wilson 1979: 184; Chandra 1981: 210.

brothers.[31] While such an imbalance certainly seems to have existed in some parts of Sirmur and Shimla districts, its causes have not been satisfactorily explained. One might further question whether polyandry was a cause or a consequence of there being fewer females in the population. Moreover, the gender imbalance argument fails to explain the practice of polyandry in places like Chini *tehsil* in Kinnaur where, in the early twentieth century, the number of females actually exceeded males.[32]

High bride-price is sometimes seen as being responsible for the practice of polyandry. James Fraser, who passed through the eastern parts of Himachal in 1815, observed:

> It is usual all over the country, for the future husband to purchase his wife from her parents, and the sum paid varies of course with the rank of the purchaser. The customary charge to a common peasant or zamindar is from ten to twenty rupees. The difficulty of raising this sum and the alleged expense of maintaining women, may in part account for, if it cannot excuse, a most disgusting usage, which is universal over the country.[33]

Even as he provided this argument, Fraser does not appear to have been fully convinced by it. Bride-price alone could not have explained the adoption of polyandry as a social norm. The high bride-price that a prospective husband was expected to pay for a bride might not, by itself, have had the capacity to fundamentally alter vital social institutions. While polyandry was sometimes customary in societies where the bride-price was very low, it was never adopted by many societies that often had to pay a very high bride-price.[34]

As a socio-economic unit, the polyandrous family certainly offered some advantages to its members. A point frequently emphasised by scholars is that it allowed for a systematic division of labour within households. It thus enabled them to fully exploit a diversity of economic resources found in the physical environment within which

[31] Parmar 1975: 89.
[32] Chatur Bhuj 1928: paras 25, 26.
[33] Fraser 1982: 206.
[34] Kapadia 1959: 71.

they were situated.³⁵ Majumdar suggested that "the number of wives can be adjusted to their economic means and personal needs."³⁶ Migratory and pastoral societies were seen as more likely to adopt polyandry because it ensured the presence of at least one husband at home while the others were engaged in periodic trading or herding activities elsewhere.³⁷ This division of labour, therefore, allowed the household a considerable degree of economic diversification. In the revenue settlement report that he prepared for Rohru *tehsil* (formerly part of Bashahr state that also included Kinnaur) in 1914, Emerson provides a very detailed and multi-causal explanation for polyandry. He ruled out gender imbalance and scarcity of land as important factors but stressed two other points. The first was the compulsion of a diversified economy that required family members to engage in a range of activities in different locations. The second point emphasised the demands for labour imposed by the state on the peasant household. He argued that "The old system, by which the state demanded the whole-time services of one man from every household for at least six months in the year, necessitated the encouragement of large joint families. A veto was therefore placed on the partition of all property and the temptation to break this prohibition was small, as division entailed the provision to the State of two men instead of one."³⁸

With regard to the state of Mandi, too, it was felt that the imposition of *begar* (forced labour) upon the peasantry by the state and its functionaries was responsible for encouraging polyandry in its Saraj area.³⁹ The connection between the forced extraction of labour by the state and the structure of the peasant family is illustrated by the case of Bashahr. In the first decade of the nineteenth century, the annual demand for *begar* was reduced by the Bashahr administration from six months to one month only. In addition, the ban on the partition of family landholdings was withdrawn. This, according to Emerson, resulted in the gradual modification – if not reduction – of polyandry. He

---

³⁵ Raha and Coomar 1987: 83; Levine 1988: 132, 159.
³⁶ Majumdar 1962: 75.
³⁷ Wilson 1982: 192.
³⁸ Emerson 1914: para 36.
³⁹ *Mandi SG* 1920: 67.

contended that the result was that there was a "widespread division of families, although, even in this case, the separation is into groups and not units."[40] The opinion amongst administrators of the time appears to have been that "the abolition of *begar* with the stimulus given to partition by the introduction of a regular revenue system will result in its [polyandry's] disappearance within a few years."[41]

Available official records seem to suggest that the efficient utilisation of family labour was a crucial consideration for polyandrous households. It enabled the family to meet the labour demands of the state and also obtain the benefit of a reasonable standard of living. The comfortable economic situation of the people of Kinnaur was noticed by W. Murray, Deputy Superintendent of the Hill States. As early as 1824, he wrote that they seemed to be "in good circumstances for their class. They have enough of the necessaries of life and not a few of the comforts."[42] These words almost unmistakably reiterate the earlier observations of J.B. Fraser that have been quoted at the onset. In the true polyandrous areas, as we noticed, the limited family labour was not all spent on agriculture. A substantial part of it went into herding and trading. Moreover, large landholdings in the higher Himalaya were not only difficult to create; they might also have been undesirable and uneconomic. The Nyinba households studied by Levine could not meet their labour needs if their landholding increased beyond a point. They believed that productivity declined if the holding got too large.[43] Polygynandry of the lower Himalaya, on the other hand, had a somewhat different approach to labour management. It has been seen by some scholars as a flexible institution, "a means of managing the ratio of workers and consumers to resources."[44] Be that as it may, there is little doubt that both polyandrous and polygynandrous households functioned as viable socio-economic units which not only survived but thrived through the centuries. They also successfully passed on to succeeding generations their household wealth and

[40] Emerson 1914: para 36.
[41] *Mandi SG* 1920: 100.
[42] Murray 1824.
[43] Levine 1988: 252.
[44] Goldstein 1987: 211.

traditional claims to resources. Customary norms were evolved and applied to ensure a smooth transfer.

Inheritance and Partition of Family Property

Himachal (not unlike most of South Asia) had a dominant oral tradition. Documentary sources from pre-colonial times about local tribal organisation and folk customs are scarce. Information of this nature was first recorded by the British from surviving social practices. These records became part of the detailed revenue-related documents known as *Riwaj-i-Am* (common tradition) or *Wajib-ul-Arz*.

It was perhaps inevitable in the process of this recording of indigenous codes and social customs by colonial administrators that they were altered, at least partially, in terms of their character and content.[45] The British were certainly familiar with the complicated nature of their task. Among the difficulties, Lyall noted, was the tendency of rival caste groups and clans "to shirk the avowal of a custom which it knows is regarded with ridicule or disdain by others of higher social standing."[46] Despite all precautions, the inherent problems of documenting oral tradition were not entirely overcome. The virtual absence of written documents compels us to use recorded traditions and customary practices, albeit with appropriate discretion.

To begin with, it appears that in a fraternal polyandrous family, the wife/wives and children all belonged to the brothers jointly. Though the right of the sons over family land was established at birth, it remained limited simply to a claim to maintenance during the lifetime of their father/fathers.[47] It was after the death of all the brothers in the older generation (who were regarded jointly as the fathers of all the children) that the issue of inheritance effectively arose. If, thereafter, the family chose to stay together, the sons would jointly claim the inheritance of their fathers. They could, and usually did, themselves continue in a polyandrous/polygynandrous relationship.[48]

[45] Bhattacharya 1996: 20–51.
[46] Lyall 1889: 149.
[47] Joshi 1929: 232–3.
[48] *Sirmur SG* 1907: 280.

In Sirmur state, at least till the early twentieth century, even sons by a woman who was not formally married into the family could rightly inherit their fathers' property.[49] This claim probably came to be increasingly disputed later. The growing influence of Sanskritisation may have engendered new ideas of marital legitimacy. By the middle of the nineteenth century, the position of illegitimate sons seems to have become considerably weaker. In Kulu, where social practices were comparable to those in Sirmur, they could now only inherit the property either with the permission of the legitimate sons or in their absence.[50]

A clearer idea of ownership rights can be obtained from an examination of the proprietary claims that arose subsequent to the partition of a family's landholding. This usually happened when one of the brothers decided to move out of the polyandrous family and demand a division of the patrimony. Presumably, such a decision would be encouraged by the availability of additional productive land or of increased resources obtained "from a household's own estate, from re-inheritance of a vacant estate, or from land newly cleared."[51] Mitchell argued that "the influx of money spent on the roads, buildings and exploitation" resulted in increased prosperity and hence the "splitting up of holdings".[52] Logically, the availability of extra resources would have been a prerequisite for partition even in non-polyandrous traditional households in other societies. Separation from a joint household was always an endeavour fraught with economic uncertainty. The inability to generate adequate and regular resources on its own sometimes resulted in the re-merger of the separating household.[53]

If partition became imperative, the custom in Himachal required that household property be shared equally amongst the sons irrespective of the number of mothers.[54] In adjacent Jaunsar-Bawar, however, the eldest and youngest brothers were customarily entitled to

[49] Ibid.: 37.
[50] Singh 2003: 42.
[51] Levine 1988: 240, 269.
[52] Mitchell 1915: 28.
[53] Tapper 1991: 130.
[54] Lyall 1889: 99; *Kangra DG* 1917: III, 194.

a slightly larger share of the family property than the others.[55] Broadly speaking, therefore, the general principle of equality amongst brothers was sought to be upheld. In so far as the claim to the children was concerned, the rules were not very clear. In a polyandrous family, the eldest brother was considered the father of all the children. However, the partitioning of a household altered the situation. At times the women could be given the right to name the father of the child. But a more accepted and less acrimonious method when the brothers had one common wife was that the eldest brother was regarded as the father of the first-born son, the second brother as the father of the second son, and so on.[56] The fact that such divisions were rare may explain why the practices associated with the claim to children were rather fluid and contested.

Even the matter of partitioning land and property became more complicated in case one or two brothers separated from the joint family while the remaining brothers continued to live together with their common wife/wives. In such a situation the share of the separating brothers was reduced, because the children in the earlier polyandrous relationship usually continued to live in the original household. Joshi, while referring to the local tradition recorded in Dehradun district, says that "If a younger brother out of four brothers separates, he cannot take away the wife or children, but the children are entitled to equal shares from the four brothers which are paid to the elder with whom they live."[57] After such a partition, if sons were born to a brother who had separated from the main family, they had no claim on the estate of the original joint household.[58] Similarly, sons born in the joint household could not inherit a share in the estate of their separated stepfather.[59] The practice in Jaunsar-Bawar was somewhat different. It seems that after the death of the separating brother, his share of the ancestral property reverted "to his children by the common wife; and his offspring by his new monogamous wife inherit

[55] Joshi 1929: 280, 281–2; Majumdar 1962: 75.
[56] *Kangra DG* 1917: II, 51–2.
[57] Joshi 1929: 233.
[58] Lyall 1889: 99.
[59] Singh 2003: 83.

only what he is able to earn or acquire after his separation from the family fold."[60] This latter practice seems to reinforce the integrity of the family as the primary and permanent social unit.

Polyandrous families in the Himalaya were clearly patriarchal. The right to inherit property, in a complete sense, was restricted to sons. This did not, however, eliminate certain well-recognised claims of the women of the family to its resources. To begin with, every woman in the household had a right to maintenance till her death.[61] But the strongest of these rights was probably the life-interest that a widow had in the estate of her husband/husbands in case there were no sons.[62] This was, of course, a right enjoyed by widows equally in non-polyandrous households. An interesting case would be that of two or more brothers who separate from the original polyandrous household along with a wife/wives. If such a wife were to survive her husbands as a widow without issue, she would be entitled to a life-interest only in one share, i.e. of the husband who died last.[63] Presumably then – in the absence of children – the remaining shares (of her husband's brothers) would be once again reattached to the original estate held by the other brothers of her husband or their sons. The right of the widow was derived from the assumption that the widow, in such instances, represented her husband.[64] As long as she continued to reside in the inherited property, her life-interest persisted. It remained so even if she took a live-in partner to assist in its management.[65] This right, however, ceased to operate if the widow either formally married her partner or left the house of her dead husband to live permanently elsewhere. Most importantly, the right to alienate the property was not normally given to widows.[66] Once again, we see that the property remained permanently linked to the original polyandrous household over the long term.

[60] Singh 1988: 171.
[61] Ibid.: 90.
[62] Lyall 1889: 72; *Mandi SG* 1920: 100, 185.
[63] Singh 2003: 82–3.
[64] Joshi 1929: 283.
[65] Lyall 1889: 72; *Kangra DG* 1917: II, 51; *Mandi SG* 1920: 100, 185.
[66] Singh 2003: 50.

As a norm, unmarried daughters had the right to reside in their father's home. They were entitled to maintenance from their father, and later from their brother or nephew – whoever was the head of the household at that point of time.[67] There was, at the same time, a general consensus that daughters and their sons could not, under normal circumstances, inherit the estate of their father or maternal grandfather, respectively.[68] This was the general rule amongst the Khasas in the Himalayan region. Only in exceptional circumstances could a daughter inherit the land and property of her father. The absence of sons was one situation in which the daughter could claim the estate. But this was only possible if she brought her husband to live in her house while her father was still alive.[69] On the other hand, if she had married earlier and already left home to live with her husband, she would be passed over by collateral relatives in the matter of inheritance. This position, which existed in the early decades of the twentieth century, appears to have changed later. It is recorded in the customary rules of Lahaul and Spiti (1945–51) that a male proprietor could gift his ancestral property to his daughter or sister and their sons but only in the absence of male lineal descendants.[70] Unmarried daughters, too, were permitted to enjoy only a life-interest in the estate. As was the custom earlier, they had no right to alienate it.

The right to alienate property in western Himalayan societies was, in fact, a severally restricted, almost non-existent, one. Even in non-polyandrous families, the father did not have the freedom to alienate land and thereby deprive his sons of their inheritance. Furthermore, the sons could not be disinherited or given unequal shares of the ancestral property by a disgruntled father.[71] The sons, on the other hand, could not claim their share of the property by insisting on a partition while the father was alive.[72] So inviolable was the collective interest of the family in the ancestral land that, amongst the Khasas in Tehri

---

[67] *Kangra DG* 1917: IV, 265; Ghosh 1987: 55–6.
[68] Joshi 1929: 236.
[69] Lyall 1889: 112; *Kangra DG* 1917: III, 194.
[70] Singh 2003: 68.
[71] Ibid.: 44.
[72] Joshi 1929: 23.

state, the sale of land appears to have been either impermissible or extremely difficult. Nor could it be mortgaged or confiscated "for the debts of the father".[73] Apart from the customary resistance to the alienation of land, the fact that there existed virtually no market for land must have made this even more difficult. In Lahaul, for example, Lyall was aware of only one instance of land sale – to Moravian missionaries – that had taken place till 1872.[74]

The Role of State, Community, and Household in Land Control

There is a broad consensus amongst scholars that absolute proprietary right over land was not a common fact in pre-colonial times. "Ownership" was at best understood through a hierarchy of rights that different social sections exercised primarily over cultivated land.[75] This was combined with several obligations that they had towards the state and the village community. As earlier mentioned, the British complicated matters by assigning exclusive proprietorship to whichever class of right-holders they found most convenient to support in an area. This led to serious disruption in many regions of the subcontinent. By the time British influence was extended to present-day Himachal, however, the colonial administration had, through a series of trials, acquired a more nuanced understanding of the issues at hand. Consequently, a graded proprietorship was created and shared between the raja or ruler of the state (*malik-i-ala* or superior proprietor) and the peasant cultivator (*malik-i-adna* or smaller/inferior proprietor).[76] The peasant households that form the subject of the present discussion belonged to the category of "inferior proprietors". Their ownership claim over the land they cultivated was constrained by certain rights that the raja (ruler) too, enjoyed over it. Colonial administrators seem to have recognised that exclusive ownership of land by an individual was not as yet a fully acknowledged

[73] Ibid.: 229.
[74] Lyall 1889: 112.
[75] Habib 1963.
[76] Singh 1998: 57–8.

norm in some societies. Unlike in many other parts of India, the rajas in Himachal were recognised as having some kind of superior – partly proprietary – right in the land.

Moreover, the pre-colonial western Himalayan states had dealt not with the individual but with peasant families. The extraction of forced labour (*begar*) was an important reason for this. In terms of its origin, it has been suggested, the state was not "the direct outgrowth of family, tribe or local community" but emerged in opposition to them.[77] It emerged as a result of military mobilisation and derived its claim over land through conquest. L.D. Joshi has argued that wherever the raja has been unsuccessful in encroaching upon the sphere of local authority, the latter retained control over the tenure under which different families possessed land. If a proprietor wished to sell a part of his land, he needed the permission of the *siana* or village headman to do so.[78] Examples of this were the Khaikari villages of present-day Uttarakhand adjoining Himachal. The customary practice in these villages, at least till the first two or three decades of the nineteenth century, was that if a family became extinct its land lapsed to the Khaikari community and not to the collaterals who may have wished to claim it.[79] Within communities, Joshi suggests the recognised landholding units were families and not individuals. For the family, therefore, the landholding was a kind of joint trust that protected the interests of all its members, especially sons.[80]

In fact, "the inseparableness of the family lands from the family" was an essential characteristic of Khasa customary law.[81] If a proprietor cultivator of a village abandoned his portion of the family land, his brothers or nephews were expected to cultivate it. In case no relatives were available, the *siana* (headman) could hand over the land to other proprietors of the village for cultivation. Failing this, a person from outside could be invited. Under no circumstances could

[77] Nisbet 1962: 100–1.
[78] Saksena 1962: 109.
[79] Joshi 1929: 195–6, 232.
[80] Ibid.: 235.
[81] Ibid.: 208.

it be handed over to a low-caste person, even if it entailed keeping the land fallow and sharing the revenue obligation amongst other upper-caste village proprietors.[82]

It needs to be recognised that, in a very rudimentary sense, household decisions were not simply economic in nature, they were also political. Hartman has argued that "it makes little sense to keep interpreting elite behaviour as political and active and peasant behaviour as economic and passive."[83] Caste, community, and kinship were vibrant decision-making social institutions. They were closely networked into the structural dynamics of pre-colonial society and state and remained so even during the colonial period, albeit in an altered manner.[84] The relationship between peasant households and the state was always particularly close; especially because land revenue was the primary source of income for the latter. Peasants were also mobilised for military assignments or for providing a host of other services required by the rulers and their administrative apparatus. The peasant–state relationship in Kulu is quite illustrative, and applies equally to the other petty principalities that once flourished across this western Himalayan region.

Peasant households in Kulu held land on condition of service to the state. The land held by many peasants of the Kanet caste was technically in lieu of military service. Low-caste Dagis were, on the other hand, required to perform menial tasks in return for the land they possessed. Each standard unit of land (called *jeola*) that was held by a Kanet household consisted of two halves. Land was measured by the amount of seed (*bhar*) required to sow a particular area. The *jeola* consisted of twelve *bhars*.[85] One half (*bartojeola*) could be held rent-free provided service was provided to the state by one male member of the household. The other (*hansilijeola*) was regularly assessed for taxation and revenue had to be paid for it to the raja. If, however, a household could provide two men for service to the state, the entire holding (*jeola*) could be converted into a *bartojeola* (i.e. rent-free).

---

[82] Saksena 1962: 102.
[83] Hartman 2004: 245.
[84] Kasturi 2002: 9.
[85] *Kangra DG* 1917: II, 150.

There was, apparently, no limit to the number of rent-paying *hansili* holdings that a family could acquire. But the labour requirements for mountain farming were enormous, and for a family to possess even two such holdings was rare. The smaller Dagi holding (called *cheti*) measured roughly one-half to one-fourth of the Kanet-held *jeola*. It was held entirely rent-free on condition of the menial services that Dagis were expected to provide.[86]

Because Kanet peasants held the largest portion of the cultivated land in the state – and the village menials held only 15 to 20 per cent of the total cultivated area in 1917 – the onus of providing *begar* also probably fell largely upon the former.[87] The state, as already mentioned, recognised the household as the primary unit for this purpose. It appeared only logical, under the circumstances, that the peasants should make a deliberate choice to live in joint families that were then regarded as single households. They could, in this manner, easily meet the state's compulsory demand for the services of one man per household. Other male members of the family were thus left free to engage in a labour-intensive agro-pastoral and/or trading household economy. The stability of the socio-political system depended upon the economic viability of households – not simply because they provided revenue, but also because they rendered services upon which the ruler was crucially dependent. There appears to have been a close relationship between the state and the peasant household. For example, we learn that polyandry in Ladakh "was found among farmers who cultivated land held directly from government and paid their taxes to it directly."[88] The higher labour demands imposed by the state on such land probably encouraged peasants to adopt polyandry as a means of freeing one male family member for state service. To take another instance, in the principality of Bashahr polyandry was a fairly common practice and (as we have noticed above) here the state did not permit the division of immovable property.[89] This, in effect, meant that peasants would be expected to live and function as

---

[86] Ibid.: 150.
[87] Ibid.: 156.
[88] Crook 1987: 46.
[89] Deuster 1996: 42.

a single household. A decline in the state's demand for labour and the subsequent permission granted for the partition of landholdings was seen by observers as resulting in a reduction in the number of polyandrous families.

Whatever factors may have prompted the initial adoption of polyandry, its continuation was evidently linked to the household economy and landholding. This becomes apparent when we examine the class/category of households amongst which it was a preferred custom. Nancy Levine categorically states that "Polyandry almost certainly was more common among the rich and landed."[90] This is supported by Wilson, who argues with respect to another region that "polyandry prevails throughout the interior of Ceylon chiefly amongst the wealthier classes..."[91] On account of their family organisation, polyandrous households had access to more family labour. They were, therefore, better placed to retain and effectively utilise a larger amount of land and resources in some kinds of areas. The greater material wealth that they accumulated gave to polyandrous families a higher social status. This enabled them to play a crucial role in the community's economic life and also occupy an important position in its political relations with the state. In the context of Tibet, Goldstein says, "Polyandry is primarily selected not for bread and butter motives – fear of starvation in a difficult environment – but rather primarily for the Tibetan equivalent of oysters, champagne and social esteems."[92] Polyandry in Ladakh, too, was closely associated with the "landed farming way of life" and was influenced by the compulsions of paying taxes on land held from the state. On the other hand, social classes with the least land did not formally adopt polyandry.[93] This pattern was equally true for Lahaul, where more of the upper-caste landowners were polyandrous than the largely landless menial classes.[94] Prince Peter has, however, contended that though it was the landowners who practised polyandry, the poorer

[90] Levine 1988: 58.
[91] Wilson 1979: 186.
[92] Goldstein 1987: 205; Levine 1988: 184.
[93] Crook 1987: 44.
[94] Ghosh 1987: 56.

people too would sometimes do so in order to "keep their meagre possessions undivided".[95]

There were also, however, some exceptions that we need to recognise. Within the region there was another form of family organisation that prevented the fragmentation of family wealth. In the adjacent area of Spiti the practice was reversed. Here only the eldest brother – who inherited the entire property – was permitted to marry, while the younger ones were required to become monks. In further contrast to the practice in Lahaul, there existed in Spiti an impoverished landless class of minstrel monks who were frequently traders and were sometimes also polyandrous.[96]

The greater social acceptability of polyandry and the prestige attached to it is illustrated by the slaves in the Nyinba village of the Nepal Himalaya studied by Nancy Levine. When slaves gained freedom and acquired enough wealth, they gave up their monogamous custom and began marrying polyandrously like their former masters.[97] Nearer our area of study, in Jaunsar-Bawar, polyandry was more common amongst high-caste landowners – Khasas and Brahmins – than amongst artisans and landless labourers.[98] It may be recalled that in Jaunsar-Bawar polygynandry was the practice. Apart from the number of wives being an indication of the wealth and social standing of the family, the practice also enabled the family to increase its labour availability in response to the requirement. Poorer peasants with small landholdings were unable to afford more than one wife. They might even have been disinclined to preserve a joint family of brothers because they had no viable inheritance in the shape of the land around which such families were invariably built.[99] It has been calculated by Raha and Coomar that in Kinnaur, till as late as the 1960s, just over 26 per cent of all marriages were polyandrous. Amongst the prosperous Rajputs, polyandrous/polygynandrous marriages were as high as about 48 per cent.[100] There were, nevertheless, many villages

[95] Peter 1963: 567.
[96] Lyall 1889: 126; *Kangra DG* 1917: IV, 266, 272.
[97] Levine 1988: 63–4.
[98] Majumdar 1962: 75.
[99] Berreman 1987: 187.
[100] Raha and Coomar 1987: 72, 78.

in Kinnaur where even the low-caste Kolis had polyandrous/polygynandrous households.[101] It is possible that in these villages even some of the lower castes possessed a reasonable amount of agricultural land. The polyandrous Kanet peasants of Saraj (Kulu) pretended to a higher status than the Kanets of Kulu proper. This was perhaps in keeping with the considerable respectability polyandry seems to have enjoyed in the region.[102] Spiti in north Himachal was the one area where the poor were inclined towards polyandry while the landowners customarily followed primogeniture.[103]

Cunningham had, in the context of Ladakh, suggested that polyandry was a system followed by the "poorer classes". Andrew Wilson, whom we have seen travelling through Himachal in the late nineteenth century, disagreed. He was of the opinion that polyandry was "found also frequently in the most opulent families." This point is perhaps borne out by his reference to the *mukhia* (headman) of the village of Pooh (Kinnaur) in whose family six brothers were married to one wife.[104] We can reasonably assume that the headman of Pooh was among the more prosperous members of the village community.

Conclusion

Customary practices like polyandry may have arisen on account of a complex combination of factors. These factors could have varied in different areas. Attempts to explain the origin of ancient practices in the absence of adequate sources is always a risky proposition. Moreover, social institutions often come to serve a purpose quite unrelated to the initial causes of their origin. The current relevance and function of a social system cannot therefore be read back into the past as the original reason for its emergence. It is easier for us, therefore, to try and understand the purposes for which polyandry came to be used in our area of study, than to trace its origins.

Irrespective of their considerable variations, both polyandry and polygynandry appear to have been, in part at least, methods of

[101] Ibid.: 91.
[102] Rose 1970: II, 458.
[103] Lyall 1889: 126; *Kangra DG* 1917: IV, 266.
[104] Wilson 1979: 187.

managing and conserving patrimonial wealth – particularly customary claims on landholdings. Rose saw polyandry as a means to "prevent the division of estates".[105] Here too the motive may normally have been to enable the family to retain a position of dominance rather than to prevent its decline into abject poverty. Family wealth was thus passed down to the succeeding generation in accordance with patriarchal rules of inheritance. While some households may have been polyandrous on account of their poverty, the larger number of such households were relatively prosperous and landowning. Polyandry was clearly something more than a rudimentary survival strategy for mountain areas with limited agricultural land.

Joint polyandrous households of landowners were also micro political units. They exerted considerable influence on matters of importance in the village community and enjoyed relatively greater prestige. Their position was further reinforced by the fact that in a political system based on the extraction of forced labour and services by the state they were better placed to meet their service obligations. They could simultaneously control comparatively more agricultural land, maintain large herds of livestock, and profitably engage in trade.

---

[105] Rose 1970: III, 13.

13

Thresholds in the Wilderness
Identities, Interests, and Modernity in Western Himalayan Borderlands

The Search for Highland Essentialities

WILLEM VAN SCHENDEL'S audacious postulation that the enormous expanse of Asian highlands – including the Himalaya, the Tibetan Plateau, and the uplands of the South East Asian peninsula – represent a distinctly identifiable region has evoked much academic interest.[1] He contended that societies in these highlands had persistently, and successfully, resisted the domination of large and powerful states at the peripheries of which they were located. Furthermore, the sparse and scattered highland population of this region exhibited greater cultural diversity than the more homogenised lowlands. To this extensive and impressive land mass, van Schendel gave the interesting name "Zomia" (originating from north-eastern India).

James Scott subsequently developed the idea of Zomia in his study of the South East Asian Massif.[2] This extensive region includes the upland territories of several countries. Scott's principal argument was

---

Published earlier as Chetan Singh, "Thresholds in the Wilderness: Identities, Interests and Modernity in Western Himalayan Borderlands", in Wahid 2016.

[1] van Schendel 2002.
[2] Scott 2009.

that the most significant social intent in the peripheral uplands was to escape domination by any state.³ It was not simply environmental conditions and cultural considerations that determined the nature of family and community institutions and economic strategies. In fact, the options available were rather restricted after people in these highlands had made this initial political choice of escaping the stranglehold of powerful agrarian states and seeking shelter in the mountains.⁴ These marginalised "shatter zones" adjoined states and provided refuge to people who were periodically buffeted by the oppressive and violent processes of "state-making and state-unmaking".⁵ A history of long-term resistance to state domination gave to highland societies the ability to change and adjust very rapidly: "turn on a dime", as Scott puts it.⁶ Resistance sustained by a social structure was easily "disaggregated and reassembled". For this purpose a "mixed portfolio of subsistence techniques was adopted as it provided greater economic advantage."⁷ Three critical ideas determined how hill people perceived themselves and structured their society: "equality, autonomy, and mobility".⁸ The adoption of an oral tradition was yet another method of escaping state control. The virtual absence of writing and texts offered "freedom of manoeuvre in history, genealogy, and legibility that frustrates state routines."⁹ According to Scott, the ambiguity accompanying oral methods of remembering created "multiple histories" that mountain people used "singly or in combination depending on the circumstances."¹⁰ It was "in their interest to keep as many of their options open as possible, and what kind of history to have is one of those options. They have as much history as they require."¹¹

[3] Ibid.: x.
[4] Ibid.: xi.
[5] Ibid.: 7.
[6] Ibid.: 24.
[7] Ibid.: 211.
[8] Ibid.: 217.
[9] Ibid.: 226.
[10] Ibid.: 329.
[11] Ibid.: 330.

Geographers, anthropologists, and historians alike have explored the idea of Zomia in a special issue of the *Journal of Global History* in 2010. Despite its theoretical appeal the concept is based on generalisations that are rather difficult to substantiate empirically. Fairly developed state formations occurred quite early within the extensive highland region defined as Zomia by van Schendel and Scott. If Zomia is conceived primarily as a region of refuge for societies that had escaped state control, the emergence of well-structured states within the region is a contradiction. One can, however, argue that state control over societies in the mountains was often quite weak, and in some places even non-existent. The lack of state intervention enabled mountain people to assert their identities and interests in opposition to the stricter "mainstreaming" efforts of the more powerful, agrarian states.

The Idea of Modern Development

The perceived isolation of mountain people from larger socio-political trends of the lowlands seemed to allow greater freedom to hill society from state control. Not surprisingly, this also gave rise to the notion that hill societies remained non-conformist or even "backward" till they were radically transformed by state-sponsored developmental activities. Change in western Himalayan societies is therefore usually seen as the result of modern development. Two sets of theoretical and methodological assumptions underlie present thinking on the impact of modernisation on the various regions of the world. This is especially true of geographical spaces (like mountains) whose isolation caused them to be mistakenly seen as unchanging and unaffected by major trends that radically transformed the world in modern times.

Development, Modernization, and Modernity

The first set of assumptions consists of three overlapping concepts: development, modernisation, and modernity. There is a logical, and perhaps even sequential, connection between the ideas of development and modernisation. With the decline and collapse of colonial empires by the mid-twentieth century the impoverishment of the peoples of the former colonies became apparent to the world. The compelling necessity for bringing about "development" in these newly liberated countries was justified by the anticipated material benefit that the "modernisation" ensuing from development would bring to them. Considerable academic work focused upon the linkages between development and modernisation. Quantifiable material change was integral to development and modernisation. The visibility of the "things" that modernisation brought to a society that it touched was an important measure of its success.

In the 1950s the embedded objective of developmental planning at the global level was to modernise previously colonised societies. This was particularly so where the burden of social tradition was regarded as a hindrance to progress. As a result "modernity" came to be regarded as "a value in and of itself".[12] It was here, too, that the relationship between development and modernity acquired greater complexity. Unlike the materially recognisable aspects of economic "modernisation", the concept of "modernity" often comes loaded with qualitative issues and asks questions dealing with values, norms, beliefs, rationality, subjectivity/individuality and a host of intangible ideas. In short, modernity engages more directly with the worldview of a society and its methods of analysis and explanation. Modernisation might successfully alter the material condition of societies. But it may not always engender in them the emergence of "modernity" as a different and systematic way of seeing, explaining, and changing the world.

The Presumed Marginality of the Western Himalaya

The second set of assumptions is directly relevant to our present purpose. In part at least, the attraction of exploring changes in social identities and in the interests of communities of the region was derived from their presumed historical marginalisation. The premise here was

[12] Oritz 2000: 255.

that because the peripheral nature of the region had inhibited change, contemporary transformations caused by "development" would, for that reason, become more apparent. This would also, therefore, make the disjuncture between tradition and modernity in such societies measureable.

These suppositions, however, require an empirical understanding of the nature of society as it might have existed before "development", and also of the changes introduced thereafter. Societies of the western Himalayan borderlands were earlier drawn into the competing interests of colonial empires and were subsequently required to follow nationally determined "developmental" activities. To discover the worldview that steered these borderland societies *before* the age of "development" and "modernisation" is a difficult task. Little has been written about popular mentalities in the western Himalaya prior to the colonial encounter – though some of the better recorded religious beliefs do reveal something about secular wisdom. More interestingly, trading and commercial activity (with its complexity of negotiations) provides some useful insights into the mind of societies that engage in it.

Early European Perspectives on the Western Himalaya

Early observations of European travellers and colonial administrators, albeit impressionistic, are quite easily available to historians today. Western Himalayan societies' introduction to modernisation and modernity began earlier than scholars have cared to notice. Prior to the concept of "modernisation", it was the colonial rulers' idea of introducing "civilisation" and its accompanying material accessories to the mountain people that influenced altruistic thinking in British India. J.G. Gerard, a British doctor stationed in Sabathu (in present-day Himachal Pradesh) in 1824, was convinced that:

> The example of European character and intelligence has not been lost upon the hill population. The Chiefs have beheld with pleasure many of the arts and sciences and the comforts of civilized life and have adopted

several useful and laudable customs. I allude here to articles of dress, household furniture, implements of husbandry, glass windows, grates and chimneys, the cultivation and cookery of the potato, medicine and chemistry, and it is quite delightful to observe the daily disuse and abandonment of hereditary prejudices and the development of energy and civilization all over the country.[13]

Gerard evidently believed that the introduction of modern science and technology would result in the dilution of traditional practices and customary beliefs that came to be classified as "hereditary prejudices". To early colonial officials this represented a change in thinking that could facilitate the transition to modernity. It appears that western Himalayan borderland societies shared certain socio-cultural characteristics that influenced how they responded to external developments. To a considerable extent, these characteristics were probably influenced by their geographical and socio-political location.

Transitory Zones and Transformation

These societies were quite clearly situated in what can be called transitory zones. The physical space they occupied compelled them to interact with, and even accommodate, the beliefs and practices of at least two major religions, cultures, and peoples. Their location at the peripheries of two dominant civilisations enabled some distinct territories of the western Himalaya (such as Kinnaur, Lahaul, Spiti, and Ladakh) to remain discrete cultural areas. Throughout the region, as well as in adjoining western Tibet, were to be found numerous locations that functioned as socio-cultural (even political) thresholds. These thresholds, as would be expected, had a dual character. They marked the point at which two grand civilisations separated. But these were also locations where the essential elements of two major cultural traditions met, transacted, and sustained a diversity of beliefs and practices.

Fisher's study of the Tarangpur traders of Nepal on the Nepal–China border area, inhabited by Magars and situated between

---

[13] Gerard 1824: 314.

the Buddhist and Hindu traditions, is a case in point. He argues that:

> The problem is not only the integration of an encysted ethnic minority into a complex society, but also the mode of accommodation reached between two major systems. The symbol systems of two different great traditions compete for commitment, so that executing the transactional chain requires a double-edged Janus-faced form of impression management – hence the present cultural heterogeneity of Tarangpur – of a society which is nominally Buddhist, strongly Hinduised and still partly tribal.[14]

The intermediate position of certain western Himalayan societies between two large cultures offered them enormous opportunities. Their location in a transition zone encouraged them to acquire multiple identities for different purposes. They needed to accommodate in their society what were apparently contradictory social and cultural arrangements. The ability to do so probably lent to them a flexibility and willingness to deal with ideas and institutions that were new and unfamiliar. This was so even as their commitment to community, village, and local religious beliefs persisted.

The larger geographical context within which major long-term historical trends occur is not always easy to identify, even though they might offer interesting explanations. Braudel's seminal study of the early modern Mediterranean world is one such outstanding example.[15] Using this study Wong argues that even for Central Asia one could adopt a similar model and "consider the cultural dynamics of regions by tracking the institutions among people crossing cultures and carrying ideas."[16] He argues that "Regions there offer a scale of observation that encourages recognition of difference *and* connection." He emphasises that "the northwestern frontier of China was a region in which four civilisations – the Han Chinese, Tibetan, Mongolian, and Islamic – have met since the sixteenth century."[17]

[14] Fisher 1987: 189.
[15] Braudel 1978.
[16] Wong 2003: 13.
[17] Ibid.: 14.

However, this meeting place had very extended linkages that went deep into the economies and societies of the neighbouring civilisations. In this extensive part of Central Asia "the connections among peoples of the region were often less important than those formed with other sedentary systems that bordered them."[18]

Ladakh Borderland: Trade and Society

Several adjoining parts of Tibet and Central Asia further north witnessed this remarkable interaction between different people of diverse backgrounds. Leh, for instance, was a place where traders – Kashmiris, Punjabis, Yarkandis, and others – from distant regions gathered to exchange goods that they had in turn brought from even more far-off markets.[19] The long and difficult journeys they undertook required an equally long period of preparation. Their extended residence in Ladakh for this purpose enabled greater social interaction and understanding.

Yarkand, in Central Asia, had a system of administration that was quite conducive for trade. Administrative control over the town was shared between a Muslim *hakim* and two Chinese *ambans*. While the *ambans* supervised customs, police and criminal justice, a chief judge appointed by the *hakim* settled civil disputes. Yarkand lay a difficult forty-day journey from Leh, and yet Yarkandi, Kashmiri, and Ladakhi traders were to be found in both places. The Kashmiris were taxed at a lower rate than the others at the customs-house. The close association of Yarkand with trade, and the transitory character of a large part of its trading population is reflected in the use of the term *musafir* (traveller). The term was used for every foreign trader resident in the town, even though some of them had been settled there long enough to have a local wife and children living with them.[20] The mixed milieu of the town is illustrated by the fact that though the governor of the city was a Chinese *amban*, the Muslim *qazi* of the town was regarded with great respect, as were the ulema. It was

[18] Ibid.: 35.
[19] Nakshahbandi 1850: 377; Vigne 1981: II, 343.
[20] Izzatullah 1843: 305; Nakshahbandi 1850: 372–85.

further noted that "whenever a dispute arises between a Mahomedan and a Chinese, it is settled according to the Mahomedan law. The Chinese are also sent to the *hakim*, and he, with common consent, settles their disputes by Mahomedan law."[21]

In fact, trade was an extremely important economic aspect of the trans-Himalayan highlands, and treaties between states refer to its regulation quite meticulously; as, for example, does the 1684 treaty between Tibet and Ladakh.[22] In adjoining Tibet, and further north in Central Asia, there were towns where trade acted as a binding factor. This was accompanied by attempts by different states to regulate routes, impose taxes and ensure some kind of administrative presence. In western Tibet, the administrators (*jongpen*) had a personal interest in trade from which they profited and this may have resulted in its close regulation. Such regulation did sometimes restrict the free movement of goods through western Tibet. An important trading town of the Changthang region of western Tibet was Gartok, which was sometimes described as not much more than a temporary trading camp. When Moorcroft visited it in July 1817, he described it as a collection of black tents and little else.[23] The smallness of the scale does not, however, detract from the fact that the trade was of great importance for the societies that engaged in this exchange. In many respects, it was crucial for their existence.

Not surprisingly, therefore, the Tibetan plateau and the mountain region bordering it in the south and west was not a "no-man's land" despite its desolate appearance. Even in this apparent wilderness there existed imagined and real thresholds where traders and travellers were carefully watched. Nain Singh and his brother who were tasked by the British with the assignment to secretly survey Tibet soon discovered how carefully the movement of people across the border was monitored. In March 1856 they first attempted to cross into Tibet through the Nepal border in the guise of Bashahris, but were turned back by an official who knew only too well that Bashahri traders did

---

[21] Nakshahbandi 1850: 383.
[22] Ahmad 1968: 353–4.
[23] McKay 1992: 410, 412, 414–15.

not use the Nepal route to enter Tibet.[24] The high passes, too, were therefore thresholds in the wilderness that were points of political and economic regulation. Even in this bleak and sparsely populated landscape, it did not take long for people to identify each other. While once again pretending to be a Bashahri travelling for business in Tibet, Nain Singh was closely questioned by suspicious Kashmiri traders who soon penetrated his disguise though they did not reveal his true identity to the Tibetan authorities.[25]

Kinnaur and Modernity

It must nevertheless be remembered that these thresholds were equally a passage for crossing from one side to the other. The societies that lived and prospered by these crossings seem to have exhibited an impressive ability to negotiate and understand diverse cultural and political nuances. Dr Gerard's early account suggests that such adaptability was to be found amongst Kinnauras.[26] He made an interesting distinction between formal education on the one hand and "civilization, morality and knowledge" on the other. The latter, according to him, had "made the greatest progress in the remote and secluded regions of Koonawur." Gerard believed that "Koonawur, in spite of the defects of the Bussahir government and its remoteness from the capital, ranks above every other State in point of intelligence, active industry and good feeling . . ." He pointed out that "there are no Brahmins in that country and there is much less of blind devotion in religion, but more of superstition. Education is there less cultivated than the actual acquirement of knowledge, which their intercourse with the Chinese, their commercial pursuits and habits of hardihood encourage and establish."[27] The lack of Brahmanical control over society in the Himalaya was seen as the window of opportunity for introducing crucial transformational changes. Through modern education and the "introduction of the morality of Christianity

[24] N. Singh 1877: 447–8.
[25] Montgomerie 2008: 431.
[26] Gerard 1824: 315.
[27] Ibid.: 315–16.

and the arts and comforts of civilization," in particular, "the moral and political improvement" of the people could be carried out.[28] Interestingly, the freedom enjoyed by women in mountain regions was seen as a something that promised "hope of future improvement".[29]

What reinforced British conviction that Himalayan society was more amenable to change was the prevalence not only of equality "to a greater degree than is to be found in any other portion of India" but also the existence of "a parity of ignorance".[30] This seemed to present a kind of clean slate opportunity to the colonial rulers to insert a greater measure of European influence. For the British it was probably easier to prevail over "irrational" belief in magic and superstition than to confront carefully formulated religious doctrines spelt out by orthodox Brahmins. Gerard's confidence in being able to effect a change in Kinnaur may have derived from his success in making small-pox inoculation acceptable in the mountainous area as early as the 1820s, while resistance to it persisted in various parts of India through the nineteenth century.[31] Many Tibetan lamas, who probably travelled through Kinnaur, were convinced of its efficacy. They had offered themselves for vaccination and even requested Gerard to carry out vaccination at the border (foreigners were not permitted into Tibet) so that others in Tibet too could benefit.[32] Gutzlaff, in fact, mentions that every year large numbers of nomadic people in the Tibet plateau areas died of smallpox.[33]

The absence of Brahmins in certain South Asian societies did not, however, invariably mean that such societies remained "simple" or "primitive" and therefore likely to succumb more easily to external intellectual and religious influences. In fact, the so-called "Hindu" belief system presented itself in diverse ways in different parts of South Asia: and the Brahmin characterised only the more formal facet of orthodox Brahmanic religion. The absence of Brahmins, therefore,

[28] Murray 1824: 274.
[29] Ibid.: 274.
[30] Gerard 1824: 314.
[31] Swinton 1824: 305.
[32] Murray 1824: 276–7.
[33] Gutzlaff 1850: 226.

did not necessarily indicate the absence of beliefs derived from the Brahmanical prescriptions. Kinnaur, even today, retains a very eclectic approach towards religion.

Markets, Money, and Exchange

The ideas of commerce and exchange permeated the structure of Kinnaura social organisation. Despite the difficult topography of the area, money and commodities were essential elements of life in Kinnaur. Travel over long distances for trade was an integral part of the annual cycle of activities and the Kinnaura capacity to negotiate in culturally diverse situations is not to be underestimated. Their ability to understand different identities and interests, too, had been remarkably sharpened over centuries. Trade routes connecting Tibet and India have existed for centuries prior to the widening of the Hindustan–Tibet road by the British. The economic and cultural baggage that passed along these routes and the opportunities for gain that this offered had always been factored into the Kinnaura worldview.

European travellers invariably refer to the trading and manufacturing activities of the Kinnauras. Among the early references, Moorcroft, on the basis of information obtained in Ladakh, writes about two kinds of local plants that were exported as "tea" in considerable quantities from Kinnaur to Ladakh.[34] Fraser mentions the production of wine, iron, lead, and copper in limited quantities – but most importantly the "fabrication of woollen cloths of several sorts, and in this they excel the inhabitants of all the countries between Sutlej and the Alaknunda."[35] Rampur is described by him as a town that "was once a flourishing place" where commodities from Kashmir, Ladakh, "Bootan" (Tibet), Kashgar, Yarkand etc., could be bought.[36] The implication seems to be that the highly exploitative period of Gorkha rule had taken a toll on its prosperity. Soon after in 1824, however, Murray, the deputy superintendent of the Simla Hill States, referred to

[34] Moorcroft 1970: 209–10.
[35] Fraser 1982: 272–4.
[36] Ibid.: 256–7.

the availability of "tea from China" and "bars of silver" from Yarkand and toys from Russia at the Rampur fair, while in Kinnaur were to be found "Mandarin chopstick, cups and saucers".[37] Rampur became once again a prosperous place where trade fairs were held thrice a year, in May, October, and December, and where "people of many countries, characters and customs" came.[38]

Not surprisingly, then, the Kinnauras were more prosperous than the peasantry in other parts of Bashahr. This prosperity was noted also by Alexander Gerard who travelled through Kinnaur in 1822.[39] He mentions two different occasions on which he ran short of money and had no difficulty in borrowing it from local Kinnauras who were very happy to loan him whatever amount he required.[40] Kinnauras obtained a good income from trade and pastoralism, and this enabled them to earn "more than enough to pay their contribution" of the revenue demanded by the Bashahr state.[41] The state was, moreover, "fully aware of the singular situation and the importance of this commerce, upon which it is so dependent."[42] The *Bashahr State Gazetteer* of 1910 (part of the *Simla Hill States Gazetteer*) while referring to the revenue settlement of Bashahr of 1894 observed that the inhabitants of Kinnaur were on "the whole better off than those of Rampur and Rohru. Good profits are made in trading, they have plenty of cattle, and they make a considerable income from fruit and forest products, as well as from wool and homespun cloth."[43] The *bandobast* report of Chini *tahsil* that was done in 1928 reiterated that the people of the *tahsil* were by and large traders and sold goods at the Lavi trade fair in Rampur after "increasing the prices by a large margin of profit".[44]

There is also an interesting reference to the existence of a committee that oversaw the transaction of trade between Kinnaura and Tibet

[37] Murray 1824: 291–2.
[38] Ibid.: 286–7; Lloyd 1840: 183.
[39] Gerard 1993: 76–7.
[40] Ibid.
[41] Ibid.: 282, 289.
[42] Murray 1824: 289.
[43] *SHSG* 1911, Bashahr: 76.
[44] Bhuj 1928: 21.

traders. Each group of Kinnaura traders had its counterpart in Tibet with which it had to transact business and the infringement of rules was punishable.[45] Nevertheless, people from Kinnaur had considerable freedom of movement in Tibet. This is proved by the fact that when the British sent an expedition to explore the eastern watershed of the upper Indus river, they had to send in a person disguised as a Bashahri trader along with a group of genuine Bashahris.[46]

The remarkable familiarity of the people of Kinnaur with fairly complex commercial transactions and their dependence on conducting business with traders from distant places situated them in a place rather different from ordinary agro-pastoral peasants of the region. Even forest produce of the area, such as *zeera* and *neoza* were successfully marketed by Kinnauras on a regular basis.[47] It is important to keep this factor in mind while attempting to understand the possible impact that developmental activity might have had on their thought processes. The "simplicity" of a pre-modern society or the theoretical "clean slate" often assumed by colonial officials because of the geographical inaccessibility of Kinnaur certainly did not exist. On the contrary, the region portrays far more intricate socio-economic characteristics than those found in some simpler peasant societies situated in close proximity to the political centre of India.

Society and Social Organisation

While taking a closer look at Kinnaur society in the context of modernisation and its trajectory towards modernity, there seem to be at least two features that merit closer examination. These were not exclusive to Kinnaura society, but they did occupy an important place in it. The first was the religious practice of Buddhism in some areas along with the institutions associated with it; and the second was the fairly common social practice of polyandry with all its economic and political implications.

The existence of Buddhism as a formal and institutionalised religion has a long history in upper Kinnaur, going back more than a thousand

---

[45] *SHSG* 1911, Bashahr: 62.
[46] Montgomerie 1870: 208.
[47] Lloyd 1840: II, 272.

years. For the colonial period, amongst the earliest references is made to it by Alexander Gerard. When he visited the village of Sangnam in 1817, he was received by about eighty Buddhist lamas and fifty or sixty nuns belonging, according to him, to "six populous villages". He further writes that the convent at Sunam had thirty-two nuns and several lamas.[48] Rose noted later that while the largest nunneries of Kinnaur were located in the villages of Kanam and Sangnam, a few *jomos* or nuns were to be found in almost every village.[49] Andrew Wilson who travelled through the region in the 1880s mentions that his baggage was sometimes carried by "lama nuns" when pressure of work had prevented the laity rendering service. Apart from cultivating the land attached to the monastery, the nuns also hired out their labour during the harvest season.[50]

But the most interesting and relevant aspect of the monastic nature of Buddhism in Kinnaur is that as a result a fair number of people in certain parts of the region were engaged in reading and writing the scriptures. Gerard says, "All lamas can read and write, and I never saw one who did not instantly recognise the few sentences in Captain Turner's Thibet."[51] The ability to at least read and write was not restricted to monks. Nuns too were encouraged to read the religious texts and would often be engaged in writing. Rose mentions that Kanet girls, who did not marry, were expected to live in nunneries and "devote their time to the study of the Tibetan scriptures".[52] Wilson saw a connection between polyandry and the existence of a large number of nuns when he argued that "Of course, there is a large number of surplus women under this polyandric system, and they are provided for in the Lama nunneries where they learn to read and copy the Tibetan scriptures, and to engage in religious services."[53]

The population of Kinnaur appears to have remained small, and an estimate of six members per household was arrived at by Alexander. Quite possibly, each (Kanet) household in upper Kinnaur would

---

[48] Gerard 1993: 21, 120.
[49] Rose 1970: III, 453.
[50] Wilson 1979: 189–90.
[51] Ibid.: 118.
[52] Rose 1970: III, 453.
[53] Wilson 1979: 189.

have one or more family members joining the religious order. They might, by that connection, also have become familiar with the merit of reading and writing – even though they did not engage directly in activities dependent upon these skills. Did these linkages, albeit tenuous, of the Kinnaura family – not merely with religion but with the world of formal learning – affect their understanding of their world and its functioning? Were smaller peasant-oriented territories within a large part of Kinnaur bound together by the larger vision of Buddhism and the secular functioning of its institutions despite the fact that they sometimes spoke different languages and dialects? Alexander Gerard explicitly mentioned the differences in the languages spoken in Kinnaur: "The inhabitants of Soognum speak a language totally different from Koonawuree and Tartar dialects . . . There are to the best of my knowledge, no fewer than five distinct tongues spoken in Koonawur . . ."[54] Did the economic activities of the monasteries – which often included trade – introduce greater social and commercial complexity in what might otherwise have remained a simple subsistence-oriented barter of products between peasant communities? Polyandrous families, I have argued elsewhere, were among the more prosperous ones in the areas where the practice existed.[55]

To complicate the situation further, there also existed a parallel hierarchy of local deities associated with each village. The Chini Tahsil Settlement Report observed that "Most of the inhabitants of this *tahsil* follow the Buddhist religion, yet they also have a different *deota* in every *chak* who is called a family *deota* (*kul deota*) and who is not like the *deota* of the entire *ghori* as is the case in Rohru and Rampur."[56] In southern Kinnaur, this hierarchy existed not within the ambit of Buddhism, but attached to the Brahmanical order. All village temples here had a number of functionaries attached to them. They managed the affairs not only of the *deota* and the temple, but also of the village itself.[57] The deity could only be approached through one or

[54] Lloyd 1840: II, 230.
[55] Singh 2011c: 98–120.
[56] Bhuj 1928: 3
[57] Rose 1970: III, 447.

the other of these temple officials. A list of temples was made by Rose and he pointed out that the deities were not all equal, that they were in fact arranged in a hierarchy that reflected their importance. The absence of Brahmins in Kinnaur has already been mentioned earlier, and not surprisingly, the *pujaris* of these temples were all Kanets.[58]

This hierarchy of *deotas* seems to be of immense significance for the administration of Bashahr state. Their connection with the monarch, who ruled on account of his claim to some amount of divinity, was quite intimate. The link between the two appears to have been renewed every year at the Fag *mela* held in Rampur – at which a large number of deities marked their presence before the ruler. This was a religio-political link that bound the ruler with his subjects through their deities. It represented the conduit through which passed subtle impulses not only of authority and consent but also of autonomy and dissent. It was the channel through which the subjects expressed their anguish and a form of disagreement that sometimes bordered on rebellion. This was, perhaps, the tried and tested means through which mountain kingdoms accommodated dissent. Are the popular agitations against large hydro-electric projects that recur in the area similar to the remnants of older forms of protest that still struggle to survive? Is the modern democratic state, with its emphasis on the individual, attempting to alter the language and idiom of autonomous decision-making of traditional village-level communities?

Some Questions about Altered Western Himalayan Identities

Modernisation (riding on the presence and overwhelming demands of the Indian state) through the scheduled tribe status and corresponding need of social mobilisation within a democratic polity has made Kinnaura ethnicity more pronounced. Perhaps Kinnaura ethnic consciousness has developed a unity today that could not have emerged in pre-modern times. But does this mobilisation involve a shift away from earlier methods of invoking the village *deota* and towards a more secular discourse within constitutional institutions? Or was the earlier

[58] Ibid.: 450, 470.

intervention of the *deota* actually political in essence and religious only in form, and therefore is its continuance even today quite logical? Does this consciousness once again reassert and consolidate traditional norms in new forms? If so, has not "development"-based modernisation stalled the emergence of modernity at least in the European sense of the "individual" and the nuclear family being the fulcrum of social organisation, and instead reinforced the traditional notion of communal, or rather, community identity?

14

Riverbank to Hilltop

Pre-colonial Towns and the Impact of British Rule on Urban Growth

Introduction: Some Methodological Issues

ARRIVING AT CRITERIA THAT distinguish urban centres from other forms of human habitation has always been a complicated and contentious task, often raising more questions than answering. Among such distinguishing criteria have sometimes been factors such as "population size, density of settlements, share of non-agricultural occupations and diversity of non-agricultural occupations."[1] Each of these factors is in turn amenable to multiple, even contradictory, interpretations and therefore remains open to reconsideration. It is neither possible nor necessary to examine them here in detail. For the present purpose, a general and broad description of what the term "town" implies might suffice. Given the fact that towns in the Himachal (North India) area of the Himalaya were not very much bigger than large villages, Braudel's classification of a town is conveniently broad enough to include a very wide range of urban settlements:

> Numbers are not the only consideration involved. The town only exists as a town in relation to a form of life lower than its own. There are no exceptions to this rule. No privilege serves as a substitute. There is no town, no townlet without its villages, its scrap of rural life attached,

First published in French as C. Singh 2003.
[1] de Vries 1984: 11.

no town that does not supply its hinterland with the amenities of its market, the use of its shops, its weights and measures, its money lenders, its lawyers, even its distractions. It has to dominate an empire, however tiny, in order to exist.[2]

But even more relevant for a study of urbanisation in Himachal are the observations of Emrys Jones, who recognises the difficulties of a situation in which "a village is almost a town, or a town nearly indistinguishable from a village." The way out of this is to "accept the local definition. A town is what is implied by the local people when they call a locality a town. If this differs from the criterion we use for statistical analysis, it is no less real."[3]

Even as we adopt this very inclusive definition of what a "town" is, it must be recognised that, unlike most villages, towns in general are dependent upon an agricultural surplus generated by peasants located outside urban confines.[4] Non-industrial societies that did not import agricultural produce could support only 13 to 15 per cent of their population as permanent urban residents.[5] A high degree of urbanisation can only be reached if the agricultural output of an individual producer meets the requirements of at least ten others, if not many more. A society with a substantial part of its population living in towns and cities was "an indication of an agriculture capable of yielding more than mere subsistence to the cultivators."[6] It has been suggested that because of their greater productivity, rice-cultivating areas have been able to support higher levels of urbanisation and that "one hectare of rice could . . . feed a population at least twice as large as one hectare of wheat."[7]

Agricultural surplus alone could hardly have been adequate to bring towns into existence. A system of socio-political organisation, and indeed an entire culture, was needed for that. In north-western Europe, towns arose around episcopal and royal residences, political

[2] Braudel 1974: 374.
[3] Jones 1969: 5.
[4] Wrigley 1990: 104; Hohenberg and Lees 1985: 17, 103.
[5] Bairoch 1990: 146.
[6] Wrigley 1990: 101.
[7] Bairoch 1990: 134, 146.

and administrative centres and even around feudal castles. It was here that inhabitants came together and engaged in productive and trading activities that catered to the requirements of the abbey, the king, or a territorial prince.[8] That much having been said, it is essential to recognise that "the economic rather than the military factor played a role in the siting of castle and trade settlement in one another's vicinity, especially since the castle functioned as a central depot for the supplies from the manor."[9] In a very obvious sense, the medieval city was an integral part of "medieval modes of rule, thought and production".[10]

The next stage in the evolution of the city, according to Lefebvre, was marked by the "critical point" when agriculture as a prime economic factor withdrew in the face of growing capitalism and its new methods of production and exchange.[11] With the emergence of urban settlements, regional resources probably came to be more effectively harnessed.[12] It has been argued that urbanisation was an "outgrowth of rural development" wherein "economic activity grows from local exchange and production for local markets to the higher stages of long-distance trade" and that in purely rural areas "a regional fair provided the facilities of a central place for this purpose."[13] This approach is associated with the "central place system" of analysis that perceives the city/town functioning as a central place for multiple purposes.[14]

There is, however, another way of looking at the problem. It is well understood that exchange and trade had the potential of penetrating and linking even towns that were located within predominantly agrarian economies.[15] This commercial interlinking of towns forms the basis of the "network system" model by which urbanisation is

[8] Verhulst 1999: 42, 43, 66–7, 69, 119–20.
[9] Ibid.: 117; Jones 1969: 25.
[10] Hohenberg and Lees 1985: 20; de Vries 1984: 7.
[11] Lefebvre 1996b: 122.
[12] de Vries 1984: 8–9, 10.
[13] Hohenberg and Lees 1985: 58, 71.
[14] Ibid.: 69.
[15] Ibid.: 62, 66; Verhulst 1999: 152.

sought to be explained.[16] The slowness of pre-modern transport and consequently the crucial role played by innumerable small towns as intermediate staging points have been pointed out by Braudel.[17] It was because of their being a part of the trade/exchange network that some towns came up at the edge of deserts and sea coasts, where the means of transportation had to be changed by traders.[18] Such towns were often situated in what has been called a "zone of contact between natural regions".[19]

Apart from being centres of religio-political authority, economic production, and commercial transactions, towns were also places where culture was constantly recreated and propagated.[20] This cultural role of urban centres had political implications. In the pre-industrial city, educational and religious organisations were a particularly important means by which the elite exercised social control, and it is hardly surprising that the heart of the city functioned as the centre of both governmental and religious activity.[21] There are therefore some things specific to urban centres and among these, Lefebvre argues, is the fact that they are situated between the "near order" and the "far order". The city, to quote him, "is a *mediation* among mediations. Containing the *near order*, it supports it; it maintains relations of production and property; it is the place of its reproduction. Contained in the *far order* it supports it; it incarnates it, it projects it over a terrain (the site) and on a plan, that of immediate life; it inscribes it, it prescribes it, *writes* it."[22]

It is obvious then that while the relative size of its population certainly helped a settlement to be categorised as an urban centre, there were several other factors that went into the making of a town. By implication, therefore, it is possible that in a predominantly rural society a settlement with a small number of inhabitants could have

[16] Hohenberg and Lees 1985: 62.
[17] Braudel 1974: 389.
[18] Jones 1969: 10.
[19] Hohenberg and Lees 1985: 49.
[20] Ibid.: 6, 38.
[21] Sjoberg 1976: 44, 46–7.
[22] Lefebvre 1996a: 100–1.

functioned as a town.²³ The situation we are dealing with in the western Himalayan region of Himachal is one in which the "town" was more a functional and less a demographic entity. Numbers and the size of settlements in Himachal may not be the most significant and influential criterion while studying urban settlements. There was, perhaps, something else that went towards making them different from the ordinary villages of the area.

The Old Tradition: Capital Towns and Markets

Present-day Himachal Pradesh was created by the merger of small western Himalayan principalities that had existed independently, or at least autonomously, for several centuries up to 1947. These montane principalities had in turn emerged after bitter skirmishes and long-drawn confrontations between petty chiefs (*ranas* and *thakurs*) who controlled small but strategic stretches of territory. This prolonged and bitter contest for supremacy resulted in the dominance of the powerful amongst them, and subsequently in the establishment of princely states.²⁴ The more extensive of these principalities were founded along the valleys of the main rivers that flowed through the region.²⁵ As a structured and clearly defined monarchical state appeared, it came to be centred on the person of the ruler (raja) and the capital town that became the focus of politico-religious authority.

If indeed there were large settlements that could possibly have been classified as towns in pre-colonial Himachal, they were almost all, barring a few exceptions, the capitals of old kingdoms. On this account, therefore, they had certain features in common. Quite expectedly, these towns were all seats of political power and in that sense represented the particular characteristic of "domination" which Braudel felt was essential to a town.²⁶ In addition to (and in support of) their position as political centres, these towns were often places

[23] Smith 1990: 28.
[24] Hutchison and Vogel 1982.
[25] C. Singh 1998: 6–32.
[26] Braudel 1989: I, 121.

where the presiding deity of the state resided.[27] The political power and religious authority thus came to be concentrated in what was in reality the solitary town in the kingdom.

The physical location of the capitals at key positions on the banks of important rivers provided them access to and control over the smaller but productive tributary valleys. It was the latter valleys, irrigated by rivulets, that were the resource base of all mountain states. One might even venture to suggest that the numerous detached valleys of the principality were "connected" with each other only through the economic and ideological mediation of the capital.

Many of these towns were also significant stages in a larger trade network that extended beyond the state boundaries, even if they themselves were not large manufacturers or consumers of merchandise. This is not to deny, of course, that in a relative sense the raja and the tiny ruling class residing in the town had the largest incomes and were the most substantial consumers in the state.

In keeping with the similar functions they performed, traditional western Himalayan towns were almost alike in physical appearance. At strategic positions were situated the raja's palace and the temple (or temples) of the presiding and other important deities of the state. A permanent and probably the largest market (bazaar) of the kingdom was located in the town and functioned as its commercial hub. Often at a short distance from the bazaar was to be found a large open space (a *chaugan* or maidan) where caravans transporting merchandise camped periodically, and where seasonal trade fairs were held.[28]

A closer scrutiny of some of the towns will serve to illustrate this better. The two principalities of Kahlur and Bashahr, which controlled much of the Satlej River valley, had their capitals at Bilaspur and Rampur respectively. Both towns lay at low elevations on the banks of the Satlej and were royal residences founded as part of the process by which monarchical states in the mountains consolidated their position.[29] The town of Bilaspur was situated on an "open, cultivated, and comparatively level ground", while all around

---

[27] *Mandi SG* 1920: 110; *Kangra DG* 1917: II, 63; *Chamba SG* 1910: 179.
[28] Kanwar 1999: 83, 92.
[29] Ibid.: 85, 86; Hutchison and Vogel 1982: II.

it stood "the mountains, bold and elevated".[30] The town, because of its location at the point where trade routes met, had its share of commercial activity. Similarly, Rampur – the capital of an extremely mountainous state bordering Tibet – lay at an altitude of 3300 feet above sea level. It appears that as the Bashahr rulers extended their influence over the narrow yet fertile valleys hidden amongst rugged mountains flanking both sides of the Satlej River, it became important for them to leave their fort-like home towns in the higher reaches of the east and establish control over key locations in the main Satlej valley. These were locations from where the resources of both sides of the river could be harnessed and through which almost all the trade passed. Rampur evidently was the most significant of such locations on the Satlej.[31] It was founded either in the late seventeenth century or sometime during the first half of the eighteenth. In so far as the town drew some of its wealth from trade, it was affected by shifts in trading activity. Fraser, who travelled through the town during the first decade of the nineteenth century, says that it was in a state of ruin as compared to its earlier prosperity.[32] It still, however, continued to function as the capital of Bashahr.

Along the valley of the River Beas were the states of Kangra, Mandi, and Kulu. The territory of Kangra (nearest the North Indian plains) was more in the nature of a mildly undulating and open valley bordered by highlands, rather than a completely mountainous terrain. As a result, the location of Nagarkot (Kangra town) and its impressive fort on the steep bank of a tributary of the Beas was influenced by considerations of military defence. This however does not appear to have hindered the appropriation of the economic resources of the kingdom by the raja. This may be because the fort (called Kangra) and the town (called Nagarkot) lay on "the low ranges which run through the centre of the district", thus making it easier to reach out to the entire area. The Beas River, on the other hand, flowed through the southern part of the Kangra territory.[33] The principality, however,

---

[30] Vigne 1981: I, 62.
[31] Kanwar 1999: 86.
[32] Fraser 1982: 256–7.
[33] *Kangra DG* 1924: 493.

passed over to Mughal control in the early seventeenth century and the fort of Kangra became the headquarters of an administrative district of the Mughal empire. The district of Kangra was perhaps the only area of Himachal where a few settlements, other than the capital town, could possibly be classified as towns. Among these were the pilgrimage centres of Jwalamukhi and the trading town of Nadaun.

Further up, along both banks of the Beas, and at a height of 2400 feet above sea level, was situated the town of Mandi, the capital of a principality of the same name.[34] The town was situated at the confluence of the Suketi rivulet with the Beas. The earliest mention of the town is found in a temple inscription dated 1442 Saka era, i.e. 1520 CE. Prior to this the Mandi ruling family had controlled only Manglaur (in Kulu) as its stronghold and later made encroachments into Suket territory in order to control the Beas valley.[35] The word "*mandi*" signifies a trading station or a market and it appears that the town of Mandi served that very purpose, both for the other areas of the state as well as for the extensive web of commercial transactions.[36] Not surprisingly, therefore, a nineteenth-century European traveller was to observe that the town "bazaar is large, and well stocked, for so insignificant a place."[37] In accordance with practices that entwined religion and political control, Mandi was also where the most important temples of the state were located. Their political role came to the forefront during the festival of Sivaratri, when the authority of the raja as the representative of the state deity was ritually renewed.

The northern principality of Kulu controlled the upper reaches of the Beas valley. Its capital Sultanpur was situated at a height of 4000 feet above sea level on a "triangular spur of table land projecting from the foot of the mountains . . . towards the conflux of the Serbari [Sarwari] and the Byas [Beas]."[38] Like many of the other kingdoms, Kulu too had originated further up in the upper Beas valley. Its early rulers had – by subjugating the numerous *ranas* and *thakurs* –

[34] *Mandi SG* 1920: 21.
[35] Hutchison and Vogel 1982: II, 177–8.
[36] *Mandi SG* 1920: 44, 50–1, 54–5; C. Singh 1998.
[37] Vigne 1981: I, 80.
[38] Moorcroft 1970: 102.

expanded their control over a large part of the Beas valley. By the mid seventeenth century they commanded the area's economic resources and had made Sultanpur the capital of the kingdom. It was probably during the shifting of the capital to Sultanpur that Lord Raghunath also came to be established as the presiding deity of the state.[39] Rituals asserting the sovereignty of Lord Raghunath and the position of the raja as his representative (even embodiment) were annually performed during Dusshehra celebrations in the Dhalpur maidan. It was here too that seasonal fairs were held. One of the important trade routes linking the North Indian plains to Ladakh, Tibet, and Central Asia passed through Sultanpur and at least part of the town's importance was derived from this fact.[40]

On the banks of the Ravi, the northernmost major river of Himachal, was situated the town of Chamba (the capital of the principality of Chamba) at a height of 3000 feet above sea level. Like Sultanpur and Mandi, even Chamba occupied terraces between the junction of two rivers, the Saho and Ravi. The raja's palace dominated the town as it overlooked the bazaar, the impressive complex of temples, and a large maidan.[41] It was the only settlement in the state that could possibly be called a town.

It must, of course, be remembered that even as we speak of towns, the population involved was rather small. Though no information is available for the period prior to British rule, censuses conducted during the colonial period give us some idea. The town of Bilaspur had a population of 3192 in 1901, which marked a fall of 2 per cent as compared to 1891. Rampur underwent a period of decline in the early nineteenth century due to a decrease in trade. This fall in population probably continued at least till the census of 1901, for the population of the town in that year stood at only 1157.[42]

In the Beas valley, the twin towns of the Kangra fort (the old town) and the town near the Kangra temple had a population of 1745 and

[39] Hutchison and Vogel 1982: II, 458.
[40] C. Singh 1998: 185, 189.
[41] Vigne 1981: 152–3; *Chamba SG* 1910: 290–1.
[42] *Simla DG* 1904: 20.

1836 respectively in 1924–5.[43] These figures appear to imply a falling population in a town that was once the centre of a fairly large and powerful kingdom. The town of Mandi, too, seems to have undergone a decline in the nineteenth century. In the early part of that century it was said to have 1000 houses; the number fell to 349 occupied and unoccupied houses in 1881.[44] Subsequently, however, the situation improved and the censuses of 1891, 1901, and 1911 all recorded an increase in the population of the state. Even the town of Mandi had a relatively large population of 7896 in 1911. However, we also learn that Mandi was the only town in the state and hardly any villages had more than 1000 residents.[45] Sultanpur, the northernmost town on the Beas, had only 200 houses in 1846, although it was believed to have had 400 houses in 1839. In 1868 the number of houses rose again to 422, with a population of about 1100.[46] These were probably rough estimates because by 1917 the population of the town stood at a respectable 3000.[47] This was almost thrice as large as that of Rampur, which was the northernmost town on the Satlej.

Chamba, we have seen, was the only mountain town on the banks of the Ravi River, and it consistently retained its prime position in the Ravi valley. Vigne, who travelled to Chamba in 1835, estimated that the town had about 1000 houses and that the population stood at around "4000 to 5000".[48] His estimate may not have been very far off the mark, because in 1904 Chamba's population was approximately 6000 souls.[49]

Before we conclude this section, a few things need to be said. The old towns of Himachal were an integral part of their immediate political and economic surroundings – natural products, as it were, of the human response to the mountainous terrain in which they were placed. Resources generated by the local economy sustained

[43] *Kangra DG* 1926: 495.
[44] Kanwar 1999: 97.
[45] *Mandi SG* 1920: 77.
[46] Kanwar 1999: 97.
[47] *Kangra DG* 1918: II, 47.
[48] Vigne 1981: I, 152–3.
[49] *Chamba SG* 1910: 290.

them. Their polity revolved around king, caste, and kinship, and their socio-religious belief system supported a society that changed ever so slowly. The arrival of the British in the western Himalaya was to turn all this on its head.

The New Order: Hill Stations and Sanatoriums

A new order of things was created with the arrival of colonialism. In Europe, the transition from "pre-modern" to "modern" often meant a shift from "pre-industrial" to "industrial", but colonial India presented a picture of far greater complexity. The "variable of Westernisation" (as different from modernisation) appeared to add more overtly an external dimension to the "internal" logic of Indian history. This made it almost impossible to distinguish between social transformations occurring as integral processes of indigenous developments and those that were brought in by colonialism. Much of what evolved during British rule was therefore the interweaving of the Western/ modern with the Indian and so-called "traditional". It has been argued that the most significant influence in this relationship was that of culture, a variable that cast a shadow over almost everything. King has emphasised the influence of three "variables" in the relationship between the colony and the metropolis: namely, "culture, technology and the power structure of colonialism."[50] An interesting consequence of this intermixing was the appearance of a peculiarly colonial phenomenon, the hill station. This development too, says King, was marked by the impact of cultural considerations. It is culture that more completely explains why the British preferred to create new towns in the hills, how they planned these settlements, and what "ethnomedical theories" went into influencing their decisions.

To begin with, however, a haphazard collection of hazy ideas and calculations underlay the establishment of hill stations in Himachal. The strategic benefit of setting up military establishments in the hills had an immediate appeal. Both Panjab and the western Himalaya

[50] King 1989: 2, 7.

could be effectively controlled by this means, and a close eye kept on the developments in trans-Himalayan areas of Central Asia and Tibet. It was during the 1820s and the 1830s that the first stations were founded in Himachal and some other parts of India.[51] It is estimated that between 1815 and 1947 about eighty hill stations were established.[52]

With an increased British involvement in the governance of a large colony, the services of an ever-increasing number of European/British officials were required. The possible effects of prolonged residence in tropical India of a person of European origin now became a matter of medical and administrative concern. A much larger number of hill stations were established in the 1840s and 1850s. This was probably because the temperate climate of the hills was seen as more suited to people of European origin, a view reinforced by ethnomedical theories that became popular in the 1860s, and which came to be reflected even in the observations of casual visitors to the hills.[53] Andrew Wilson, who travelled to Simla and through its surrounding areas in the 1880s, approved of the practice of the British Indian government shifting up to Simla in summer. He felt it was "of great importance that its members should not be unnecessarily exposed to the depressing and destroying influence of the Indian hot season and rains."[54] In fact, it was thought that "tropical degradation" posed a major threat and prevailing wisdom "precluded the possibility of European settler populations surviving over several generations *as* Europeans."[55] If ever there was a possibility of Europeans settling permanently in India, it could only be in the hills. It was even suggested that a Scottish and Irish peasantry could be settled in the Himalaya. In fact, after 1857, there was a marked increase in European settlements in the highlands.[56]

More specifically, the hills were originally seen as being relatively free from disease. The elevated location of many of the hill stations

[51] Kennedy 1996: 13.
[52] King 1976: 157.
[53] Ibid.: 108.
[54] Wilson 1979: 41.
[55] Kennedy 1996: 33.
[56] Ibid.: 151, 154.

placed them beyond the reach of malaria. For primarily medical reasons, therefore, it was recommended that "one-third of the establishment of European troops in India should preferably be permanently located in the hills." It is certainly true that the mortality rate of European soldiers in the British Indian army was much higher than that of its Indian soldiers. King also argues that "without the existence in India of a European military force the modern hill station would not have developed."[57] Andrew Wilson even went so far as to argue that "the British soldier improves greatly in strength and appearance on these heights"![58] With the outbreak of cholera and typhoid in some of the stations, however, it became abundantly obvious that they were not insulated from all diseases. Their importance as suitable "places of convalescence" then became the rationale for their existence rather than as settlements devoid of any disease whatsoever.[59] An entire population with a distinctly alien culture seems to have come up in the hill towns overlooking the North Indian plains. As Wilson travelled up to Simla, he first passed through Kasauli, "a depot for the convalescents of European regiments". Thereafter, he went past Sanawar, an "Asylum for boys and girls of European or mixed parentage", and two "sanitariums" (Dagshai and Sabathu) that were also "military depots" for British soldiers.[60] By the late nineteenth century the numerous hill stations that dotted the hilltops had become a dominant feature of the area.

Chief among these towns was Simla, an uninhabited spot on a forested ridge, when in 1817 it first caught the fancy of the Gerard brothers who were surveying the Satlej valley. In 1822 Lt Kennedy (Assistant Political Agent for the Panjab Hill States) built the first permanent house.[61] Because of its location at a height of 7500 feet above sea level, individual Europeans recovering from illness had, by 1824, begun building houses with the permission of the local rulers to whom the territory belonged.[62] Lord Amherst was the first gover-

[57] King 1976: 109, 158.
[58] Wilson 1979: 33.
[59] Kennedy 1996: 29.
[60] Wilson 1979: 33.
[61] *Simla DG* 1908: 120.
[62] Ibid.: 14.

nor general of India to visit Simla in 1827, and the very next year Lord Combermere, the commander-in-chief of the army, arrived with his entire senior staff. A house was later built in 1829 for Governor General William Bentinck, though he was able to come up to Simla for the first time only in 1832.[63] Because of its increasing attraction as an escape from the discomfort of the plains during the summer and monsoon months, the British government entered into negotiations with the rajas of Patiala and Keonthal in whose territory Simla and its surrounding areas fell. Thereafter, sixteen villages were acquired for establishing a settlement primarily for Europeans.[64] As early as 1831, about sixty houses for Europeans existed in the town,[65] and by the 1860s approximately three hundred European cottages had been built.[66] By 1901 Simla's population was counted at 13,960.[67] This, of course, was during summer. The 1880s witnessed the construction of huge and impressive buildings such as the Viceregal Lodge, the Army Headquarters, the Telegraph Office, and numerous others for housing important departments of the imperial government that moved up in summer. Equally impressive buildings were erected for local government – a hospital, court house, town hall, police stations, etc. Indeed, it appeared as if "a massive shift in the geography of power" had taken place "from the plains to the hills".[68] Within a short span of half a century a city had been created on a mountain, a city from where Britain's Indian empire was ruled.

Simla was the prime but not the only town in Himachal to be linked directly with the imperial system. It was in fact too large and too important to stand alone. Several other smaller stations arose simultaneously and appeared to arrange themselves in a kind of hierarchy. This was a stratification that Dane Kennedy says reflected the nature of the "British colonial community at large".[69] As early as 1815

[63] Ibid.: 120.
[64] Ibid.: 14.
[65] Wilson 1979: 61.
[66] Kennedy 1996: 163.
[67] *Simla DG* 1908: 20.
[68] Kennedy 1996: 163, 173.
[69] Ibid.: 11.

the British had decided to retain certain tracts of territory in the hills that they felt were important for military purposes. On a hilltop (at a height of 4500 feet) in one such tract was set up the military station of Sabathu. Much of this territory was taken over as compensation for the services rendered by the British for restoring the rule of the local hill rulers after expelling the Nepalese occupation forces. For some of the additional territory acquired in Sabathu a compensation of only Rs 80 per annum was paid to the *rana* of Kuthar. Till 1842 it was garrisoned by a battalion of Gorkha soldiers who had enlisted with the British after their defeat in the Gorkha war. Subsequently a British infantry regiment was stationed there. Sabathu now began to take on the appearance of a European settlement with houses for British officers, "a small Roman Catholic Church and a school-house used as a Protestant Church." By 1901 the town, with a population of 2177, was as large as some of the older towns of the western Himalaya.[70] Of course, most of it was made up of soldiers.

A similar area consisting of five villages was obtained without compensation in 1847 from the maharaja of Patiala. The military cantonment of Dagshai that was established on a hill overlooking the tract here stood at a height of 6087 feet above sea level. It was garrisoned by a British Infantry regiment and its population had by 1901 increased to 2159. Sixteen years later (1863–4) more land was acquired from the *raja* of Baghat on the road leading towards Simla. Though this was initially used as a rifle range for the Sabathu battalion, it had by the early years of the twentieth century come to be used "as the summer head-quarters of a British Infantry Regiment".[71]

Immediately adjoining Simla was the military station of Jutogh, used as a summer cantonment by "two batteries of British Mountain Artillery and two companies of British Infantry."[72] After the revolt of 1857 and subsequent to a survey in 1859–60 by the military department, military stations in the mountains of north-west India seemed to gain importance. In the north-west of Himachal, the cantonment

[70] *Simla DG* 1908: 15, 20, 118.
[71] Ibid.: 119.
[72] Ibid.: 117.

of Dalhousie was established in 1860. By "the 1870s, a sixth of the British forces in India were located in hill cantonments, and two decades later the proportion was nearer a quarter."[73]

An important feature of the Himalayan hill stations was that they came up on ridges that were uninhabited, or almost so. This does not mean that these were originally unutilised spaces. Village gods (temples), sacred groves, pastures, and forests belonging in common to villages situated further down the mountainside often occupied such areas.[74] Nevertheless, the setting up of new towns in apparently unoccupied territory did seem to give their creators ostensibly "clean" beginnings free from "Indian" influence. It was here (insulated from the older cities and away from their homeland) that a British population appears to have engaged in the endeavour to devise a community that was demographically similar to the one at home – including a larger number of British women and children – than were to be found in other Indian towns.

Towards this end, and in order to conform to the social norms that existed then in Britain, were established institutions such as the church, the club, the library, the theatre, the racecourse, and occasionally the museum.[75] All these institutions represented everything that was middle class in metropolitan society because, obviously, there was no European working class in India. The nearest thing to a European working-class enclave was the cantonment that housed the lower-class British soldiery, situated at a distance from the "civil stations". King argues that there existed a "colonial third culture" that was neither completely British nor completely Indian, but basically of the British in India. His contention is that "the urban universe of the colonial third culture consisted of three basic parts, the *cantonment*, the *civil station* . . . and the city (*native city* or *native quarter*)."[76] But it was sought to segregate even the cantonments of the hills from the local native population. To use the words of a Royal Commission, the isolation of cantonments was viewed as an advantage for keeping

[73] Kennedy 1996: 156, 158.
[74] C. Singh 1998: 101–11.
[75] King 1989: 11.
[76] Ibid.: 79, 80.

at bay "two at least of the greatest banes of cantonment life on the plains, the poisonous spirituous liquor of the bazaars and the venereal infection . . . a few sentries ought to be sufficient to guard a well-chosen hill station from these great evils."[77]

Hill stations came at a cost, and adjoining areas and the hill peasantry paid a part of this. Timber from the forests around Simla was extracted on a large scale for the construction of buildings not only in Simla but also in Dagshai and Sabathu.[78] An estimated 250,000 cubic feet of timber per year was used in Simla during the large-scale construction of the 1880s; and till the end of the nineteenth century 85,000 cubic feet was annually consumed.[79] The hill principality of Keonthal touching Simla had by the end of the nineteenth century "practically no old deodar, all having been sold to Simla traders."[80] Even after the towns had come into existence the continued requirement of enormous amounts of fuel wood, especially in large stations like Simla, put unprecedented pressure on the forest. Water was a particularly scarce commodity, more so for settlements perched upon hilltops. Once again, resources were harnessed at the cost of the neighbouring villages. Springs and rivulets were taken over and water pumped up to the station. In order to supply water to Simla, the land of some villages situated on a higher connected ridge to the north-east was acquired (and the villagers moved out) for creating a "water catchment area". Water was collected from numerous small springs in this area and channelled down to the town.

It was not only on natural resources that enormous demands were made. An army of Indian labourers performed the menial jobs and also the exacting physical toil (as *chaprasis*, sweepers, building- and road-construction workers, porters, rickshaw pullers, to mention a few) in order to support a much smaller European population. An estimate made in the 1880s suggested that there were in Simla for "about fifteen hundred Europeans . . . as many thousand natives."[81]

[77] Ibid.: 117.
[78] Kanwar 1999: 122.
[79] Kennedy 1996: 53.
[80] *SHSG* 1911, Keonthal: 9.
[81] Wilson 1979: 62.

Bringing Lord Auckland up to Simla took 1500 coolies. Ten years later Lord Dalhousie used the services of 9000 labourers.[82] Kanwar has even suggested that by the late nineteenth century there were usually 4000 Europeans in Simla who required the services of 30,000 Indians.[83]

A system of forced labour (*begar*) for various purposes had existed in the Himalayan states for a very long time. The raja was entitled to demand such labour from his subjects for both official and personal use, while state functionaries could call for labourers (*begaris*) only during the course of official work. The custom of *begar* was certainly exacting, but even for the common peasant this normally entailed only a few days of work in a year and did not require him to be away from his fields for very long.[84] With the continuous arrival of British officials from the early eighteenth century onwards, the demand for *begar* became oppressive. The subsequent creation of hill stations and the annual retreat to the mountains of the viceroy, the commander-in-chief and an army of secretaries made *begar* unbearable. Even after forced labour was abolished, the continuing and enormous requirement for labour often entailed coercing peasants to leave their fields and work as porters for long periods of time.

The colonial government had created a network of hilltop towns. Such settlements had been unknown to the western Himalaya. Not only were these towns alien, they were also oppressive and unsustainable: in almost every sense they lay beyond the rationality of mountain society. The occupation of mountain ridges went against the cultural and religious sensibilities of hill folk, the strangeness of the European lifestyle to its social surroundings was all too obvious, and the economic and ecological pressure that the new ruling class exerted on the natural environment was unprecedented. No Himalayan town could have survived under such circumstances. But the hill stations flourished, not because they were sustained by the small and local socio-economic system of the mountains, but because they lavishly exploited the vast resources of the entire British Indian empire.

[82] Kennedy 1996: 177.
[83] Kanwar 1999: 109.
[84] Negi 1995.

Ironically, these hill towns were sustained by the resources of the dusty plains, the marshes, and the tropical forests of India – the very places from whose discomfort and inhabitants the British sought to escape. But escape was hardly possible. So many "natives" were needed to keep the sahibs in splendour and comfort that a tiny India replicated itself in and around each of these towns. The hill stations were therefore neither British nor Indian, nor indeed even Himalayan. They arose, in fact, from a fascinating time-specific combination of political expediency, ethnomedical theories, colonial ideology, and the nostalgia of an alien population living far away from home.

Bibliography

Abul Fazl. 1978. *Ain-i-Akbari*, tr. H.S. Jarrett, ed. Jadunath Sarkar, New Delhi: Oriental Books Reprint Corporation, reprint, 3 volumes.

———. 1979. *Akbarnama*, tr. H. Beveridge, New Delhi: Ess Ess Publications, reprint, 3 volumes.

Ahmed, Z. 1968. "New Light on the Tibet-Ladakh-Mughal War of 1679–84", *East and West*, 18 (3–4): 340–61, stable URL: http://www.jstor.org/stable/ 29755343.

Alan R., H. Baker, and Derek Gregory (eds). 1984. *Explorations in Historical Geography*, Cambridge: Cambridge University Press.

Allix, A. 1929. *L'Oisans au Moyen-Age, étude de géographie historique en haute montagne d'après des documents inédits suivie de la transcription des textes*, Paris, pp. 110, 145–53.

An Appeal for the Mountains: Mountain Agenda. 1992. Bern: Switzerland Mountain Agenda, Centre for Development and Environment, Institute of Geography, University of Bern.

Anderson, Benedict. 1991. *Imagined Communities*, London and New York: Verso.

Anderson, J.D. 1917. *Final Settlement Report of the Simla District, 1915–16*, Lahore.

Anderson, Malcolm. 1996. *Frontiers, Territory and State Formation in the Modern World*, Cambridge: Polity Press.

Applegate, Celia. 1999. "Europe of Regions: Reflections on the Historiography of Sub-National Places in Modern Times', *The American Historical Review*, vol. 104, no. 4 (October 1999), pp. 1157–82.

Asad, Talal. 1977. "Equality in Nomadic Social Systems? Notes Towards the Dissolution of an Anthropological Category", in Claude Lefebvre (ed.), *Pastoral Production and Society*, Cambridge: Cambridge University Press.

Asboe, W. 1937. "Agricultural Methods in Laoul, Western Tibet", *Man*, 37, May.

Atkinson, Edwin T. 1976. *Religion in the Himalayas*, New Delhi: Cosmo Publications (originally published as *The Himalayan Gazetteer*, vol. II, chs VIII, IX, and X).

Babur, Zahiruddin. 1979. *Baburnama*, tr. Annette Susannah Beveridge, New Delhi: Oriental Books Reprint Corporation, 2 volumes published together (first published 1922).

Bairoch, Paul. 1990. "The Impact of Crop Yields, Agricultural Productivity and Industrial Costs on Urban Growth between 1800–1910", in Ad van der Woude, Akira Hayami, and Jan de Vries (eds), *Urbanization in History: A Process of Dynamic Interaction*, Oxford: Clarendon Press.

Baker, Alan. 1984. "Reflections on the Relations of Historical Geography and the Annales School of History", in Alan R.H. Baker and Derek Gregory (eds), *Explorations in Historical Geography*, Cambridge: Cambridge University Press.

Baker, Alan R.H., and Derek Gregory (eds). 1984. *Explorations in Historical Geography*, Cambridge: Cambridge University Press.

Baker, D. 1991. "State Policy, the Market Economy and Tribal Decline: The Central Provinces, 1861–1920", in *Indian Economic and Social History Review*, vol. 28, no. 4.

Barnes, G.C. 1889. *Report of the Land Revenue Settlement of the Kangra District, Punjab* (report completed in 1850 and first published in 1855), reprint, Lahore: Civil and Military Gazette Press.

Bascom, William. 1984. "The Forms of Folklore: Prose Narratives", in Alan Dundes (ed.), *Sacred Narrative: Readings in the Theory of Myth*, Berkeley and Los Angeles: University of California Press.

Basu, Sajal. 1992. *Regional Movements, Politics of Language, Ethnicity-Identity*, Shimla: Indian Institute of Advanced Study and Delhi: Manohar Publications.

Bates, S.H., and D.G. Bates. 1974. "The Origins of Specialized Nomadic Pastoralism: A Systemic Model", *American Anthropology* 39 (2): 186–93.

Beals, Alan R. 1964. "Conflict and Interlocal Festivals in a South Indian Region", in Edward B. Harper (ed.), *Religion in South Asia*, Seattle: University of Washington Press, pp. 99–113.

Berkes, F., I. Davidson-Hunt, and K. Davidson-Hunt. 1998. "Diversity of Common Property Resource Use and Diversity of Social Interests in the Western Indian Himalaya", *Mountain Research and Development* 18 (1): 19–33.

Bernbaum, Edwin. 1990. *Sacred Mountains of the World*, San Francisco: Sierra Club Books.

———. 1997. "The Spiritual and Cultural Significance of Mountains", in B. Messerli and J.D. Ives (eds), *Mountains of the World: A Global Priority*, New York/London: The Parthenon Publishing Group.

Berreman, Gerald D. 1960. "Cultural Variability and Drift in the Himalayan Hills", *American Anthropologist*, New Series, vol. 62, no. 5 (October).

———. 1963. "Peoples and Cultures of the Himalayas", *Asian Survey*, vol. 3, no. 6 (June).

———. 1964. "Brahmans and Shamans in Pahari Religion", in Edward B. Harper (ed.), *Religion in South Asia*, Seattle: University of Washington Press.

———. 1987. "Himalayan Polyandry and the Domestic Cycle", in M.K. Raha and P.C. Coomar (eds), *Polyandry in India*, Delhi: Gian Publishing House.

Berti, Daniela. 2006. "Ritual Kingship, Divine Bureaucracy, and Electoral Politics in Kullu", *European Bulletin of Himalayan Research*, 29–30, Summer.

Bhattacharya, Neeladri. 1996. "Remaking Custom: The Discourse and Practice of Colonial Codification", in R. Champakalakshmi and S. Gopal (eds), *Tradition, Dissent and Ideology: Essays in Honour of Romila Thapar*, Delhi: Oxford University Press.

Bijalwan, Asharam. 2003. "Rawian Anchal ka Samagra Itihas", Ph.D. thesis submitted to Kumaon University, Nainital.

Black-Michaud, Jacob. 1986. *Sheep and Land: The Economies of Power in a Tribal Society*, Cambridge: Cambridge University Press, and Editions de la Maison des Sciences de L'Homme.

Bommes, Michael, and Patrick Wright. 1982. "'Charms of Residence': The Public and the Past", in Richard Johnson, *et al.* (eds), *Making Histories: Studies in History-writing and Politics*, Centre for Contemporary Cultural Studies, London: Hutchinson & Co.

Braudel, F. 1966. *La Méditerranée et le monde méditerranéen à l'époque de Philippe II*, Paris, vol. I.

———. 1974. *Capitalism and Material Life, 1400–1800*, tr. Miriam Kochan, London: Fontana/Collins.

———. 1978. *The Mediterranean and the Mediterranean World in the Age of Philip II*, tr. Sian Reynolds, London: Fontana/Collins, 2 volumes (first published in France in 1949).

———. 1989. *The Identity of France: History and Environment*, tr. Sian Reynolds, London: Fontana Press, vol. I.

Brower, B. 2000. "Sheep Grazing in National Forest Wilderness: A New Look at an Old Fight", *Mountain Research and Development*, 20 (2): 126–9.

Brown, C.W. 1987. "Ecology, Trade and Former Bhotia Identity", in M.K. Raha, *The Himalayan Heritage*, Delhi: Gian Publishing House.

Chadda, Maya. 1997. *Ethnicity, Security and Separation in India*, Delhi: Oxford University Press.

Chakrabarti, Kunal. 1992. "Anthropological Models of Cultural Interaction and the Study of Religious Process", *Studies in History*, vol. 8, no. 1, January–June, pp. 123–49.

Chakravarty-Kaul, M. 1998. "Transhumance and Customary Pastoral Rights in Himachal Pradesh: Claiming the High Pastures for Gaddis", *Mountain Research and Development* 18 (1), pp. 5–17.

Chamba SG: Chamba State Gazetteer (1904). 1910. Punjab States Gazetteer, vol. XXII, Punjab Government, by A. Samuel T. Weston, Lahore: The Civil and Military Gazette Press.

Champakalakshmi, R., and S. Gopal (eds). 1996. *Tradition, Dissent and Ideology. Essays in Honour of Romila Thapar*, Delhi: Oxford University Press.

Chandra, Ramesh. 1981. "Sex Roles Arrangement to Achieve Economic Security in North Western Himalaya", in Christopher von Furer-Haimendorf (ed.), *Asian Highland Societies: An Anthropological Perspective*, New Delhi.

———. 1987a. "Polyandry in the North-Western Himalaya: Some Changing Trends", in M.K. Raha and P.C. Coomar (eds), *Polyandry in India*, Delhi: Gian Publishing House.

———. 1987b. "Sex Roles Arrangement to Achieve Economic Security in North Western Himalaya", in M.K. Raha and P.C. Coomar (eds), *Polyandry in India*, Delhi: Gian Publishing House.

Chatur Bhuj. 1928. Report Tarmim Bandobast Tahsil Chini (Tahsil Chini Settlement Report), typescript, Hindi translation of the original Urdu by Daulat Ram Tegta, 1970.

Chauhan, Kuldeep. 2004. "Feud between Devotees Intensifies", *The Tribune*, Chandigarh, 25 October.

Chauhan, Surendra. 2000. "Dev Boindra", in Jagdish Sharma (ed.), *Himachal Pradesh ki Lokgathaien*, Shimla.

Clarke, Peter (ed.). 1976. *The Early Modern Town: A Reader*, London: Longman and the Open University Press.

Coldstream, J. 1913. *Final Report of the Third Revised Settlement 1910–1913 of the Kulu Sub-Division of the Kangra District*, Lahore: Punjab Government Press.

Comaroff, John, and Jean Comaroff. 1992. *Ethnology and Historical Imagination*, Boulder and Oxford.

Conzelmann, Elizabeth. 2006. "A Royal Ritual of Mandi State", *European Bulletin of Himalayan Research*, 29–30 Summer.

Crook, John H. 1987. "Polyandry in Ladakh", in M.K. Raha and P.C. Coomar (eds.), 1987b, *Polyandry in India*, Delhi: Gian Publishing House.

de Vries, Jan. 1984. *European Urbanization, 1500–1800*, Cambridge, Massachusetts: Harvard University Press.

der Woude, Ad van, Akira Hayami, and Jan de Vries (eds). 1990. *Urbanization in History. A Process of Dynamic Interaction*, Oxford: Clarendon Press.

Deuster, R.H. *Kanawar*. 1996. Shimla: Himachal Pradesh Academy of Arts, Culture and Language. First published 1939.

Diack, A.H. 1898. *Final Report of the Revised Settlement of the Kulu Sub-Division of the Kangra District*, Lahore: Civil and Military Gazette Press.

Dickens, Peter. 1996. *Reconstructing Nature: Alienation, Emancipation and the Division of Labour*, London: Routledge.

Drekmeier, Charles. 1962. *Kingship and Community in Early India*. Stanford: Stanford University Press.

Duby, G. 1984. "L'état de la vallée de Barcelonnette au moyen-âge", *Sabença de la Valeia*, Barcelonnette.

Dughlat, Mirza Muhammad Haidar. 1972. *Tarikh-i-Rashidi: A History of the Mughals of Central Asia*, tr. E. Denison Ross, ed. N. Elias, London.

Dundes, Alan (ed.). 1984. *Sacred Narratives: Readings in the Theory of Myth*, Berkeley and Los Angeles: University of California Press.

Emerson, H.W. 1914. Rohru Tahsil Settlement Report. Unpublished manuscript in Himachal Pradesh Government Secretariat Library, Shimla.

Ensminger, J., and A. Rutten. 1991. "The Political Economy of Changing Property Rights: Dismantling a Pastoral Commons", *American Ethnologist*, 18 (4), pp. 683–99.

Feldhaus, Anne. 2003. *Connected Places. Region, Pilgrimage and Geographical Imagination in India*, New York: Palgrave Macmillan.

Fisher, James F. 1985. "The Historical Development of Himalayan Anthropology", *Mountain Research and Development*, vol. 5, no. 1, February.

———. 1987. *Trans-Himalayan Traders: Economy, Society and Culture in Northwest Nepal*, Delhi: Motilal Banarsidass.

Fontaine, L. 1996. *History of Pedlars in Europe*, tr. Vicki Whittaker, Durham, N.C.: Duke University Press.

———. 1998. "Données implicites dans la construction des modèles migratoires alpins à l'époque moderne", *Histoire des Alpes*, no. 3, pp. 25–35.

———. 2003. *Pouvoir, identités et migrations dans les hautes vallées des Alpes occidentales (XVIIe–XVIIIe siècle)*, Grenoble.

———. 2005. "Montagnes et migrations de travail (XVe–XXe siècles). Un essai de comparaison globale", in *Revue d'histoire moderne et contemporaine*, 52/2, pp. 26–48.

Fortier, J. 2001. "Sharing, Hoarding, and Theft: Exchange and Resistance in Forager–Farmer Relations", *Ethnology* 40 (3), pp. 193–211.

Foucault, Michel. 1980. *Power/ Knowledge. Selected Interviews and Other Writings, 1972–1977*, ed. and tr. Colin Gordon, New York: Pantheon Books.

Fox-Genovese, Elizabeth, and Eugene D. Genovese. 1989. "Social Classes and Class Struggle in Geographic Perspective", in Eugene D. Genovese and Leonard Hochberg (eds), *Geographic Perspectives in History*, Oxford: Basil Blackwell.

Frank, Andre Gunder. 1992. "The Centrality of Central Asia", *Studies in History*, vol. 8, no. 1, p. 93.

Fraser, James Ballie. 1982. *The Himala Mountains*, Delhi: Neeraj Publishing House. First published 1820.

Furer-Haimendorf, Christoph von. 1988. *Himalayan Traders: Life in Highland Nepal*, New Delhi: Times Books International. First published 1975.

——— (ed.). 1981. *Asian Highland Societies: An Anthropological Perspective*, New Delhi: Sterling Publishers.

Galaty, J.G., and D.L. Johnson. 1990. "Introduction: Pastoral Systems in Global Perspective", in J.G. Galaty and D.L. Johnson (eds), *The World of Pastoralism: Herding Systems in Comparative Perspective*, New York: The Guilford Press, pp. 1–31.

Garrett, H.L.O. (tr. & ed.). 1971. *Punjab a Hundred Years Ago; As Described by V. Jacquemont (1831) and A. Soltykoff (1842)*, Patiala: Department of Languages, Government of Punjab.

Gellner, Ernest. 1983. "The Tribal Society and Its Enemies", in Richard Tapper (ed.), *The Conflict of Tribe and State in Iran and Afghanistan*, London: Croom Helm.

Genovese, Eugene D., and Leonard Hochberg (eds). 1989. *Geographic Perspectives in History*, Oxford: Basil Blackwell.

Gerard, Alexander. 1993. *Account of Koonawar in the Himalaya*, ed. George Lloyd, New Delhi: Indus Publishing Co. First published 1841.

Gerard, J.G. 1824. "Letter of Dr J.G. Gerard, Assistant Surgeon, 1st Nusseeree Battalion, to Captain C.P. Kennedy, Assistant Deputy Superintendent, Soobathoo, dated 20 November 1824", in *Punjab Government Records*, Lahore: Punjab Government Press, 1911, 8 vols, 10 parts: vol. I, *Delhi Residency and Agency Records, 1807–1857*.

Ghosh, T.K. 1987. "Persistence of Lahaul Polyandry and Decline", in M.K. Raha and P.C. Coomar (eds), *Polyandry in India*, Delhi: Gian Publishing House.

Giersch, C. Patterson. 2010. "Across Zomia with Merchants, Monks and Musk: Process Geographies, Trade Networks, and the Inner-East-Southeast Asian Borderlands", *Journal of Global History*, vol. 5.

Glatzer, B., and M.J. Casimir. 1983. "Herds and Households among Pashtun Pastoral Nomads: Limits of Growth", *Ethnology* 22 (4), pp. 307–25.

Godelier, Maurice. 1978. *Perspectives in Marxist Anthropology*, tr. Robert Brain, Cambridge: Cambridge University Press.

———. 1986. *The Mental and the Material: Thought, Economy and Society*, tr. Martin Thorn, London: Verso.

Goldstein, Melvyn C. 1987. "Pahari and Tibetan Polyandry Revisited", in M.K. Raha and P.C. Coomar (eds), *Polyandry in India*, Delhi: Gian Publishing House.

Gonda, J. 1976. *Visnuism and Sivaism: A Comparison*. New Delhi: Munshiram Manoharlal. First published 1970.

Goswamy, Karuna, 2006. "Narsingh/ Narsingh Bir and Kulu: A Preliminary Inquiry into Cultural Processes", unpublished paper presented at the Fellows' Seminar, Indian Institute of Advanced Study, Shimla.

———. 2007. "Some Thoughts on Kulu: The Nature and Formation of a State", unpublished paper presented at the Fellows' Seminar, Indian Institute of Advanced Study, Shimla.

Grimm, Jacob. 1883. *Teutonic Mythology*, ed. and tr. James Steven Stallybrass, London: George Bell and Sons.

Guha, J.P. (ed.). 1979. *The Voyages of Thevenot and Careri*, published as vol. II of *India in the Seventeenth Century*, New Delhi: Associated Publishing House.

Guha, Ramachandra. 1989. *The Unquiet Woods: Ecological Change and Peasant Resistance in the Himalaya*, Delhi: Oxford University Press.

Guha, Sumit. 1999. *Environment and Ethnicity in India, 1200–1991*, Cambridge: Cambridge University Press.

Guillet, David. 1983a. "Towards a Cultural Ecology of Mountains: The Central Andes and the Himalayas Compared", *Current Anthropology*, vol. 24, no. 5, December, pp. 561–7.

———. 1983b. "Reply" to comments by Ricardo A. Godoy, Christian E. Guksch, Jiro Kawakita, Thomas F. Love, Max Matter, and Benjamin S. Orlove in *Current Anthropology*, vol. 24, no. 5, December.

Gutzlaff, Ch. 1850. "Tibet and Sefan", *Journal of the Royal Geographical Society of London*, 20: 191–227 (see p. 226), stable URL: http://www.jstor.org/stable/179803.

Habib, Irfan. 1963. *The Agrarian System of Mughal India, 1556–1707*, Bombay: Asia Publishing House.

Hamilton, A.P.F. 1932. *Revised Working Plan for the Kanawar Forests (Sutlej Valley) of the Upper Bashahr Division*, Lahore.

Hann, C.M. 1993. "From Production to Property: Decollectivization and the Family-Land Relationship in Contemporary Hungary", *MAN*, 28 (2), June.

Harcourt, A.F.P. 1870–1. "On the Himalayan Valleys: Kooloo, Lahoul and Spiti", *Proceedings of the Royal Geographical Society of London*, 15 (5), pp. 336–43.

———. 1972. *Himalayan Districts of Kooloo, Lahoul and Spiti*, Report completed in 1870. Reprint, Delhi.

Harper, Edward B. (ed.). 1964. *Religion in South Asia*, Seattle: University of Washington Press.

Hartman, Mary S. 2004. *The Household and the Making of History: A Subversive View of the Western Past*, Cambridge: Cambridge University Press.

Heesterman, J.C. 1998. "The Conundrum of the King's Authority", in J.F. Richards (ed.), *Kingship and Authority in South Asia*, Delhi: Oxford University Press.

Herzfeld, Michael. 1990. "Pride and Perjury: Time and the Oath in the Mountain Villages of Crete", *MAN* (n.s.), vol. 25, no. 2, June.

Higham, John. 1994. "The Future of American History", *Journal of American History*, vol. 80 (March), pp. 1289–1309.

Hindustan Times, Chandigarh edition. (A daily newspaper. Reports published in the Chandigarh edition have been used. The dates of the specific reports used are mentioned in the main text.)

Histories des Alpes. 2008. Special Issue: "Andes-Himalayas-Alpes", no. 8, Zurich: Chronos Verlag.

Hobsbawm, E.J. 1991. *Nations and Nationalism since 1870: Programme, Myth, Reality*, Cambridge: Cambridge University Press (Canto Edition).
Hoekveld, Gerard A., and Gerda Hoekveld-Meijer. 1995. "The Region as Cloister: The Relation Between Society and Region Reconsidered", *Geographfiska Annaler Series B, Human Geography*, vol. 77, no. 3 (1995), pp. 159–76.
Hohenberg, Paul M., and Lynn Hollen Lees. 1985. *The Making of Urban Europe, 1000–1950*. Cambridge/London: Harvard University Press.
Holland, Stuart. 1976. *The Regional Problem*, London: Macmillan Press.
Humphrey, C. 1985. "Barter and Economic Disintegration", *Man*, New Series 20(1), pp. 48–72.
Hutchison, J., and J. Ph. Vogel. 1982. *History of the Panjab Hill States*, Shimla: Department of Languages and Culture, Himachal Pradesh, 2 vols. First published 1933.
Ibbetson, Denzil. 1970. *Panjab Castes*, Patiala: Department of Languages, Punjab Government. First published 1883.
Inden, Ronald B. 2000. *Imagining India*, London: C. Hurst & Co. (Publishers) Ltd.
Izzatullah, M. 1843. Travels beyond the Himalaya, *Journal of the Royal Asiatic Society of Great Britain and Ireland*, 7 (2), pp. 283–342, stable URL: http:// www: jstor.org/stable/ 25207596.
Jahangir, Nuruddin. 1978. *Tuzuk-i-Jahangiri*, tr. Alexander Rogers, ed. H. Beveridge, New Delhi: Munshiram Manoharlal, reprint, 2 vols.
Johnson, Richard, Gregor McLennon, Bill Schwarz, and David Sutton. 1982. *Making Histories: Studies in History-writing and Politics*, London: Centre for Contemporary Cultural Studies, Hutchinson & Co.
Jones, Emrys. 1969. *Towns and Cities*, London: Oxford University Press.
Joshi, Jaishree. n.d. "A Historical Study of Jubbal During the 19th Century", unpublished M.Phil. dissertation, Himachal Pradesh University, Shimla.
Joshi, L.D. 1929. *The Khasa Family Law in the Himalayan Districts of the United Provinces*, Allahabad: Government Press.
Journal of Global History, 2010. 5. London School of Economics.
Kangra DG: Gazetteer of the Kangra District: Part II to IV: Kulu and Saraj, Lahaul and Spiti (1897). 1899. Compiled by A.H. Diack, Lahore: Civil and Military Press.
Kangra DG: Kangra District Gazetteer (Parts: II—Kulu and Saraj; III—Lahul; IV—Spiti, 1917). 1918. Punjab District Gazetteers, vol. XXX A, Lahore: Superintendent, Government Printing, Punjab.

Kangra DG: Kangra District Gazetteer (1924–25). 1926. Punjab District Gazetteers, vol. VII, part A, Lahore: Superintendent, Government Printing, Punjab.

Kanwar, Pamela. 1999. *Essays on Urban Patterns in Nineteenth Century Himachal Pradesh*, Shimla: Indian Institute of Advanced Study.

Kapadia, K.M. 1959. *Marriage and Family in India*, Bombay: Oxford University Press.

Karan, Pradyumna P., and Cotton Mather. 1976. "Art and Geography: Patterns in the Himalaya", *Annals of the Association of American Geographers*, vol. 66, no. 4, December.

Kashyap, P.C. 2000. *Living Pre-Rigvedic and Early Traditions of Himalayas*, Delhi: Pratibha Prakashan, pp. 120–1.

Kasturi, Malavika. 2002. *Embattled Identities: Rajput Lineages and the Colonial State in Nineteenth Century North India*, New Delhi: Oxford University Press.

Kennedy, Dane. 1996. *Magic Mountains: Hill Stations and the British Raj*, Delhi: Oxford University Press.

Keonthal SR. 1914. Abbreviation for Keonthal Revenue Settlement Report, Simla District, 1901, mimeograph version in English, Panjab Hill States Agency Records, basta 1, no. 15, H.P. State Archives.

Khoury, Philip S., and Joseph Kostiner (eds). 1991. *Tribes and State Formation in the Middle East*, London: I.B. Tauris & Co.

King, A.D. 1976. *Colonial Urban Development: Culture, Social Power and Environment*, London: Routledge & Kegan Paul.

———. 1989. "Colonialism and the Development of the Modern Asian City: Some Theoretical Considerations", in K. Ballhatchet and J. Harrison (eds), *The City in South Asia: Pre-Modern and Modern*, London: Curzon Press.

Kirk, G.S. 1984. "On Defining Myths", in Alan Dundes (ed.), *Sacred Narratives: Readings in the Theory of Myth*, Berkeley and Los Angeles: University of California Press.

Klass, Morton. 1995. *Ordered Universes: Approaches to the Anthropology of Religion*, Boulder & Oxford: Westview Press.

Knight, David B. 1982. "Identity and Territory: Geographical Perspectives on Nationalism and Regionalism", *Annals of the Association of American Geographers*, vol. 72, no. 4 (December), pp. 514–31.

Kobayashi, Audrey. 1989. "A Critique of Dialectical Landscape", in Audrey Kobayashi and Suzanne Mackenzie (eds), *Remaking Human Geography*, Boston: Unwin Hyman.

Lefebvre, Claude. 1979. "Introduction: The Specificity of Nomadic Pastoral Societies", in *Pastoral Production and Society*, Cambridge: Cambridge University Press.

——— (ed.). 1977. *Pastoral Production and Society*, Cambridge: Cambridge University Press.

Lefebvre, Henri. 1991. *The Production of Space*, tr. Donald Nicholson-Smith, Oxford, UK/Cambridge, USA: Blackwell.

———. 1996a. "The Specificity of the City", in Henri Lefebvre, *Writing on Cities*, selected, translated and introduced by Eleonore Kofman and Elizabeth Lebas, Oxford: Blackwell Publishers.

———. 1996b. "Around the Critical Point", in Henri Lefebvre, *Writings on Cities*, selected, translated, and introduced by Eleonore Kofman and Elizabeth Lebas, Oxford: Blackwell Publishers.

Lévi-Strauss, Claude. 1978. *Structural Anthropology*, tr. Monique Layton, Harmondsworth: Penguin/Peregrine, 2 vols.

———. 1996. "Introduction", in A.C. Burguiere, Klapisch Zuber, M. Segalan, and F. Zonabend (eds), *A History of the Family: Vol. I, Distant Worlds, Ancient Worlds*, Cambridge: Polity Press.

Levine, Nancy E. 1988. *Dynamics of Polyandry: Kinship, Domesticity, and Population on the Tibetan Border*, Chicago: University of Chicago Press.

Lewis, Bernard. 1975. *History Remembered, Recovered and Invented*, Princeton: Princeton University Press.

Lloyd, George (ed.). 1840. *Narrative of a Journey from Caunpoor to Boorendo Pass in the Himalaya Mountains by Major William Lloyd and Captian Alexander Gerard's Account of an Attempt to Penetrate by Bekhur to Garoo and the Lake Mansarowara, With a Letter from the Late J.G. Gerard Detailing a Visit to the Shatool and Boorendo Passes*, London: J. Madden & Co., 2 vols.

Lovell, Nadia (ed.). 1998a. *Locality and Belonging*. London: Routledge.

———. 1998b. "Wild Gods, Containing Wombs and Moving Pots: Emplacement and Transience in Watchi Belonging", in Nadia Lovell (ed.), *Locality and Belonging*, London: Routledge, pp. 53–77.

Luchesi, Brigitte. 2006. "Fighting Enemies and Protecting Territory: Deities as Local Rulers in Kullu, Himachal Pradesh", *European Bulletin of Himalayan Research*, 29–30 Summer, pp. 62–81.

Ludden, David. 1989. *Peasant History in South India*, Delhi: Oxford University Press.

Lyall, J.B. 1889. *Report of the Land Revenue Settlement of Kangra District, Punjab, 1865–72*, Lahore: Civil and Military Gazette Press. First

published 1874. Edition published in 1889, including the settlement report of G.C. Barnes, has been used.
Majumdar, D.N. 1962. *Himalayan Polyandry: Structure, Functioning and Culture Change—A Field Study of Jaunsar-Bawar*, Bombay: Asia Publishing House.
Mandelbaum, David G. 1964. "Introduction: Process and Structure in South Asian Religion", in Edward B. Harper (ed.), *Religion in South Asia*, Seattle: University of Washington Press.
———. 1982. "The Nilgiris as a Region", *Economic and Political Weekly*, vol. 17, no. 36 (September 1982), pp. 1459–67.
Mandi SG: Mandi State Gazetteer, 1904. 1908. Lahore: Punjab Government.
Mandi SG: Mandi State Gazetteer, 1920. 1920. Lahore: Punjab Government.
Marriott, McKim. 1955. "Little Communities in an Indigenous Civilization", in McKim Marriott (ed.), *Village India: Studies in the Little Community*, Chicago and London: University of Chicago Press, pp. 171–222.
Martin, John E. 1986. *Feudalism to Capitalism: Peasant and Landlord in English Agrarian Development*, Hampshire & London: Macmillan Press Ltd.
Mathieu, J. 2009. *History of the Alps 1500–1900: Environment, Development, and Society*, Morgantown WV.
Mathieu, Jon. 1999. "Alpine History, AD 1200–1900, Some Remarks on Methods and Models", in Philippe Della Casa (ed.), *Prehistoric Alpine Environment, Society, and Economy*, Papers of the International Colloquium PAESE 1997 in Zurich; also published in Rudolf Habelt (ed.), *Universitatsforschungen zur prahistorischen Archaologie*, Bonn, vol. 55.
———. 2000. "From Ecotypes to Sociotypes: Peasant Household and State Building in the Alps, Sixteenth–Nineteenth Centuries", *The History of the Family*, vol. 5, no. 1.
McDonald, James R. 1966. "The Region: Its Conception, Design and Limitations", *Annals of the Association of American Geographers*, vol. 56, no. 3 (September), pp. 516–28.
McKay, A.C. 1992. "The Establishment of the British Trade Agencies in Tibet: A Survey", *Journal of the Royal Asiatic Society*, Third Series, vol. 2, no. 3 (November), pp. 399–421, stable URL: http://www.jstor.org/stable/25182574.
Messerli, B., and J.D. Ives (eds). 1997. *Mountains of the World: A Global Priority*, New York/London: The Parthenon Publishing Group.

Michaud, Jean. 2010. "Editorial – Zomia and Beyond", *Journal of Global History*, vol. 5.

Mitchell, Alan. 1915. *Report on the Administration of Bashahr, 1914–15*, Shimla: Liddell's Printing Works.

Molnar, A. 1981. "Economic Strategies and Ecological Constraints", in C. von Furer-Haimendorf (ed.), *Asian Highland Societies: An Anthropological Perspective*, New Delhi: Sterling Publishers.

Montgomerie, T.G. 1870. "Report of the Trans-Himalayan Explorations Made During 1868", *Proceedings of the Royal Geographical Society of London*, 14 (3), pp. 207–14, stable URL: http://www.jstor.org/stable/1799050.

———. 2008. "Report of a Route Survey made by PUNDIT ___, from Nepal to Lhasa and thence through the Upper Valley of the Brahmaputra to its Source", in U. Bhatt and S. Pathak (eds), *Asia ki Peeth Par: Pandit Nain Singh Rawat: Jeewan, Anweshan Tatha Lekhan*, Nainital: Pahar, pp. 447–509, first published in the *Journal of the Royal Geographical Society*, London, 1877.

Moorcroft, W., and G. Trebeck. 1970. *Travels in the Himalayan Provinces of Hindustan and the Punjab; in Ladakh and Kashmir and Bokhara by Mr William Moorcroft and Mr George Trebeck from 1819 to 1825. Prepared for Press by H.H. Wilson*, Patiala: Department of Languages, Punjab Government, first published Calcutta: Asiatic Society, 1837.

Moore, Harry Estill. 1938. "Social Scientists Explore the Region", *Social Forces*, vol. 16, no. 4 (May 1938), pp. 463–74.

Mountain Research and Development. 2006. Special Issue: *Religion and Sacredness in Mountains: A Historical Perspective*, vol. 26, no. 4, November.

———. 1985. Vol. 5, no. 1, February, Special Issue: *Convergences and Differences in Mountain Economies and Societies: A Comparison of the Andes and Himalaya*, pp. 1–111.

Muir, Richard. 1997. *Political Geography: A New Introduction*, Hampshire: Macmillan Press.

Murphy, Alexander B. 1990. "Historical Justifications for Territorial Claims", *Annals of the Association of American Geographers*, vol. 80, no. 4 (December), pp. 531–48.

Murray W. 1824. From Lieutenant W. Murray, Deputy Superintendent, Shimla Hill States to C. Elliott, Agent to the Governor-General, Western Provinces, dated Camp Subathoo, 6 July 1824, in *Punjab Government Records*, Lahore: Punjab Government Press, 1911,

8 vols, 10 parts; vol. I, *Delhi Residency and Agency Records, 1807–1857*, pp. 251–99.

Nakshahbandi A.S. 1850. "Route from Kashmir via Ladakh to Yarkhand", tr. J. Dowson, *Journal of the Royal Asiatic Society of Great Britain and Ireland*, 12, pp. 372–85, based on Persian MS, dated 1846, stable URL http://www.jstor.org/stable/25228626.

Negi, Jaideep. 1995. *Begar and Beth System in Himachal Pradesh: A Study of Erstwhile Shimla Hill States*, New Delhi: Reliance Publishing House.

Nisbet, Robert A. 1962. *Community and Power*, New York: Galaxy Books.

Nizamuddin, Ahmad. 1990 & 1992. *Tabaqat-i-Akbari*, tr. Brajendranath De and Baini Prashad, Delhi: Low Price Editions, vol. I: 1990; vol. II: 1992.

Orlove, Benjamin S., and David W. Guillet. 1985. "Theoretical and Methodological Considerations on the Study of Mountain Peoples: Reflections on the Idea of Subsistence Type and the Role of History in Human Ecology", *Mountain Research and Development*, vol. 5, no. 1, February, Special Issue: *Convergences and Differences in Mountain Economies and Societies: A Comparison of the Andes and Himalaya*.

Ortiz, R. 2000. "From Incomplete Modernity to World Modernity", *Daedalus* 129 (Winter 1): *Multiple Modernities*: 249–60, stable URL: http://www. jstor.org/stable/20027922.

Parmar, B.S. 1959. *Report on the Grazing Problems and Policy of Himachal Pradesh*, Shimla: Forest Department, Himachal Pradesh.

Parmar, Y.S. 1975. *Polyandry in the Himalaya*, New Delhi: Vikas.

Peabody, Norbert. 1991a. "*Kota Mahajagat* or the Great Universe of Kota: Sovereignty and Territory in Eighteenth Century Rajasthan", *Contributions to Indian Sociology* (n.s.), vol. 25, no. 1, pp. 29–56.

———. 1991b. "In Whose Turban Does the Lord Reside?: The Objectification of Charisma and the Fetishism of Objects in the Hindu Kingdom of Kota", *Comparative Studies in Society and History*, vol. 33, no. 4, October, pp. 726–54.

Pelto, Pertti J., and Greta H. Pelto. 1975. "Intra-Cultural Diversity: Some Theoretical Issues", *American Ethnologist*, vol. 2, no. 1, February Issue: *Intra-Cultural Variation*.

Pemble, John. 1971. *The Invasion of Nepal: John Company at War*, Oxford: Oxford University Press.

Peter, Prince. 1963. *A Study of Polyandry*, The Hague: Mouton & Co.

Phillimore, P. 1981. "Transhumance and Environmental Damage: A Re-examination of Flock Population Trends among Pastoralists in Himachal Pradesh", Paper presented at 7th European Conference on Modern South Asian Studies, SOAS, London, quoted in M.J. Casimir and A. Rao, "Vertical Control in the Western Himalaya: Some Notes on the Pastoral Ecology of the Nomadic Bakrwal of Jammu and Kashmir", *Mountain Research and Development*, 1985, 5 (3), pp. 221–32.

Popular Memory Group. 1982. "Popular Memory: Theory, Politics, Method", in Richard Johnson, Gregor McLennon, Bill Schwarz, and David Sutton, *Making Histories: Studies in History-writing and Politics*, Centre for Contemporary Cultural Studies, London: Hutchinson.

Radhakrishna, M. 1989. "The Criminal Tribes Act in Madras Presidency: Implications for Itinerant Trading Communities", in *Indian Economic and Social History Review*, vol. 26, no. 3, 1989, pp. 269–95.

Raha, M.K. 1987. *The Himalayan Heritage*, Delhi: Gian Publishing House.

———, and P.C. Coomar. 1987. "Polyandry in a High Himalayan Society: Persistence and Change", in *Polyandry in India*, M.K. Raha and P.C. Coomar (eds.), Delhi: Gian Publishing House.

——— (eds). 1987. *Polyandry in India*, Delhi: Gian Publishing House.

Ramdayal, ed. and tr. 1973. "Dhar Deshu", in *Himachali Lok Gathaein*, Shimla: Public Relations Department, Himachal Pradesh, pp. 230–1.

Rangarajan, M. 1996. *Fencing the Forest*, New Delhi: Oxford University Press.

Rao, Aparna, and Michael J. Casimir (eds). 2003. *Nomadism in South Asia*, Delhi: Oxford University Press.

Rathore, Bhuvaneshwari. 2000. "Pandmayan", in Jagdish Sharma (ed.) *Himachal Pradesh ki Lok Gathaein*, Shimla: Himachal Art, Culture and Language Academy.

Ratnagar, Shireen. 1991. "Pastoralism as an Issue in Historical Research", *Studies in History*, 7, 2, n.s.

Redfield, Robert. 1989a. *Little Community and Peasant Society and Culture*, Midway Reprint, 1989, first published 1960, Chicago and London: University of Chicago Press.

———. 1989b. "Peasant Society and Culture", in Robert Redfield, *Little Community and Peasant Society and Culture*, Robert Redfield, Midway Reprint, 1989, first published, 1960, Chicago and London: University of Chicago Press.

"Report on Lapsed and Reserved Territory in the Protected Sikh and Hill States and on the Latter Generally, 1824". 1824. Being Chapter VIII of *Punjab Government Records*, Lahore: Punjab Government Press, 1911, 8 vols, 10 parts; vol. I, *Delhi Residency and Agency Records, 1807–1857*, pp. 229–324.

Rhoades, Robert E., and Stephen I. Thompson. 1975. "Adaptive Strategies in Alpine Environments: Beyond Ecological Particularism", *American Ethnologist*, vol. 2, no. 3, August.

Richards, J.F. (ed.). 1998. *Kingship and Authority in South Asia*, Delhi: Oxford University Press.

Ringrose, David. 1989a. "Towns, Transport and Crown: Geography and the Decline of Spain", in Eugene D. Genovese and Leonard Hochberg (eds), *Geographic Perspectives in History*, Oxford: Basil Blackwell.

———. 1989b. "Social Classes and Class Struggle in Geographic Perspective", in Eugene D. Genovese and Leonard Hochberg (eds), *Geographic Perspectives in History*, Oxford: Basil Blackwell.

Rizvi, J. 2001. *Trans-Himalayan Caravans: Merchant Princes and Peasant Traders in Ladakh*, New Delhi: Oxford University Press.

Rodgers, W.A. 1991. "Environmental Change and the Evolution of Pastoralism in South Asia", *Studies in History*, 7, 2, n.s.

Rose, H.A. 1970. *A Glossary of the Tribes and Castes of the Punjab and North-West Frontier Province (Based on the Census Report for the Punjab, 1883* [by Denzil Ibbetson] *and the Census Report for the Punjab, 1892* [by Edward Maclagan], Patiala: Department of Languages, Government of Punjab, 3 vols.

Rosser, Colin. 1969. "A 'Hermit' Village in Kulu", in M.N. Srinivas (ed.), *India's Villages*, Bombay: Asia Publishing House, first published 1955.

Roy Burman, B.K. 1993. "Tribal Population: Interface of Historical Ecology", in Mrinal Miri (ed.), *Continuity and Change in Tribal Society*, Shimla: Indian Institute of Advanced Study.

Rustomji, N.K., and Charles Ramble (ed.). 1990. *Himalayan Environment and Culture*, Shimla: Indian Institute of Advanced Study.

Saberwal, V.K. 1999. *Pastoral Politics: Shepherds, Bureaucrats, and Conservation in the Western Himalaya*, New Delhi: Oxford University Press.

Saksena, R.N. 1962. *Social Economy of a Polyandrous People*, Bombay: Asia Publishing House. First published 1954.

Salzman, P.C. 2002. "Pastoral Nomads: Some General Observations Based on Research in Iran", *Journal of Anthropological Research*, 58 (2), pp. 245–64.

Salzman, Philip S. 1967. "Political Organization Among Nomadic Peoples", *Proceedings of the American Philosophical Society*, vol. 111, no. 2, April.

Sanan, Deepak, and Dhanu Swadi. 1998. *Exploring Kinnaur and Spiti in the Trans-Himalaya*, New Delhi: Indus Publishing Co.

Sax, William. 2006. "Rituals of the Warrior *Khund*", *European Bulletin of Himalayan Research*, 29–30, Summer, pp. 120–34.

Schendel, Willem van. 2002. "Geographies of Knowing, Geographies of Ignorance: Jumping Scale in Southeast Asia", *Environment and Planning D: Society and Space*, 20, 6.

Scoones, I. 1999. "New Ecology and the Social Sciences: What Prospects for a Fruitful Engagement?", *Annual Review of Anthropology*, vol. 28.

Scott, James C. 2009. *The Art of Not Being Governed: An Anarchist History of Upland Southeast Asia*, New Haven & London: Yale University Press.

Shabab, Dilaram. 1999. *Kulu: Himalayan Abode of the Divine*, New Delhi: Indus Publishing Company.

Sharma, Ashwini. 2007. "Deities not to take sides, put BJP on backfoot", *Indian Express*, Chandigarh, 11 November 2007.

Sharma, B.R. 1990. "The Institution of the Village Gods in the Western Himalayas", in N.K. Rustomji and Charles Ramble (eds), *Himalayan Environment and Culture*, Shimla: Indian Institute of Advanced Study.

Sharma, Jagdish (ed.). 2000. *Himachal Pradesh ki Lokgathaien*, Shimla.

Sherring, Charles A. 1998. *Western Tibet and the British Borderland: The Sacred Country of Hindus and Buddhists with an Account of the Religion and Customs of its Peoples*, New Delhi: Asian Educational Services. First published London, 1906.

Shneiderman, Sara. 2010. "Are the Central Himalaya in Zomia? Some Scholarly and Political Considerations across Time and Space", *Journal of Global History*, vol. 5.

SHSG 1911. Abbreviation for *Punjab States Gazetteer: Vol. VIII—Simla Hill States 1910*, Lahore: Government of Punjab, The Civil and Military Press, Samuel T. Weston, 1911. The gazetteers of twenty hill states are included in this volume and each gazetteer has separate pagination.

Simla DG. 1889. Abbreviation for *Simla District Gazetteer, 1888–89*, Lahore: Punjab Government.

Simla DG. 1908. Abbreviation for *Simla District Gazetteer, 1904*. Lahore: Punjab Government.

Singh, B. 1952. *Final Report of the Fourth Revised Settlement of the Kulu Sub-Division of the Kangra District, 1945–52*, Chandigarh: Controller of Printing and Stationery, Punjab.

Singh, Bachittar. 2003. *Rewaj-i-Am (Kulu, Lahaul, Spiti Settlement, 1945–51)*, Shimla: Himachal Academy of Arts, Culture and Language.

Singh, C. 1988. "Conformity and Conflict: Tribes and the 'Agrarian System' of Mughal India", *Indian Economic and Social History Review*, vol. 25, no. 3, pp. 319–40.

———. 1991. *Region and Empire: Panjab in the Seventeenth Century*, Delhi: Oxford University Press.

———. 1995. "Forests, Pastoralists and Agrarian Society in Mughal India", in David Arnold and Ramachandra Guha (eds), *Nature, Culture, Imperialism: Essays on the Environmental History of South Asia*, Delhi: Oxford University Press, pp. 21–48.

———. 1997. "A Strategy of Interdependence: Gaddi, Peasant and State in Himachal", in Dev Nathan (ed.), *From Tribe to Caste*, Shimla: Indian Institute of Advanced Study, pp. 374–86.

———. 1998. *Natural Premises: Ecology and Peasant Life in the Western Himalaya, 1800–1950*, Shimla: Indian Institute of Advanced Study and New Delhi: Oxford University Press.

———. 2002. "The *Dhoom* in Himachal Pradesh: Community Consciousness, Peasant Resistance or Political Intrigue?", in Laxman S. Thakur (ed.), *Where Mortals and Mountain Gods Meet*, Shimla: Indian Institute of Advanced Study.

———. 2003. "Du fon des vallees aux sommets. Les villes precoloniales de l'Himachal et l'impact de la domination britannique sur la croissance urbaine", *Histoire des Alpes*, 2003/8, Special Issue: *Andes-Himalaya-Alpes*, Zurich: Chronos Verlag.

———. 2004. "Between Two Worlds: The Trader-Pastoralists of Kinnaur", in Rudolph Heredia and Shereen Ratnagar (eds), *Mobile and Marginalized Peoples: Perspectives from the Past*, New Delhi: Manohar, pp. 35–64.

———. 2006. "Long-Term Dynamics of Geography, Religion and Politics: A Case Study of Kumharsain in the Himachal Himalaya", *Mountain Research and Development*, vol. 26, no. 4, November, pp. 328–35.

———. 2008a. "The Place of Myth, Legend & Folklore in Western Himalayan History", in Surinder Singh and Ishwar Dayal Gaur (eds), *Popular Literature and Pre-Modern Societies in South Asia*, New Delhi: Dorling Kindersley.

———. 2008b. "Pastoralism and the Making of Colonial Modernity in Kulu, 1850–1952", in *Nomadic Peoples*, Special Issue: *Mountain Pastoralism and Modernity: Historical Approaches*, vol. 13, no. 2.

———. 2011a. *Recognizing Diversity: Society and Culture in the Himalaya*, Shimla/Delhi: Oxford University Press.

———. 2011b. "Introduction: Recognizing Himalayan Diversity", in

Recognizing Diversity: Society and Culture in the Himalaya, Delhi: Oxford University Press.

———. 2011c. "Polyandry and Customary Rights in the Western Himalaya", in Singh (ed.), *Recognizing Diversity: Society and Culture in the Himalaya*. New Delhi: Oxford University Press, 98–120.

———. 2013. "Constructing the State in the Western Himalaya", *Journal of Punjab Studies*, 20: 1 & 2, pp. 3–21.

Singh, Durga. 1901. Abbreviation for *Report Bandobast mai Iqrarnama-i-Riyaya wa Wajib-ul-Arz, Riyasat Keonthal, Zila Shimla* (Urdu version), *Keonthal State Settlement Report*, Shimla: Army Press.

Singh N. 2008. "Extracts from a Diary kept by Pundit____, during his Journey from Nepal to Lhasa, and from Lhasa through the Upper Valley of the Brahmaputra to the Source of that River near Mansarowar Lake", in U. Bhatt and S. Pathak (eds), *Asia ki Peeth Par: Pandit Nain Singh Rawat: Jeewan, Anweshan Tatha Lekhan*, Nainital: Pahar, 447–509. First published in the *Journal of the Royal Geographical Society*, London, 1877.

Singh, N.K. and Rajendra Joshi (eds). 1999. *Religion, Ritual and Royalty*. Jaipur: Rawat Publications.

Singh, Sarva Daman. 1988. *Polyandry in Ancient India*, reprint, Delhi: Motilal Banarasidass. First published 1978.

Sirmur SG: Gazetteer of Sirmur State (1904). 1907. Lahore: Punjab Government.

Sjoberg, Gideon. 1976. "The Nature of the Pre-industrial City", in Peter Clarke (ed.), *The Early Modern Town: A Reader*, London: Longman and the Open University Press.

Smadja, Joelle (ed). 2014. *Territorial Changes and Territorial Restructuring in the Himalaya*, New Delhi: Adroit Publishers.

Smith, Anthony D. 1987. *The Ethnic Origin of Nations*, New York: Basil Blackwell.

Smith, Carol. 1990. "Types of City-size Distributions: A Comparative Analysis", in Ad van der Woude, Akira Hayami, and Jan de Vries (eds), *Urbanization in History. A Process of Dynamic Interaction*, Oxford: Clarendon Press.

Soja, Edward W. 1990. *Postmodern Geographies: The Reassertion of Space in Critical Theory*, London/New York: Verso.

Srinivas, M.N. 1965. *Religion and Society among the Coorgs of South India*, Bombay: Asia Publishing House. First published 1952.

Sutherland, Peter. 2006. "T(r)opologies of Rule (*Raj*): Ritual Sovereignty and Theistic Subjection", *European Bulletin of Himalayan Studies*, 29–30, Summer.

Swinton, G. 1824. Secretary to Government in the Political Department, Fort William to C. Elliot, Agent to Governor General, Delhi, dated 27th August 1824, in *Punjab Government Records*, Lahore: Punjab Government Press, 1911, 8 vols, 10 parts: see vol. I: *Delhi Residency and Agency Records, 1807–1857*.

Talbot, Cynthia. 1995. "Inscribing the Other, Inscribing the Self: Hindu–Muslim Identities in Pre-Colonial India", *Comparative Studies in Society and History*, 37: 1: 1995, pp. 692–722.

Tambiah, Stanley J. (ed.). 1985. *Culture, Thought and Social Action: An Anthropological Perspective*, Cambridge, M.A.: Harvard University Press.

Tapper, Nancy. 1991. *Bartered Brides: Politics, Gender and Marriage in an Afghan Tribal Society*, Cambridge: Cambridge University Press.

Tapper, Richard. 1991. "Anthropologists, Historians and Tribesmen", in Philip S. Khoury and Joseph Kostiner (eds), *Tribes and State Formation in the Middle East*, London: I.B. Tauris & Co.

——— (ed.). 1983. *The Conflict of Tribe and State in Iran and Afghanistan*, London: Croom Helm.

Thakur, L.S. 1996. *Architectural Heritage of Himachal Pradesh*, Delhi: Munshiram Manoharlal.

Thapar, Romila. 2004. "The Scope and Significance of Regional History", in *Ancient Indian Social History: Some Interpretations*, New Delhi: Orient Longman Pvt. Ltd, pp. 317–32.

The State of the World's Mountains – A Global Report. 1992. London/New Jersey: Mountain Agenda, Zed Books.

The Tribune, Chandigarh. (News daily; dated references in the main text.)

Thevenot, Jean de. 1686. *The Travels of Monsieur de Thevenot into the Levant*, London: H. Clark.

Thomas, G. Powell. 1846. *Views of Simla*, London.

Thompson, E.P. 1977. "Folklore, Anthropology and Sociology", *Indian Historical Review*, vol. III, no. 2, January.

Trompf, G.W. 1989. "Macrohistory and Acculturation: Between Myth and History in Modern Melanesian Adjustments and Ancient Gnosticism", *Comparative Studies in Society and History*, 31:4.

van der Veer, P. 1998. "The Global History of Modernity", *Journal of the Economic and Social History of the Orient* 41 (3), pp. 285–94.

———. 1999. "All That Is Solid Melts into (Thin) Air", *Journal of the Economic and Social History of the Orient*, 42 (4), pp. 566–8.

van Schendel, W. 2002. *Vide supra* "Schendel".

Vansina, J. 1965. *Oral Tradition: A Study in Historical Methodology*, London: Routledge & Kegan Paul.

Verhulst, Adrian. 1999. *The Rise of Cities in North-West Europe*, Cambridge/Paris: Cambridge University Press and Editions de la Maison des Sciences de l'Homme.

Vigne, G.T. 1981. *Travels in Kashmir, Ladak, Iskardo, The Countries Adjoining the Mountain-Course of the Indus and the Himalaya, North of the Punjab*, 2 vols, reprint, New Delhi: Sagar Publications, New Delhi. First published in the mid nineteenth century.

Vitali, Roberto (ed.). 1996. *The Kingdom of Gu.ge Pu.hrang. According to mNga'.ris rgyal.rabs by Gu.ge mkhan.chen Ngag.dbang graps.pa* [sic], Dharamsala.

Vogel, J. Ph. 1911. *Antiquities of Chamba State*, part I, Calcutta: Superintendent Government Printing.

Vyathit, G.S. 1984. *Folklore of Himachal Pradesh*, New Delhi: National Book Trust.

Wahid, Siddiq (ed.). 2016. *Tibet's Relations with the Himalaya*, Delhi: Academic Foundation.

Warren, A. 1995. "Changing Understanding of African Pastoralism and the Nature of Environmental Paradigms", *Transactions of the Institute of British Geographers*, New Series, 20 (2), pp. 193–203.

Washbrook, D. 1997. "From Comparative Sociology to Global History: Britain and India in the Pre-History of Modernity", *Journal of the Economic and Social History of the Orient* 40 (4), pp. 410–43.

———. 1998. "The Global History of 'Modernity': A Response to Reply", *Journal of the Economic and Social History of the Orient* 41(3), pp. 295–311.

———. 1999. "... and Having Melted into Thin Air, Then Rains Down Again", *Journal of the Economic and Social History of the Orient*, 42 (4), pp. 569–74.

Whitehead, Henry. 1921. *The Village Gods of India*, Madras/Calcutta: Oxford University Press.

Wilson, A. 1979. *The Abode of Snow: Observations on a Tour from Chinese Tibet to the Indian Caucasus, through the Upper Valleys of the Himalaya*, Kathmandu: Ratna Pustak Bhandar. First published London: G.P. Putnam's Sons, 1886.

Wong R.B. 2003. "Between Nation and World: Braudelian Region in Asia", *Review* (26) 1, pp. 1–45, stable URL: http://www.jstor.org/stable/40241564.

Worster, Donald. 1994. *Under Western Skies: Nature and History in the American West*, New York/Oxford: Oxford University Press.

Wrigley, E.A. 1990. "Brake or Accelerator? Urban Growth and Population Growth before the Industrial Revolution", in Ad van der Woude, Akira Hayami, and Jan de Vries (eds), *Urbanization in History: A Process of Dynamic Interaction*, Oxford: Clarendon Press.

Zimmer, Oliver. 1998. "In Search of Natural Identity: Alpine Landscape and the Reconstruction of the Swiss Nation", *Comparative Studies in Society and History*, vol. 40, no. 4, October.

Index

aal (lineage) 37, 213
agriculture 21, 36, 109, 124, 125, 128, 129, 131, 132, 139, 140, 148, 162, 171–3, 183–6, 194, 196, 198, 200, 208fn68, 221, 254–5
agro-pastoralism 8, 9, 24, 25, 36, 38, 127–8, 130, 132, 136, 139–40, 167, 172–4, 184–6, 188, 194, 200, 207, 208fn68, 214–15, 230, 248
Ajai Pal, Raja 111
Ajbar Sen, Raja 60
Ajit Singh, Raja 120
allegiance 36, 42, 47, 53, 62, 66–7, 72, 74–5, 83, 108, 126fn8, 212
alpine pastures 143–4, 153, 156, 157, 187, 188, 192–3, 204
Alps 24, 166, 167, 169–71, 174, 178–80
alpwirtschaft 25
Ambala 150
amban 242
Ambika Devi (temple) 61
Andes 24, 25
Asur Danun 108
Auckland, Lord 270

badhi (carpenter) 163
Baghal state 111, 122
Bagi 84
Bahadur Singh, Raja 59

Bahu Sen, Raja 69fn28
Bajaura 60, 61
Balag 47, 48
Balbhadra, Raja 59
Balu Nag (*deota*) 51, 52, 113
Bambu Rao 85
ban (forest grazing area) 158–60, 161, 161, 188, 202
ban-kharetar (hayfields in the forest) 202
Banar (*deota*) 106
Bangahal 157, 159
banjar ghasni (hayfield) 142
Banjar (Kulu) 51, 53fn63, 113
banwaziri (forest tax) 160
Bareog (*deota*) 85
bartojeola (landholding) 229
Bashahr (state) 38, 45, 58, 60, 62, 63, 70, 74, 83, 99, 101, 102–4, 105, 108, 121, 128–9, 135–8, 141, 142, 144–5, 146, 150, 152, 171, 175, 177, 247, 251, 258, 259
Bashahri (traders) 243–4, 248
Bashera 86
Bashik (*deota*) 105
Baspa (river/valley) 128, 138, 143, 151
Batahuli (Old Mandi) 60
batkaru (tax) 157
Beas (river) 59, 60, 61, 100, 157, 175, 177, 259, 260–1, 262

295

begar (forced labour) 121, 122, 220, 221, 228, 230, 270, 270
Behangamani 69fn28, 100, 103
Bengal 18, 22, 26
Bentinck, William 226
Bhabra 108
Bhagwati (devi) 85, 86fn28
Bhakar 4, 74
Bhakaru (*see also* Bhokru) 107
Bhaler (clan) 42, 73
bhandar (granary) 43, 108fn37
Bhattiyat 156
bheral berha (sub-lineage) 37–8, 213
Bhima Kali 63, 102, 136
Bhokru (*see also* Bhakaru) 108
bhor (deity assisting a superior *deota*) 86, 86fn27, 107
Bhotu (*deota*) 105
Bijai Pal 111
Bijat (*deota*) 74, 83, 111
Biju (*deota*) 73, 74, 83, 110, 111
Bilaspur 60, 143, 258
boiree (*vairi*) 47, 48
Brahmanical 9, 40, 50, 56, 60, 64, 66
Brahmanisation 59, 62, 75
Brahmanism 57, 62, 80, 90, 135, 137, 152
Brahmaur 58, 61, 63fn17, 69fn28, 154–6, 162
bride-price 27, 217, 219
Buddhism 151, 152, 248–50
Buddhist 63, 135, 141, 151, 152, 175, 241, 249, 250
Buddhist monasteries 151, 175
Burha Dev (*deota*) 84

cantonments 267–9
capital towns 60, 152, 257
caste 22, 26, 27, 28, 29, 40, 41, 43, 45, 62, 62fn11, 66fn25, 67fn27, 68, 80, 83fn14, 86, 87, 98, 107, 115, 124, 136–8, 140, 155, 162–4, 169, 170, 178, 209, 213, 222, 229, 231, 232–3, 262
Central Asia 147, 148, 241–3, 261, 264
Chagaon 54
Chaini/Chehni 51, 59, 113
Chajoli 84fn21
Chalda (Mahasu *deota*) 105, 106, 109
Chaldu *see* Chalda
Chamang (weavers) 136
Chamba-Lahaul 215
Chamba 9, 58, 59, 60–1, 62, 62fn11, 63, 69fn28, 154–5, 157, 158, 159, 160, 161, 177, 187, 189, 192, 205, 215, 261, 262
Champavati (devi) 63
Chamunda Devi 61fn10
Chandeshwar 107, 108
Chandra valley 189, 204
Changthang 134, 243
Chasralu 105–6
chaugan 258
chawl (oath) 120
Chebishi 84fn21, 85, 86
Chehni *see* Chaini
chela (oracle) 44
Chhabalri 43
Chhabrog 43
Chhatrarhi 61
Chhibar (clan) 41
Chhichhar forest 85
chiefdom 58, 68–71, 73, 74, 77, 80–1, 86fn25
chiefship (*see also* chiefdom) 8, 136
Chini 132, 138fn42, 143, 219, 247, 250
Chohag 75fn43

cholera 265
Chur Chandni 108
Chur Dhar 107–8, 121
Churah 61fn9, 156
Churu 107
clan 36, 37, 39, 41–2, 45, 48, 50, 62, 63fn17, 66fn25, 72–5, 78, 80, 82, 90, 136–7, 213, 222
Combermere, Lord 266
community 34–55, 64, 69–70, 77, 79, 87, 97, 115, 119, 122, 123, 130, 136, 137, 141, 159, 160, 162–3, 170, 171, 187, 196, 202, 203, 211–13, 216, 227, 228, 229, 233. 236, 241, 268
cultivation 129, 130, 131, 171, 186, 189, 196, 198, 207, 208, 228, 248

Dagon 42, 73
Dagshai (cantonment) 265, 267, 269
Dakhani Mahadev 61
Dalai Lama 135
Dalhousie (cantonment) 268
Dalhousie, Lord 270
Dashal 61
Dashehra 51
Dattatreya temple 61
Dehra 162
Deo Chand 41, 73
deota (see also *devta*) 40, 42–54 *passim*, 65–8, 71–4, 80–5, 87–90, 109, 111, 113, 121, 151, 250–2
Deothal village 110
Dev Boindra (*deota*) 111
development 11, 53, 55, 131, 175, 205, 237–9 *passim*, 248, 252, 255
Devi Kundin 111

Devi Ram 108
Devjani village 109, 110
devta (see also *deota*) 40, 54, 65, 115
Dhalpur Maidan 113, 261
dhandak (peasant protest) 118
Dhanu Deo (*deota*) 43, 73
dhar (grazing area) 156–9, 162
Dhar Deshu 47, 48fn50
dharma 78
Dharta 42
Dhauladhar 154
Dithu (*deota*) 85
diversity (general) 21, 32, 126; geographical 20; social/cultural 30, 32, 214, 216, 235, 240; economic 219, 253
Dodra 42, 43
Domang (smiths) 136
Dudan village 111
Dum (*deota*) 73, 74, 83, 87–9 *passim*
dum (peasant protest) 50, 114, 118–23

ecological adaptation 25, 29
ecological 7, 15, 24, 25, 26, 28, 29, 123, 127, 128, 151, 167, 176, 184, 187, 270
ecology 7, 25, 128
environment/environmental 2fn3, 3, 13, 15–18 *passim*, 23, 24, 26, 30, 33, 34, 36, 53–4, 81, 84fn21, 110, 111, 115, 119, 130, 139, 167, 170, 207, 219, 231, 236, 270
ethnicity 8, 19, 70, 251
ethnie 18, 22, 36, 50
Europeans 264, 265, 266, 269, 270

Fag *mela* 251

INDEX

family 25, 30, 36, 115, 132, 133, 135, 139, 140–2, 158, 159, 170, 178, 179, 180, 186, 191, 211–17, 219, 220–6, 228, 230, 231–3, 234, 236, 250, 252
family deity 63, 65, 71, 83, 84, 118
Fateh Singh 121
folklore 6, 31, 47, 69, 76, 77, 91, 95, 96, 110, 112, 212, 213
Forest Act 201, 206
forest regulations 198, 201, 205
French Alps 167, 178, 180

Gaddi (shepherding tribe) 154–65
Garhwal 60, 105, 118, 150
Garoo (*see also* Gartok) 147–9 *passim*, 176
Gartok (*see also* Garoo) 147–9 *passim*, 176, 243
gatti (oath) 120
geography/geographical factors 1, 3, 9, 13, 15–17, 18, 19–23, 32–5, 56–75, 77, 78, 114, 119, 137, 150, 176, 181, 198, 213, 237, 240, 241, 248
gharu-kharetar 202
ghori (revenue district) 38, 65fn21, 250
Giri river 66fn25, 70, 81
Gorkha 246, 267
Gosain traders 177, 178, 179
gotra 37, 162
Guga Pir 107, 110
Gujjar/Gujar 6, 160, 161, 184
gur (oracle) 44, 47, 53

Hali 163
hansilijeola (landholding) 229
Hatkoti 60, 106
hegemony 56, 66–8, 79, 80fn9, 90, 118

hierarchy social/political 7, 49, 50, 55, 79, 117, 136, 137, 141, 214, 227; of *deotas* 46, 52, 57, 65, 68, 74, 75, 80, 84, 85, 86, 87, 90, 97, 113, 151, 152, 212, 250, 251
hill station 71, 263–5, 268–71
Hinduism 27, 56, 57, 64, 65, 66fn25, 68, 74fn42, 82fn10, 97, 151
Hira Sen, Raja 60
hiundasis 155
Homiyan Mian 48
Hoshiarpur 150, 177, 181
household 10, 114, 139fn46, 140–1, 185, 196, 212–15, 217, 219, 220–1, 223–7, 229–31, 233, 234, 249
Huna Rishi 105, 106
Hurla Khad 59

identity 2, 5, 6, 13, 16–17, 18, 19–23, 37, 39, 43, 50–1, 70, 75, 77, 84fn21, 110, 118, 126fn8, 127, 155, 162, 163–4, 212, 237, 238, 241, 244, 246, 251, 252
inheritance 158, 159, 212, 222, 223, 226, 232, 234
Inner Saraj 178, 190, 192, 195, 197, 198, 200

Jad/Zad 137
Jagat Singh, Raja 59, 101
jagati pat 52
Jagatsukh 59, 60, 61, 189
Jai Chand 147
Jamlu (*deota*) 65fn22, 121
Jamrot 42
Jataon village 111
Jatil 41, 74
Jau (*deota*) 74, 83

Jaunsar-Bawar 213, 216, 217, 223, 224, 232
Jawala Singh (*wazir*) 122
jeola (landholding) 229, 230
Jipur (*deota*) 42, 71, 72fn56, 73, 81
Jit Danon 111
Jiwa Nand 122
jongpen (Tibetan admininstrator) 243
Jubbal state 74, 83
Junga (*deota*) 41, 42, 48, 71–5, 81–4
Jutogh (cantonment) 267
Jwalamukhi 178, 260

Kahlur state 58, 60, 258
Kalaur (*deota*) 42, 73
Kalian Sen 59
Kanam 141, 249
Kanawar (*see also* Kinnaur) 130, 135fn54, 137fn41
Kanet (peasants/caste) 41–3, 45, 50, 72–4, 82fn11, 90, 107, 111, 118–19, 122, 136–8, 157, 229–30, 233, 249, 251
Kaneti (*deota*) 42, 43
Kangra (town/district) 8, 43, 44, 58, 150, 154–65 *passim*, 177, 181, 184–7 passim, 192, 193, 194, 202, 203, 204, 216, 259, 260, 261
Kapur Singh (*wazir*) 120
Karcham-Wangtoo 54
kardar 44, 138fn44, 177
Karna (*deota*) 109
Kasauli (cantonment) 265
Kashgar 148, 246
Kashmir 16, 18, 26, 60, 105, 106, 107, 110, 191, 242, 244, 246
Katain 74, 83
Kawar 42

Kennedy, C.P. 153, 265
Keonthal state 41–3 *passim*, 45, 47, 48, 70, 71–4, 76–84, 266, 269
Khaikari 228
Khampa 140, 145
Khandai village 106
Khanoga (clan) 41, 73
Khas/Khasa 37, 45, 226, 228, 232
khat 37, 66fn25
Khatris 66fn25, 163
khumbli (council) 38
khumri (council) 37
khund (warrior clan) 38, 45, 46, 48fn50
Kiar 43
Kinnaur (*see also* Kanawar) 53, 54, 101, 124, 128, 129–53, 170–8 *passim*, 212–15 passim, 217, 219, 220, 221, 232–3, 240, 244–51
Klainu Deo (*deota*) 43
Kochi 129
Kogi 43
Koli 43, 45, 136, 138fn44, 163, 233
Korgan Deo (*deota*) 43
Kot Ishwar Mahadev 74, 83, 84, 86–9
Kotguru 111
Kothi Mandholi 84, 89fn54
kothi 44, 157, 193
Koti 42, 42fn51, 43, 71, 72, 73, 74, 81, 83
Kotkhai 74, 83, 111
Kukti pass/village 157, 162
Kulu shepherds 191, 193, 204
Kulu 38, 43, 44, 51, 52, 53, 58–63 *passim*, 67, 68, 69fn28, 85, 99, 100–3 *passim*, 108, 113, 120,

143, 157, 158, 170, 175–8, 183–207, 212, 216, 217, 223, 229, 233, 259
Kumharsain 74, 76, 81, 83, 84–9
Kuthar state/rana 110, 111, 267
Kutlehr state 71, 72fn56, 81

Ladakh 146, 147, 148, 175, 177, 191, 192, 230, 231, 233, 240, 242, 243, 246, 261
Ladakhi 175, 242
Lahaul/Lahul 61fn9, 147, 148, 170, 171, 175, 176, 178, 187–94, 197, 204, 205, 212, 215, 217, 226–7, 231–2, 240
Lahauli / Lahaula traders 176, 191
Lakshana Devi (temple) 61, 61fn7
Lalita Varman, Raja 59
lamas 135, 175, 245, 249
lambardar 38
landholding 24, 36, 114, 214, 220, 221, 223, 228, 231, 232, 234
landownership 210, 212
Lata (*deota*) 86–7
legitimacy 68–9, 70, 83, 98, 103, 152, 160, 223
lohar (blacksmith) 137fn42, 163

Madho Rai, Lord 60, 103
Mahasu (*deota*) 64fn18, 104–8, 109, 110
Maheshwar Devta 54
Mahi Prakash, Raja 47, 48
Mahlog state 111
maidan (open ground) 113, 258, 261
Maindrarath 106
Makarsa 59, 100

Malendi 84, 85, 86–7
Malendu (*deota*) (*see also* Marechh) 84fn21, 85, 86–7
malundi/mahlundi 156, 159
Mananeshar (*deota*) 84fn21, 87
Mandi 58–60 *passim*, 62–4, 66fn25, 68, 69fn28, 103, 119, 121, 122, 143, 157, 188, 193, 259, 260, 261, 262
Manglaor/Manglaur 59, 69fn28, 260
Mani Mahesh 61
Mansarover 85
Manuni (*deota*) 42, 73
Marechh (*deota*) 84, 85, 86
mawannas (chiefs) 86
Meruvarman, Raja 58
migration 16, 39, 118, 144fn59, 145, 157–8, 162, 164, 166–70 *passim*, 172, 174–5; types of 179–82
migratory flocks 131, 132, 145, 173
migratory practices 167–71, 174
modernisation 2, 237, 238, 239, 248, 251, 252, 263
modernity 116, 201, 208, 209, 235, 237–8, 239, 240, 244, 248, 252
mountain societies 9, 23, 24, 25, 27, 28, 31, 32, 77, 166, 167, 174, 175, 179, 181
muafi 44

Nadaun 111, 185, 260
Nagarkot (old Kangra town) 259
Naggar 59, 61, 63
Nahan 48, 111, 121
Nain Singh (explorer) 243–4
Narain Sen, Raja 60
Narasimha (temple) 61

Nepal 16, 26, 29, 71, 146, 148, 151, 191, 212, 214, 117, 232, 240, 243, 244, 267
Nihagu (deota) 75fn43
Nirath 61, 62
Nirmand 60, 61, 62
Nisung 149, 176
nomadic/nomadism 10, 26, 36, 124, 126, 127, 148, 155, 169, 183, 245
nomads 124, 125, 126, 140, 148
nuns/nunneries (see also *zomos*) 141, 249
Nurpur 154, 156, 161, 185

opium 177, 178, 179
Ores (carpenters) 136
Outer Saraj 195, 196, 197, 198, 200

Pabasi (*deota*) 105
Pabbar (river) 60, 105
Pahari 26, 27, 28
Palwi 47
Pandavas 99, 102, 103, 106
Pangi (Chamba) 61fn9, 132, 156, 161fn31
Paras Ram 121
Parbati (river/ valley) 100, 192
Parol 59, 195
Parsuram 61
partition (of family property) 141, 202, 205, 212, 214, 218, 220, 221, 222, 223, 224, 226, 231
pastoralism/pastoralists 17, 21, 36, 48fn50, 81, 109, 119, 124–53, 154, 155, 158, 160, 161, 164, 170–4, 183–209, 220, 247
Pathankot 156
Patiala state/raja 42, 150, 266, 267
Phagu 73, 74, 83

Pharal 86
phati (revenue district) 38, 193, 204
polyandrous/polyandry (system/ family) 37, 210–34, 250
polygynandry 216, 217, 221, 232, 233
Pooh 137, 233
popular memory 5, 92, 93, 94, 116
Punar 71, 74fn43
Punjab Land Revenue Act 205

Raghunath, Lord 51, 59, 62fn12, 63fn17, 67, 68, 99, 101, 103, 113, 261
Rajput 6, 27, 45, 62fn11, 63fn17, 66fn25, 107, 137, 137fn42, 163, 232
rana 9, 58fn5, 59, 59fn6, 60, 66, 69fn28, 71, 73, 81, 82, 86, 88, 89, 90, 119, 257, 260
Rathi 163
Ravi river/valley 58, 60, 61, 69fn28, 155, 261, 262
Rawain 109
Rawal (clan) 42
Rawin 71
Rihara 163
Rupi 59, 178, 185, 188–90, 192–200 *passim*

Sabathu (cantonment) 239, 265, 267, 269
Sahilvarman, Raja 58
Sainj (Keonthal) 48
Sainj (Kulu) 192
Samsu (*deota*, Duryodhana) 109
sanatarium 265
Sangnam (*see* Sonam) 249
Sarajis 178

Sarkaghat 122
Satlej river/valley 48, 54, 60, 61, 70, 81, 85fn23, 128, 146, 147, 149, 171, 175, 176, 177, 258, 259, 262, 265
Shadga 108
Shainshar Kothi 59
Shainti (clan) 42, 73
Shakti Devi 61, 83, 84
Shaneti (*deota*) 42, 72
Shangri state 85, 85fn23
Sharal 43
Sharali Deo (*deota*) 43
Sharmala 84, 87, 89fn53
Shaya 107
sheep-rearing 130, 133
shepherding 132, 133, 155, 173, 185, 192, 198
shepherds 132, 144, 145, 155–7, 159–61, 164, 188–9, 191–4, 201, 204–7
Sher Kalia (*deota*) 106
Shimla/Simla (district/town) 8, 38, 41, 43, 65fn21, 71, 86fn25, 104, 121, 143, 178, 200, 212, 216, 217, 219, 264–7 *passim*, 269–70
Shimla/Simla Hill States 64fn18, 70, 81, 86fn25, 105, 129, 151, 153, 172, 256
Shipki 147
Shrigul (*deota*, see also Srigul) 64fn18
Shringa Rishi (*deota*) 51, 52, 113
Sialkhar 147
siana/seana/sayana 38, 66, 228, 37, 38
Sidh Sen, Raja 59
Sihal 84, 87
Simla (see Shimla)
Sip Deo (*deota*, Sipur) 42fn31, 43, 72fn36
Sipi 163
Sirmur (state/area) 42, 43, 47, 48, 58, 64fn18, 66fn25, 104, 107, 108, 111, 121, 143, 212, 216, 217, 219, 223
Siva 61, 63, 63fn17, 64, 64fn18, 65fn20
Sivaratri 51
small-pox 245
Sobha Ram (of Gandhiani) 122
Solan 143
Sonam nunnery (see Sangnam) 141
sowana 160.
Spiti 145, 188, 189, 190, 191, 197, 204, 226, 232, 233, 240
Sri Vidya (devi) 63
Srigul (*deota*, see also Shrigul) 104, 107–11, 121
Suket state 42, 43, 59, 69fn28, 143, 260
Sultanpur 59, 60, 67, 68, 260, 261, 262
Sur Prakash, Raja 111
Suraj Sen, Raja 60, 103

talang sa (householder) 141
Tara 83
thada 48
thakurai 59, 68, 69, 70, 71–5, 77, 80, 81–4
Thangi village 149
thok 37
Tholing 125
Tibetan plateau 30, 85, 133, 134, 146, 173, 174, 191, 235, 243
Tika 72, 73, 82, 82fn12
Tirthan (river) 192

trade 33, 60, 166–8, 191, 192, 195, 198, 210, 234, 242–4, 246–7, 250, 255, 256, 258, 259
traders 132, 232, 240, 248, 269
trader pastoralists 124–53
trakar (mid-hill pasture) 156
Trans-Himalayan trade 146, 175, 177
transhumance/transhumant 9, 24, 25, 124, 154, 155, 164, 168, 170, 187, 189, 191, 192, 196
tribal 21, 124–5, 126fn8, 155, 158, 162, 163, 169, 222, 241
tribe 28, 65fn20, 73fn40, 124–6, 139, 140, 147fn66, 163, 164, 169–70, 214, 228, 251
trini/tirni (grazing tax) 161, 162fn31
Tripura Sundari 63
trongba (household) 214–15
Tulsu Negi 120–1
Turi (village musician) 43
typhoid 265

Upardes 84, 87
urban 15, 17, 26, 55, 175, 179, 181, 209, 210, 253–71

Vaisnavism 62–3
Vakya Tandi 113
village gods 39, 40, 41, 42, 64, 64fn20, 65fn21, 72–5, 84, 90, 152, 268
Vishnu/Visnu 51, 61, 62, 62fn11, 62fn12, 63, 65fn20, 80

wajib-ul-arz (customary rules) 188, 222
warisi (inheritance in forest pasture) 158–61, 204
Western Tibet 125, 137, 139, 147, 150, 240, 243

Yarkandi traders 148, 175, 191, 242, 246, 247

Zomia 29–33, 235, 237
zomos (*see also* nuns) 141

www.ingramcontent.com/pod-product-compliance
Lightning Source LLC
Chambersburg PA
CBHW051804230426
43672CB00012B/2628